21st CENTURY BUDDHISM

by

Dr. Daney Dumdeang

21st CENTURY BUDDHISM THESIS

Presented to the Faculty of the Graduate School
of the University of British Columbia
for the advanced degree

by

Sompong Gunavaro Dumeang

Copyright © 2025

by Dr. Daney Dumdeang

All rights reserved.

ISBN: 979-8-89324-968-2

No part of this book may be reproduced, stored in a retrieval system, or transmitted in any form or by any means—electronic, mechanical, photocopying, recording, or otherwise—without prior written permission of the publisher, except for brief quotations used in reviews or articles.

The opinions expressed by the Author are not necessarily those held by the Publishers.

The information contained within this book is strictly for informational purposes. The material may include information, products, or services by third parties. As such, the Author and Publisher do not assume responsibility or liability for any third-party material or opinions. The publisher is not responsible for websites (or their content) that are not owned by the publisher. Readers are advised to do their own due diligence when it comes to making decisions.

Published by Franklin Publishers

Printed in the United States of America

For permissions, inquiries, or additional copies, contact:

Franklin Publishers

www.franklinpublishers.com

Dedicated this Book to

My Dear Mother

Mrs. Intrara Dumdeang

Acknowledgments

Although I have personally lived among the Thai and Thai-Chinese people for almost two decades, I have never looked so carefully into their ancestral worship as I have done for this paper. I would like to express my deep thanks to my wife, Mrs. Glory (Nungtalogawithoon) Thomas, and to a personal friend, Mr. Sompong Dumdeang, Ph.D., for their assistance in strengthening my knowledge in this field. Without their valuable input, the paper could not have been written.

Thank You Note From The Author

The author would like to thank the following people:

Dr. Joseph Richardson, who invited him to join the Religious Studies Department at the University of British Columbia, Vancouver, Canada, and appointed him to the Tibetan Studies PhD program committee while he was concurrently lecturing at the University of Washington in Seattle, Washington.

Dr. P. Yesu Ratnam, the former GSM director in India, who coordinated my manuscript with the GSM Board members. I am deeply sad that he passed away recently and cannot see this revised work published in the USA. I know his spirit will receive my thoughts of gratitude for his excellent help while he was alive. He remains in my heart forever.

I also thank my wife and daughter for being part of Dr. Yesu's orphan children program in India.

I thank the Buddhist Society in Sri Lanka for encouraging my book to continue to be read all over the Asian nations.

I thank my parents, who gave me birth, took care of me, and had me follow the steps of our family tradition. Without both of you, I would not be here today.

I thank my first guru, Arjarn Boon Sirm Therako, who taught me the basic foundation of Buddhist traditional education and astrology.

I thank Arjarn Pra Kroo Udom Kanatjikarn, who was my preceptor and ordained me as a young Buddhist novice monk, and later as a Buddhist monk.

I thank Arjarn Prom, Arjarn Sathain, Arjarn Buddhadasa Bhikkhu, and Arjarn Chao Khun Panyanonda, who were all part of my Buddhist life.

I thank the Patriarch Somdej Buddhajarn (Chao Khun Kiaw Upaseṇo), president of the Buddhist University, who believed in me. He assigned me many different Buddhist tasks, including appointing me as a leader and director of the *Dhammacārika* program to teach various mountain tribespeople in communist-sensitive areas of Northern Thailand, a project sponsored by a UN program.

I thank Pope Benedict XVI, who spiritually encouraged me, recognized my Buddhist work, and gave me strong spiritual strength and support.

I thank Sophie from Franklin Publishers, who recognized my work and supported my idea to continue publishing this book.

I thank David, who gave me the greatest support in publishing a better version of my book, *Buddhism*.

I thank father Arjarn FaTai at the Chinese World Buddhist Society, who fully supported my work.

I thank Luk Dej Sangsri, who coordinated the retyping of this entire book, and Tom Ropradit, for making the manuscript able to be republished.

Last and not least, I thank my beautiful wife, Patty; my three children; my eight grandchildren; my daughter-in-law; all my friends, close and faraway, whose names are unmentioned; and my entire audience who has fully given me support.

May God bless you all.

Dr. Daney Dumdeang Dumdeang Foundations / ECO

A Note for the Author's Family

When I showed my daughter a picture of us in Cambodia, where we visited the most significant Buddhist ruins in the world, I was glad I was there with her. The trip to Thailand, Cambodia, and Sri Lanka in November 2005 was in honor and memory of our "father-daughter trip." The publisher put her (photo?) in the introduction of the book. When she saw it, she said, "Great, Papa, but it is in Thai. I can't read it. Maybe you could translate it for me sometime." I did translate the appendix and showed it to Tommy, and then to Myla, as well as the rest of the family.

While revising this (my best-selling book), I have also had the opportunity to add and check for suitable material that may be helpful for Thai society, especially regarding the violence in southern Thailand. I do not know if my translation will be sent to press; I still have doubts. However, I have summarized it for my family, at least, as I feel that it is my obligation.

I considered this the appropriate time to include a number of additions I had been waiting to implement in order to make the book as complete as possible. To this end, I added an important teaching known as "The Buddhist's Life," which was written by me when my daughter was one month old. I recorded it from a lecture I gave at different universities and at the World Buddhist center, to which I was invited by Princess Poon Pismai Diskul (the daughter of Rama V). I feel that it is more beneficial to readers.

The origin of this book was a summary given as an appendix to a book of the same title. My book was taken from "A Discourse and Blessing Given on the Occasion of Leaving the Monkhood" for a monk who had been ordained temporarily according to Thai tradition. Some faithful Buddhists asked to print the discourse and blessing as a gift of Dhamma for the New Year of 1994.

When the Director-General of the Department of Local Administration, Ministry of the Interior, asked to print that summary as a gift of Dhamma for the New Year of 1988, I carried out some improvements in terms of content and style. I made it more concise, easier to read, and more complete by bringing it more into line with the new "Buddhist's Life Standards"—which I love to call the conclusion of Philosophy. I will summarize the contents of this book more when I feel better.

A practicing Buddhist may use "The Buddhist's Life Standards" as primary standards for leading his life, and then proceed to the qualities and practices given in the "Guidance for Living" to bring his life to greater virtue, success, benefit, and eventually, perfection. I here express my appreciation to my team working in Thailand, especially Prasop, Jaruex, Pramaha Jarearn, etc., for their hard work. To my wife, my children, and my grandchildren: I am thankful for their support and cheerfulness, which give me delight and pride in my work for Buddhists in Thailand and around the world.

More direct content: In relation to the practical affairs of everyday life, religions may take two approaches: one is to ignore them completely, concentrating wholly on the higher aim of merging with GOD or realizing ultimate truth; the other is to go into great detail about such matters, telling us how to organize our will, what foods to eat, and what clothes to wear. These seem to be two extremes.

To me, as the author of this book and my previous hundred books and uncountable articles, Buddhism is a teaching of moderation (the Middle Path of Purity, you may say). As in other things, the Buddhist teaching steers a middle course, in this case between the two extremes of blindly ignoring practical daily affairs and laying down a code of rigid and inflexible rules. The Buddhist teachings offer guidelines for behavior based on timeless truths—the positive weal created by compassionate, wise relationships—and aimed at the ultimate goal of spiritual freedom: living in the world and yet above it.

"The Buddhist's Life Standards" arose in response to the need to stress the importance of Buddhists having some principles to adhere to and earnestly practice. This is to be achieved by reviving and advocating the principles of practice described by the Buddha in the *Sigālovāda Sutta* (D. III. 180-193)—which I translated from the Pali language to Thai when I was a young monk...—as regulations which Buddhists may hold to and practice as general standards for conducting their lives, and by which they may together contribute to a good, happy, and prosperous society.

This would be in conformity with the original acknowledgment, recorded in the commentary, of the *Sigālovāda Sutta* as the "layman's code of discipline" (*Gihi-vinaya*), or the model for a householder's conduct, to go alongside the "monk's code of discipline" (*Bhikkhu-vinaya*).

The whole content of "The Buddhist's Life Standards" is to be found within *A Handbook for Living*. The former can be taken as the Buddhist's minimal standards for conducting his life, while the latter is a compilation of general Dhamma principles for leading a virtuous life and may be regarded as an extension of the former.

A practicing Buddhist may use "The Buddhist's Life Standards" (which is my most favorite book because it is so precise, and has been honored as a bestseller for psychologists and other medical fields to assist their work and be away from depression when they lose their patience. I learned this from a Head Doctor at a general hospital while I was the caretaker for my son, Peter, who had dengue fever. I was ignored and had forgotten my (role as a) writer for the last four decades)... as preliminary standards for leading his life, and proceed to the qualities and practices given in *A Handbook for Living* to bring his life to greater virtue, success, benefit, and eventually perfection (*Nirvana* or *Nibbāna* = complete freedom).

Ancestral Worship In Thailand

As a nation, Thailand is composed of a variety of socio-ethnical elements, all of which worship ancestors in different manners. The fundamental religion is Theravāda Buddhism. It is worshipped by 94% of the population.[1] The actual employment of the religion in ancestral worship varies from that of folk religion in the rural community to the formal hierarchy of the *WAT* (temple) in urban settings. Set apart from Thai Buddhism, yet influential over all parts of the worship, is the Thai-Chinese Buddhist thought brought into the cities by the influx of Chinese immigrants, who compose some 70% of the population of Bangkok, Haad Yai, and Chieng Mai. The predominant sociological emphasis is that of a Thai and Thai-Chinese population focused around Buddhism, a philosophy from India initially introduced to the Thai population in China some 1,500 years ago.[2]

The vast amount of Buddhist variance makes a definition of ancestral worship difficult. Whereas Chinese ancestral worship is distinctly different, there still remain similarities between the two systems that make it effective to write this paper based on the Chinese research material available in our libraries. As is true of the Chinese, Thai worship is broken into two distinct categories. The first is that of domestic worship, and the second is extra-domestic worship. This paper will begin with a statement on the encouragement of ancestral worship by Buddhism. After a brief discussion of mourning and burial ceremonies, the writing will then observe the patterns of domestic and extra-domestic ancestral worship as it is employed on a daily basis. The paper will also include an overview of two of the major festival ceremonies and will conclude with a description of the funeral preparations of a wealthy Thai family. The direct analysis of Thai ancestral worship will be drawn from personal interviews held with Glory Thomas (my Thai-Chinese wife) and Mr. Sompong Dumdeang (a Thai now residing in Portland, Oregon, who was a Buddhist monk for twelve years).

The Buddhist religion, in and of itself, encourages the concept of ancestral worship. Buddhism denies an existing eternal soul and, at the same time, denies the materialistic view that there is no afterlife.[3] Yet, Gautama Buddha (*Phra Phuttha Chao*), the original teacher, taught concerning bodily reincarnation, assuming that he had lived some five hundred lives in different forms. Death, then, must be definable as a process of life, and the focus of our lives is to be placed on the merits of our current existence. Gautama Buddha taught that death is caused by "loss of merit" (by our bad deeds), "loss of life" (because of the completion of time), or "untimely death" (death due to violence or psychic power).[4] To be prepared for this death and the possibility of reaching *Nirvana* (*Niphan*), man is to meditate on death, and in this way eliminate lustful states of mind and gain holiness.[5]

Furthermore, the Buddha suggests that a pure mind is gained through respect for those already dead. Such respect eliminates the possibility of retribution being paid back upon the living due to a lack of reverence. A final justification for the death-worship phenomenon is noted in Buddhist writings, which suggest that to be faithful in the veneration of the Buddha will bring both confidence in this life and an assurance toward the way of salvation, which is to be known in *Niphan*.[6]

Concerning the issue of death and spirit existence after death, the following religious pattern is predominant. The living person is composed of two parts: the body and the soul (*Vinyan*). Upon death, the *Vinyan* leaves the body to exist in another world, the spirit world. The *Vinyan* will descend into hell and there remain for the time necessary to be properly punished for earthly sins, that is, the "loss of merits." When payment for the sins is complete, the *Vinyan* will then prepare for bodily reincarnation to again strive toward the perfect life. Should the death have occurred due to evil deeds or by an "untimely death," the *Vinyan* will become a ghost (*Pii*). The *Pii*, which is eliminated from the possibility of reincarnation because of the circumstances of death, will roam the locality in which death occurred to bring evil actions against the family.

The ancestral ghost world is filled with numerous different characters. There are the *Pii Tani* (a female spirit forced to live in a banana plant), the *Pii Krasue* (a female spirit that flies through the night as a wreath of fire), the *Pii Tai Hong* (a man, woman, or child who has died due to violence), the *Pii Dip* (a devilish spirit that lives in a coffin by day and in the streets by night), the *Nang Nak* (a female spirit of a mother who died while giving birth), and a vast number of others.[9] All are to be worshiped and paid homage so as to prevent unnecessary interference in daily life. In comparison to these evil spirits stand the *Vinyan*, awaiting bodily reincarnation, and the Gautama Buddha, who has gained entrance into *Niphan*. In *Niphan*, Buddha is never born again, never dies, and exists in what appears to be a real and living dream.[10]

Before moving into the death-mourning element, it is important to summarize the philosophical dilemma involved. The dilemma is the issue of mortality and immortality. Whereas the Buddhist hope is to reach *Niphan*, there is no real proof that *Niphan* can be reached. This then leaves man in a mortal body which will retain its mortal nature through reincarnation. Yet, should the "loss of merit" or "untimely death" have been the cause of death, the *Vinyan* becomes a *Pii*, which seems to gain a spirit immortality in a negative fashion. The *Pii* is mortally dead but is immortally tied to the earth as an agent of evil power. Probably the best manner in which to define the religious "Wheel of Hope" is as follows: Man can gain the state of *Niphan* (or what the Chinese call "Western Heaven"[11]) and become what might be called a universal soul. Mortal man who dies as a *Vinyan* awaits re-entry into the living area so that he may again advance toward "the way" that Gautama Buddha felt he had gained. And the ghost, *Pii*, lives in an immortal death of trouble and sorrow.

To (address the) calamity of death, Thai culture requires that all men become Buddhist monks (temporarily). By this means, the monk is imagined to establish his good merits. This will give an assurance of reaching *Vinyan* status and a swifter opportunity toward bodily reincarnation. Further, the holding of the monkhood for from three days to one month is of advantage to the family. Specifically, this is to the advantage of the elders of the family who may be reaching the "loss of life" period of their existence.[12] This will be discussed fully in the section concerning domestic ancestral worship.

The most basic (worship) is for the relief of the intrusion of the evil spirits, *Pii*. This worship is followed by constructing a spirit house, *San Jaew*, outside of the house. This spirit house is to provide convenient housing for an evil ancestral spirit of the family and/or for other spirits that might be roaming in the vicinity. At the *San Jaew*, an offering of uncooked rice, water, seasonal fruit, and incense is offered on a daily basis. Each week on the monk's day, *Wan Phra*, a special offering will be provided. Likewise, on any special festival day, such as New Year's, a sacrificial offering will be placed before the shrine.

The more sophisticated family and the business establishment will employ the *San Jaew* in a slightly different fashion. In these instances, the persons involved will go to the *WAT* and ask the monks to come and perform a ritual chant around the *San Jaew*. The family or business pays for the house to become the enshrinement of a monk of important name who has died recently. The house will then be encircled with a *Sai Sin* (silk string) so as to assure the business or family that the spirit of the monk will remain in the *San Jaew*. This is believed to overcome the power of the *Pii* that might be familiar with the area in which the house or business is located. Before this *San Jaew*, the same daily ritual is performed as is done before the common domestic spirit house.

Domestic worship of the *Vinyan*, the second type of domestic worship, is done inside the house. ... (When a crisis occurs, a shaman is consulted to determine) what is needed to make the spirit happy. After the request of the spirit is known, the payment is made in a manner similar to that of the Chinese. The family will collect whatever the spirit requests and will conduct a ritual burning ceremony. The *Vinyan* or *Pii* is then assumed to be pleased enough to bring a halt to the crisis. However, to prevent the reoccurrence of the circumstances, the family will conduct the ritual on a monthly basis on each full moon in the future.[15] For further assurance, the family will also begin to do other good deeds in areas they feel might appease the ancestral spirit.

When a parent of the family dies, a young child between the ages of seven and sixteen is sent to the *WAT* to be ordained as a monk. The child monk (*Nain*) is believed to provide the parent the way in which to move conveniently into the other world. The child is young and considered to be of good merit-standing, so the deceased parent can "grasp hold" of his robe and be led toward the other world. It is imperative for a family to have a child become a monk before an elder in the family dies. Should a parent die before a son becomes a monk, the parents and family have failed to *tham bun* (do good). If there has been no monk in the family, the elder has no access to the other world. This implies that the parent, with no monk's robe to grasp, will become a *Pii* rather than a *Vinyan*.[16]

The process of extra-domestic ancestral worship relates to the worship of Gautama Buddha and Buddhist monks. It is conducted in the same fashion as the domestic ritual, although sometimes the complete body of a chicken will be added to the altar. On *Wan Phra*, I have noticed that special attention is given to the Buddha altar and the sacrifices of veneration that are given. The Buddha is venerated for having reached *Niphan*, and other great monks are honored for having possibly reached *Niphan*. The special attention to extra-domestic worship may take place in the home or before the Buddha image in a *WAT*. The people will help pay for the construction of a temple so as to gain merit toward *Niphan*. The family, at the time of a death, will also seek to make a special offering to a *WAT* or to a specific monk and in this way assure the good fortune of the deceased.

Before concluding the essay, it is best to observe two special festivities that are used as part of ancestral worship. The first is the Thai New Year. On April 13th of each year, the *Songkran* (water festival) takes place. On this day, the family will welcome the incoming of the new year by repeating the water cleansing ritual done at the time of the cremation. Outside of the house, a *tham bun* is performed by offering every spirit water. Usually, this means the sprinkling of water over all members of the family as a type of baptism. In modern Thailand, since the introduction of water balloons and motor transportation, this gay festivity has often caused not a baptism, but violent deaths and injuries. As a living person, it is important to watch out for flying balloons filled with water, or you might quickly become a *Vinyan* or a *Pii*.

The second festivity of importance is that of Chinese New Year, known as *Prapheni Wai Pii* (the day to honor the ghosts). On this day, the family will prepare a banquet of food for spirit worship. A table is set in the *Hong Rap Khaek* (living room), and an abundance of food is set on the table. Incense is then lit, and the family proceeds out of the house to throw dry rice over, under, and around the house to invite the spirits to come to the feast. After approximately one hour, the time needed for the incense to burn, the family will re-enter the house to serve themselves and their neighbors with the food. There is an old Thai myth that says the spirits can be seen on this day. To see the spirits and to know who they are, you may enter the living room nude, and you will be able to watch them as they eat.

The most accurate way to illustrate the enormous impact that ancestral worship has throughout each vein of Thai culture is to observe the actions of a wealthy family as they prepare for the cremation of an elder. In a wealthy family, the mourning period can range from seven days to three years. On the first day after the death, the family will begin the construction of a paper house of enormous dimensions. The house will include furniture, luxury items, automobiles, and paper-doll servants. Beyond these items, the family will also fill several suitcases with counterfeit money and collect the favorite sentimental jewelry of the deceased. On the day of the cremation, the paper house and all the accessories will be burned, either in front of the house or on the grounds of the temple at which the cremation is to take place.

Even at the conclusion of the cremation, the mourning period is still considered to be in effect. At the conclusion of this period, the family will go to the *Maa Pii* (shaman) to prepare for a séance. The séance is conducted to find what the spirit, which is supposed to be in the other world, needs to remain happy. After the séance, the family will begin to pay tribute through all manners of domestic and special rituals as laid out earlier in the essay. On the full moon day, any items of special interest that were made known in the séance will be burned. Further, if the ancestor had been a monk, the family will purchase a Buddha image to serve as the quarters in which the *Vinyan* will reside and will place this image on the family altar or in the *Hong Phra* (Buddha room).

To better support this final setting, I would like to relate to you (a story) concerning the home in which I resided while in Bangkok. The house was what had once been a mansion but was now a ruin. The story of the house was that the ancestor who had lived there had asked, through a *Maa Pii*, that the house be left for him to live in alone. In obedience to this belief, the family had moved out of the house. When the Peace Corps came into the country as volunteers, the family decided that the house could be rented to them at no harm. As a Peace Corps volunteer, I lived in the house on several occasions over a five-year period. Never once did I or any other person living there experience any encounter with the *Vinyan* or *Pii* that supposedly lived in the house.

Preface

The contents of this book are gleaned from the Pali Tipiṭaka (some parts from Sinhalese, Tamil, and Sanskrit languages) and Commentaries, the texts of Theravāda Buddhism (please see the full contents of my *21st Century Buddhism*, which was published a few years ago). This is the Buddhism which is lived and practiced today in Thailand, Sri Lanka, Burma, Laos, and Cambodia. (My book is also used as curriculum for a PhD program at Rangoon University and has been used as a spiritual "Holy Book"... by a large group of men every Sunday at a popular hotel for a "Tipiṭaka-Bible reading" to heal their AIDS disease, and they have been healed.)

The teachings are over 2,500 years old, but they are far from outdated. In today's egalitarian society, in which we find all our traditional roles either torn down or under question, and in which—in spite of a flood of "enlightened" ideals—our lives are more confused than ever, the Buddhist teachings, dating back to a time when things were much simpler, are like...

Many people today look on life in all sectors as a struggle between conflicting interests: the "boss" against the "workers"; the "government" against the "people"; the "rich" against the "poor"; and even "women" against "men" or "children" against "parents"; "Muslims" against "Buddhists" (for example, since the revival of a separatist Muslim insurgency in early 2004), on and on, with no end. Or "students" against "teachers" (such as at Virginia Tech), "husband" against "wife," etc.

When the aim of life is seen as material wealth or power, society becomes a struggle between conflicting personal interests, and we are in need of an ethic to protect those interests. It is a "negative ethic." Society is based on selfish interests—"the right of each and every person to pursue happiness"—and an ethic, such as "human rights," is needed to keep everybody from cutting each other's throats in the process.

Table of Contents

INTRODUCTION

The terms "Buddhism" and "Buddhist Philosophy" have been used in such a variety of ways that a preliminary discussion of these terms is needed. For the most part, when we hear the word "Buddhism," we associate it with either: a) the teachings of Gautama Buddha, or b) the teachings of one of the schools within the Hīnayāna or Mahāyāna traditions. It is not wrong to define Buddhism in this way; it is merely insufficient.

"Buddhism" is, of course, an English word. It refers in a general way to the religion of the Buddha, much as the word "Hinduism" refers to the religion of the Hindus. In Pali, the canonical language of early Buddhism, the equivalent word is *Buddhasāsana*, which means "the teaching of all knowers of all ages." The original sense appears in the *Samantapāsādikā*, in the *Pātimokkha* section of the Pali Vinaya collection, as:

Avoiding the acts of all evil deeds, Committing the act of all good deeds, Purifying your hearts—these (all of these three commitments) are the teaching of all Buddhas (knowers).[1]

Sabbapāpassa akaraṇaṁ, kusalassa upasampadā, Sacittapariyodapanaṁ, etaṁ buddhāna sāsanaṁ.

According to the last phrase of this Pali gatha, *etaṁ buddhāna sāsanaṁ* ("this is the teaching of the Buddhas"), "Buddhism" refers to the teachings of all Buddhas, or "enlightened ones," of the past—including Gautama, the historical Buddha—and even the future Buddha, Maitreya.[2]

The terms Hīnayāna and Mahāyāna are not helpful to us in our understanding of essential Buddhism. The Buddha himself attained supreme enlightenment and taught the way to all mankind. "Two pillars are supporting the great edifice of Buddhism: *Mahāprajñā*, great wisdom, and *Mahākaruṇā*, great compassion. The wisdom flows from the compassion and the compassion from the wisdom, for the two are one."[3]

In a further statement attributed to the Buddha from Thai sources, he says, "All my teachings of *dhamma* fall into these categories:

Sandiṭṭhiko - that which is visible, belonging to this life

Akāliko - that which is immediate and timeless

Opanayiko - that which leads inward

Paccattaṁ - that which is individual, single, particular

These *dhammas* are inseparable, established in their own nature (*svabhāva*), and not divisible into separate schools. Thus, all Buddhas have two fundamental duties:

a) to develop from ordinary manhood into Buddhahood through the perfection of *dhammas* and to teach all mankind; and b) to follow and practice all the *dhammas* practiced by enlightened ones in the tradition of the Buddhas.

Hence, all *dhammas* permanently retain their own natures. They do not change, however much men try to redevelop them or make them appear different. It is true that there are political and cultural differences between the areas where Hīnayāna and Mahāyāna Buddhism developed; the former in Thailand, Burma, Cambodia, Laos, and Ceylon, and the latter in Tibet, Mongolia, Japan, Vietnam, and Korea. The expression may be different, but the *dhamma* is one.

By the same token, I have tried to avoid using the term "Theravāda Buddhism" in any way that designates a unique kind of Buddhism. Similarly, the names of Asanga or Nagarjuna indicate historical developments; furthermore, both Hīnayāna and Mahāyāna Buddhism teach the momentary tenet. The Buddhist *Anicca* doctrine is the theory of impermanent *dhamma*; one perceives *anicca* (impermanence) as *nicca* (permanence) due to delusion. Hume thought one perceived a "self" or "soul" (rather than "no-self" or "no-soul") because of "impressions" and "ideas" (impressions of sensation and/or reflection). Hume believes that all moral beliefs, impressions, and ideas lead us to identify ourselves as possessing an "I-ness."

For instance, he explains in Books I and II (of *A Treatise of Human Nature*) that "impressions of reflection" are: 1) non-rational in origin, and 2) contributed by the mind to experience, rather than derived directly from perception. Hume uses "impressions of reflection" to explain his original empirical belief, which can be very difficult to follow. He further thinks that we believe in the existence of the "self" because "belief" arises from "impressions" of causal necessity, and this impression of causal necessity arises from the "mechanism of sympathy." The mechanism of sympathy results from the nature of what the mind does with its contents. "Belief," says Hume, "is more properly an act of the sensitive, than of the cogitative part of our natures."[8]

Returning to an Eastern context, all three "stems" of Buddhism—Hīnayāna, Sāmkhya Mahayana, and Nihilistic Mahayana—are similar. Semi-Mahayana Buddhism was formulated by Vasubandhu from Harivarman's ideas. This school holds that the real thought of Hīnayāna Buddhism provides wisdom not through the negative thesis that material substances are unreal, but through the positive thesis that *ideas* (the originally-referred-to data of the senses in the aesthetic continuum) are real. Consequently, from this system arose the "Nihilistic Mahayana" Buddhism of Nagarjuna. He believed that the final state of sense and introspection, *Nirvana*, did not leave one with absolutely nothing. The nothingness of Nagarjuna was only partially understood by Tao(ism). Tao perceived that "What it is" can be derived from deduction. Westerners, nevertheless, misinterpret the conception of *Nirvana* of the three schools as a contradiction. However, the three systems of Buddhism have a logical relationship, which is similar to the related philosophies of Hobbes, Berkeley, and Hume. As indicated above, Hume's philosophy is especially compatible with early Theravāda Buddhism.

Hīnayāna Buddhism was established by early Buddhist elders,[9] particularly by Harivarman, who believed that neither the mental nor the material substance of common sense exists. “Mental” and “material” refer to the transitory succession of immediately introspected data in the aesthetic continuum. Harivarman’s notion is obviously similar to Hume’s philosophy.

Furthermore, Hume’s viewpoint of the self as a (bundle of) impressions and ideas is similar to the concept of the five *skandhas* in Buddhism, which (in aggregate) create the “I-ness” (*Ahamkara*, or “I-creator”). Hence, there are only phenomena of the mind (mental phenomena); indeed, the mind itself is empty (*Sunyata*) of defilement (*Upadana*). Consequently, when the mind is empty, one can be absolutely delivered from the unfree condition (*Samsara*). The mind is then formless, sightless, and wishless. This is the concept of *Nirvana*. The meaning of the “self” is extinct, and the “world” is no longer extant; therefore, this state transcends all words and concepts.

The philosophy of Hume states that there is no self in material substance; there are only impressions and ideas (real and unreal). And if delusion exists, it is real. The Buddha taught that delusion is unreal. Therefore, when there is delusion, “I-ness” (*Ahamkara*) exists, but it is unreal. When one has attained wisdom, there is no delusion and therefore no “I-ness”; this (state of non-delusion) is real. Wisdom is the process by which delusion is dynamically changed and overcome through the principle of the Four Noble Truths. There is no longer delusion. This relates to the twin doctrines of impermanence and no-self. The Buddha taught that the conditioned world is delusion (*Avidya*), fundamentally full of undesirable, unlasting appearances. Freedom and salvation (enlightenment) can only be found by escaping to the unconditioned world called *Nirvana*. Everything else is unreal.

The Buddha resisted the doctrine of permanence and emphasized that all entities are impermanent. He banished permanent substance (*atta*) from his metaphysics. The transcendental utopian goal, *Nirvana*, exists not as a substance (as *Arahantaship* wrongly became identified), but as a state—a permanent state. Hume similarly conceived personal identity as (a bundle of) simple impressions. Conversely, the Buddha defined life as more than just impressions, ideas, and delusions. He defined real life as *Nirvana*. To reach *Nirvana*, one must destroy delusion according to the principle of the Four Noble Truths; Buddhism is a religion of practice. Buddhism is a secular philosophy that leads one toward freedom by working on the elements of the causal chain, culminating in the destruction of bondage and the attainment of freedom.

I am highly grateful to the G.S.M. President and important members: Mrs. P. Aruna and Dr. Rev. P. Yesu Ratnam, Director; Mr. Jetla Venkateswara Rao, Secretary; Mr. Kallakuri Satyanarayana Rao, Advisor; Mr. Nanduri Kamaju; and Jetla Ramakrishna Paramahamsa for their cooperation in printing and delivering this book.

Dr. Daney Dumdeang

Founder, President, Chairman of the Board

DUMDEANG REALTY CO.

P.O. Box 2265, OR 97208 U.S.A.

CHAPTER I

The Philosophy In Practice

In this chapter, I will analyze Buddhist philosophical issues in both a practical and theoretical sense. Theory without practice is empty, and practice without theory is meaningless. Thus, the two must work in concert to fulfill a philosophical goal.

To make this discussion intelligible and logical, certain questions must be raised. Do we have to believe that the only way to achieve complete freedom from suffering in Buddhism is to practice the Four Noble Truths? Is one who follows the Four Noble Truths able to distinguish between the mundane and the super-mundane (*Nirvana*) world (i.e., both physical and mental phenomena)? Is the truth of the Four Noble Truths only a transcendent phenomenon? If it is not merely a transcendental phenomenon, how can we demonstrate it, in the fullest sense, to those not practicing the Four Noble Truths? All of these questions should be re-examined, but we do not need to answer them all, for they are merely related to philosophical games. I shall now set these questions aside until later.

Let us first examine the etymological content. Perhaps this will help us understand Buddhism, since philosophy is based on language and grammar, as well as the mental phenomena studied by the science of logic.

Let us begin with the word "philosophy." What does this word mean in the context of Buddhist philosophy? The Pali word for philosophy is *Paññā*, which means wisdom and intelligence. Likewise, the Sanskrit *Prajñā* is the same; *Paññā* and *Prajñā* are noun forms. The Pali verb *paññāyati* means "to be known, to be perceived, to appear to exist; to be well-known." The Sanskrit verb is *prajñāyate* (pra = complete plus jñā = to know).

The word *paññā* has a variety of connotations when combined with other words. For example, *paññācakkhu* [1] means "the eye of wisdom" (one of the five kinds of extraordinary sights of a Buddha). *Paññāratana* [2] means "the gem of reason or knowledge."

Our analysis is of the word "philosophy" (*paññā*) in the nominative case. *Paññā* may be used as an adjective as well as a noun. The term *Buddhi* (intellect) is related in meaning to *paññā* and *Bodhi*. The word *Bodhi* is from the same root as the word "Buddha" and means "enlightenment." I, however, prefer to translate the word *bodhi* as "All-Enlightened One." Hence, the term "Buddhist" (which the author relates to *Buddhi*) as used in the phrase "Buddhist Philosophy," functions as the adjective (*visesana*) for the noun "philosophy" (*paññā*).

The Greek word *philosophia* means "love of wisdom"; *philos* means "love" and *sophia* means "wisdom." Therefore, as the dictionary says, philosophy is "the science which aims at the explanation of all the phenomena of the universe by the ultimate cause" and "the calm and unexcitable state of mind of the wiseman." Hence, the phrase "Buddhist philosophy," or (*Buddhi-Paññā*), literally means "the wisdom of the all-enlightened one." Some Westerners perceive *buddhi* to mean "intuition"—the "immediate apprehension by the mind without reasoning"—by which one attunes one's limited human consciousness to the spark of the Light or Spirit, or the Buddha within.

Etymologically, the word *paññā* (as related to *buddhi*) requires an object; it requires a "whatness." It is equivalent to the incomplete English sentence, "X knows...?" The verb "to know" requires an object, because the meaning of "knowing" is incomplete [3]—in the same way that "to think" and "to understand" are incomplete and require complementary words or objects. "To know" requires an action or description that is the "whatness." In the case of *paññā*, an object is required, and that object is the *Cattāri Ariyasaccāni* (the Four Noble Truths), the basic discussion of this chapter.

I would further like to analyze the word "Buddhist." A "Buddhist" is one who can obtain the wisdom of the Four Noble Truths. All Enlightened Ones are those who have the "eyes of *Dhamma*" (*Dhammacakkhu*), [4] namely, regarding their conduct of action and perfection of merit (some authorities call this the perfection of the three vehicles: *Sāvaka* (Arahant), *Paccekabuddha*, and *Bodhisatta*). These enlightened ones primarily and ultimately attain *Nirvana* in both forms: [5]a) the form in which the five group elements (*khandhas*) remain after enlightenment (*Sa-upādisesa-Nibbāna*), [6]and b) the form in which the five group elements do not remain after enlightenment (*Anupādisesa-Nibbāna*). [7] I will later discuss the attainment of *Nirvana* more completely.

We can simply summarize the essential meaning of Buddhism by asking and answering two questions:

1. **What is Buddhism?** Buddhism is the science by which one is released from suffering. [8]

2. **How can one release suffering?** One can be relieved from suffering by practicing (following) the Four Noble Truths. [9]

In brief, the (practice of the) Four Noble Truths consists of the truth of morality, meditation, and wisdom, which is sometimes called "the old learned Buddhism." [10] These are, however, not only Buddhist practices, but common to all religions.

The Eightfold Noble Path [11] is the path the Buddhist follows which leads to the extinction of all suffering. It consists of: Right View, Right Intention, Right Speech, Right Conduct, Right Livelihood, Right Effort, Right Mindfulness, and Right Concentration. [12] Only by following the Eightfold Path can human beings end their suffering and realize (obtain) *Nirvana*.

Before presenting the chief doctrine of the Four Noble Truths, I shall offer a critique of its philosophical analysis. I am more concerned with the doctrine of the Four Noble Truths than with any other aspect of Buddhism.

The teachings of all Indian philosophies, Buddhist and non-Buddhist, are known as *dhammas*. The practice of *dhammas* applies to the laity on the social, mundane level and to the monks on the super-mundane level. The monk is one who gives up the material world, practices *Dhamma* on the super-mundane level for ultimate deliverance or renunciation, and teaches the way of *Dhamma* to the laity. Non-Buddhists, like Jains who practice *dhamma*, are also monks. They believe that only monks can be liberated from *samsara*; thus, their *dhamma* concerns the monk rather than the laity. This social discrimination caused the Buddha to critique the social caste system, [13] for He maintained that *Dhamma* concerns all mankind. Mahāyāna Buddhism later developed from Hīnayāna, and in Mahāyāna, *Dhamma* closely concerned the laity as well as the monk.

In Buddhism, *dhammas* for society (for the laity) refer to the concept of duty. Duty means the practice of life. Hence, when one practices *Dhamma*, one interacts with things commonly thought of as "other than oneself." *Dhamma* is thus the moral conduct by which one reaches the ultimate goal, much like Kant's "duty" or "moral habit," which became one of his crucial doctrines. Besides following *Dhamma*, Buddhists practice *artha* and *kāma* [14] and believe it is their duty to guide themselves and their families to a calm and peaceful spiritual life. I will later discuss the super-mundane notion of *Dhamma*.

Dhamma in this thesis is treated in relation to science and its philosophy, metaphysics, morals (ethical science), and epistemology, according to various sources of the Buddhist canon. [15]I shall review *Dhamma* from an "emotive" standpoint, [16] avoiding technicalities as far as possible. I will concentrate on key *suttas*—i.e., the *Dhammacakkappavattana Sutta* and the *Anattalakkhaṇa Sutta*—which are the chief doctrines of Thai Theravāda Buddhism.

What is *Dhamma* on the super-mundane level? It is the most important Dhammic practice. In brief, one must practice moral habits (*sīla*), meditation (*samādhi*), and wisdom (*paññā*), and ultimately overcome *māyā* (illusion) through the development of insight-wisdom, as guided by the *paññā* of *vipassanā-bhāvanā* (insight meditation). When one practices these states of *Dhamma*, one's mind becomes purified and freed from the conditioned world (the world of *samsara*), and one becomes an *Arahant*. Thus, one attains *Arahantship* by practicing the Four Foundations of Mindfulness (*Satipaṭṭhāna*).

This is the one way to achieve *Nirvana*: "the one path to Deliverance," the *Ekayāna Magga* (as said in Pali). Of the three highest saintships, the Theravāda Buddhist prefers the one who achieves *Nirvana* as an *Arahant* above any other. *Arahants* are those who have reached *Nirvana*, the "Supreme Goal," the "Highest Fruit of the Eightfold Noble Path." [17]

Buddhaghosa says that "*bhikkhu samma viharati*"; (Muller argues) that this is one "who having himself entered the Noble Path, leads his brother into it, and this, no doubt, is good Buddhism. However, it is a practical application of the text, a theological exegesis, and not a philological explanation. Even so, it seems to lay stress too much on 'bereft' and too little on 'Arahant'." [18]

Satipaṭṭhāna includes four kinds of meditation on mindfulness. In English, *Satipaṭṭhāna* closely translates to the "Establishment of Mindfulness." *Satipaṭṭhāna* was proclaimed by the Buddha, meaning it is the highest *Dhamma* for the one path to deliverance.

The four kinds of Establishing Mindfulness are:

1. **Establishing Mindfulness on the Physical Body (*Kāyānupassanā*):** This includes 14 ways of reflection on the body. Two are: a) meditation on respiration (*Ānāpānasati*), and b) meditation on the physical composition of the parts of the body (*Kāyagatāsati*). [19] Through this practice, one comes to realize that there is no "soul" in the body. Then we can know that we are naturally empty, or *anattā*; then there is no desire in the body (sexual desire, *kāma-tanhā*). It helps us destroy craving (desire) and attachment to false views. This meditation helps us gain more power in our effort toward reaching salvation (*Nirvana*).

This meditation is (for overcoming) what is perceived in the body as the "Hallucination of Wholesomeness" (*Subha-saññā Vipallāsa*). [20]

2. **Establishing Mindfulness on Feelings (*Vedanānupassanā*):** This involves nine kinds of reflection, primarily to counteract the feelings (sensations of rise and fall) that arise at various moments in one's life. This *Satipaṭṭhāna* helps destroy the "Hallucination of Happiness" (*Sukha-saññā Vipallāsa*). [21]

3. **Establishing Mindfulness of Thought (*Cittānupassanā*):** This helps destroy ill will, greed, jealousy, etc. This meditation guides us to destroy the "Hallucination of Permanence" (*Nicca-saññā Vipallāsa*). [22]

4. Establishing Mindfulness on Phenomena (Dhammānupassanā): This is the field of the constituents of enlightenment and truth. For example, it is the reflection on the Ariyasacca (Noble Truths)—the search for the four forms of suffering, which include: 23

a) Suffering

b) The cause of suffering

c) The cessation of suffering

d) The way to the cessation of suffering

This Satipaṭṭhāna helps the practitioner destroy the idea that "there is a soul" (or the "Hallucination of Self," Atta-saññā Vipallāsa). 24

One who practices *Satipaṭṭhāna* seriously is never a slave to false views. Thus, he is more advanced in reaching *Nirvana* directly. This the Lord Buddha stressed as the only path to the complete freedom of mankind. Mindfulness (*Sati*) is the control required to act and reach the highest path:

"The one and only path, Bhikkhus ('Buddhist monks'), leading to the purification of beings, to passing far beyond grief and lamentation, to the dying out of ill and misery, to the attainment of the right method, to the realization of Nirvana, is that of the Fourfold Setting-up of Mindfulness." [25]

When one attains *Nirvana*, one has reached perfection; that is to say, one is free. Free from what? This freedom, in brief, is freedom from attachment (*Upādāna*), [26]which results in the realization that there is no "I-ness" or "my-ness," but rather *anattā* (no-self). [27] Thereby, one is free from the structure of suffering and removed from all worldly conditions. This merit derives basically from the practice of meditation; for one who searches for the cause of things also comes to understand the nature of cause-effect relationships, known as the Law of Dependent Origination (*Paṭiccasamuppāda*), or the Wheel of Law (sometimes called the Twelve Chains of Gautama). [28]

One who correctly practices the basic elements of the teaching—*Sīla*, *Samādhi*, and *Paññā*—reaches *Nirvana*. [29] The result of reaching *Nirvana* enlightens him to see "I-ness" as "no-ness." This "giving up attachment to the five *skandhas*" [30] appears in the same man who, at first, is an ordinary man and who, finally, is transformed by his *Nirvana*.

Who is Buddha? Buddha is *a* man, but *the* man who won *Nirvana*. The *Tathāgata* is the *Puggala* (person), the prototype of all *puggalas*. As Stcherbatsky states, the *Vātsīputrīyas* intended "to support the doctrine of a supernatural surviving Buddha from the philosophical side." [31] Thus, the person who had not yet reached *Nirvana* and who then reached *Nirvana* is one and the same.

No matter whether one has the experience of *Nirvana* in the present or future, that experience is carried from the past (previous life) and is not isolated from any previous experience. Every event is related to every other. The *Pratītyasamutpāda* theory, for example, is the basic teaching of Buddhism. The question is, "Why do I not know, myself, that I was another form of being before this form of being?" The answer is: because of delusion (ignorance does not allow us to know). Another question is, "Was I enlightened in a previous life?" The answer is yes. But again, we do not know because of delusion

(*Avijjā*). [32]The Buddha gives us the evidence: "this sage Sunetra, who existed in the past, that Sunetra was I." [33] Linguistically and psychologically speaking, the word "I" means the universal person rather than the individual person. Since all of the psycho-physical events have changed, it can only be the "person" himself who makes the Buddha and Sunetra identical. Similarly, when the Buddha says, "in the past I have had such a body," the word "I" can refer only to a particular person, [34] not to an eternal "self."

One who attains *Nirvana* also experiences the rise and fall (the nature) of physical and mental forms (elements). Having experienced that the five *skandhas* are momentary existence and delusion—unreal and "no-self" [35]—one sees that the "self" and "soul" are only the union of mind (*mana*) and matter (*rūpa*). In short, one understands that the mark of impermanence is in all phenomena. There is (only) suffering (*dukkha*) and no identity, such as a "soul" or "self" (*anattā*). [36] The egolessness of self (phenomena) becomes clear. This clarification, the Buddhist calls the *Dhammacakkhu*, the Eye of Wisdom.

The *Arahant* is one who has overcome the *Tilakkhaṇa* (Three Marks) of nature. He is then free; that is to say, he controls himself from universal conditions. He is unmovable by any phenomena, since he understands himself as "the orientation character (of the game of nature)." He is free to understand the conditions of the Twelve Chains... free from the conditioned world, (having entered) the unconditioned world. The Four Noble Truths that he made an effort to follow now reside within him. Freedom corresponds with universal power. He works to overcome all attachments and thereby achieves complete freedom. He is also free from the law of *Karma*: what is done by him is beyond what is universally determined; it is neither an increase nor a decrease of good (*kusala*) or bad (*akusala*). There is no (new) cause or effect. This is "neitherness" (*abhayagrit*). He has nothing more to do according to social status.

As the Buddha uttered after he became enlightened: "*Aneka Jāti Saṁsāra...*" which translates as:

Many a House of Light hath held me seeking ever him

who wrought these prisons of the senses, sorrow-fraught;

sore was my ceaseless strife! But now, Thou builder of this

Tabernacle—Thou! I know Thee! Never Shalt Thou build again

these walls of pain, nor raise the roof-tree of deceits, nor lay

fresh rafters on the clay; broken thy house is, the ridge-pole split!

Delusion fashioned it! Safe pass I thence—

Deliverance to obtain.

(Sir Edwin Arnold, Light of Asia) 37

We should note that *Dhamma*, in brief, has two notions. The first is *Saṅkhatadhamma* (the conditioned nature; that which is created by internal and external causes depending upon each other—relativism). [38] My translation is "imperfect in nature" or "conditioned nature." In the analysis of this word, *saṁ-* is a prefix. It has many meanings, but here it means "together" or "connection." It is synonymous with the Sanskrit word *sama* (which means "even" or "in the same way") and the Pali word *samanta* (which means "all together"). *Khata* comes from the root word *kara*, which means "to perform." In Sanskrit, *kṛta* (is the past participle of *kṛ*). The author notes a grammatical rule of *ākhyāta* (declension). In Pali, it is said that *kara* can change when a prefix or suffix is added. Here we have *saṁ-* as a prefix and *-ta* as a suffix. The suffix *-ta* makes the verb *kara* (from the root *karoti*) a past participle, changing it into a noun meaning "that which is made, done, composed, or performed." These root words are combined with *dhamma* for proper use. Hence, *Saṅkhatadhamma* is here divided into two categories:

a) inanimate beings (unmovable beings): mountains, oceans, buildings, farms, etc.; and

b) animated beings (movable things): i.e., humans, animals, etc. 39

Saṅkhatadhamma regards animate beings as consisting of the five *skandhas*, viz., *rūpa* (form), *vedanā* (feeling), *saññā* (perception), *saṅkhāra* (mental formations), and *viññāṇa* (consciousness). [40]These groups of elements are real in conventional reality (*sammuti-sacca*) and are perceived by the common person (*puthujjana*), but they are not real in the absolute reality (*paramattha-sacca*), which is perceived by the *Ariyas* (Noble Ones). [41]

Who are the *Ariyas*? They are saints who fall into one of four categories, or degrees, depending on their level of enlightenment. They are: [42]

1. **1st degree - *Sotāpanna*:** "the state of entering into the stream of wisdom." The saint who has attained this cannot have more than seven births among men and angels before entering *Nirvana*. [43]
2. **2nd degree - *Sakidāgāmī*:** "he who must come back once." After attaining this degree, there will be only one more birth among men or angels before reaching *Nirvana*. [44]
3. **3rd degree - *Anāgāmī*:** "he who will not come back." There will be another birth, but not in the world of sensuality. From the heavens of the *Brahmās*, *Nirvana* will be attained. [45]
4. **4th degree - *Arahatta*:** "the venerable." This is the perfect saint who will pass to *Nirvana* without further birth. [46]

This source is from the *Siamese Pathammā Somphothiyān Katha*. [47]

Since we have seen how words can combine in Pali grammar, we can provide an English translation as follows: *Saṅkhatadhamma* is a natural state. All aspects of nature are related, or, as Western thinkers clarify, are "relatively real." The aspects of nature perform together. The elements of nature produce themselves, in regard to nature's processes, into cognition via six subjective and six objective "bases" (*āyatana*). [48] This is illustrated below:

I. Six Internal Bases (*Adhyatma-Āyatana*) [49]	II. Six External Bases (*Bāhya-Āyatana*) [50]
sense of vision (eye)	color, shape, sight
sense of audition (ear)	sound
sense of smelling (nose)	odor
sense of taste (tongue)	taste
sense of touch (body)	tangibles
faculty of the intellect (*mana*)	non-sensory objects (*dhamma*)

All of these classifications (categories one to six) function together in correspondence; i.e., color is the function of the eye. This phenomenon is represented in the function of the mind according to the five *skandhas*. The *skandhas* are regarded by the six internal bases and the six external bases. For example, if the eye perceives a good color or shape, the mind registers a good feeling (*Sukha-ārammaṇa*: produces pleasure); [51]if the eye perceives a bad color or shape, unpleasant feelings arise in the mind (*Dukkha-ārammaṇa*). [52] (Each of the internal and external bases has independent and primary authority; i.e., the eyes have the authority to see, but the nose does not. This is why Pali terms these phenomena *Indriya* (Faculty). For example, *Cakkhu-indriya* means the "Eye Faculty" or independent authority of the eye. [53]) This phenomenon occurs for the *Puthujjana* (mundane people), but not for the *Ariyas*, because their minds have gone beyond pleasure and displeasure. Therefore, they have neither *Sukha-ārammaṇa* nor *Dukkha-ārammaṇa* and are called *Abyākata* (Neutral). Hence, the internal and external bases create 64 elements (6 internal bases + 6 external bases = 12; 12 x 5 *skandhas* = 60; 60 + 4 *Mahābhūta* (great elements: fire, air, earth, water) = 64). [54]

Some authorities divide the *Saṅkhata Dhamma* into 18 classes (*dhātu*) of elements represented in the composition of an individual stream of life (*santāna*) (and) the different planes of existence. The six

Visayas (objects) are regarded in relation to the six *Indriyas* (receptive faculties), but *ārammaṇa* (objects) are attributes in regard to the six *Viññāṇas* (consciousnesses).

The second notion of *Dhamma* is *Asaṅkhatadhamma*—the independent, natural reality. (As may be noted, this second notion of *Dhamma* is the negative of the first. The prefix *a-* means "no" or "isolated.") [55]

When we start to travel, we have a will or direction of where to go, and then we have attention according to our will. The will brings us where we want to be. This is the destination of the world traveler. In the same way, Buddhists have an internal and ultimate goal, both in life and after the end of life. This goal is the result (and suppression) of the world process. Some Westerners call this "Utopia" or "absolute freedom." However, Buddhists refer to this as *Nirvana*, which is characterized by absolute calm and the destruction of all worldly conditions. Specifically, all co-origination is extinguished, replaced by immutability. All of this is the notion of *Asaṅkhatadhamma*. [56]

Therefore *Asaṅkhatadhamma*, generally speaking, is synonymous with *Nirvana*. The question, then, is: "How can one reach *Nirvana*?" In short, one must cut off desire and practice the morality and *kamma* which is called the Eightfold Noble Path. After practicing this, one experiences one's practice (of the Four Noble Truths) as insight. This aspect of practice is common to many approaches to life. It is called by Buddhists the *Cattāri Ariyasaccāni*. This system of teaching cannot be taught; each person has to realize it for himself. I will discuss this further in the next chapter.

Theravādin Buddhists find the essence of *Dhamma* in the first sermon of the Buddha, entitled "Setting in Motion of the Wheel of the Dhamma." [57] This first sermon is known as the *Dhammacakkappavattana Sutta* (Turning the Wheel of the Dhamma). In the *Dhammacakkappavattana Sutta*, the Buddha taught the Four Noble Truths: [58]

1. This is the truth of suffering. [59]

2. This is the truth of the cause (arising) of suffering. [60]

3. This is the truth of the cessation of suffering. [61]

4. This is the truth of the path which leads to the cessation of suffering. [62]

The First Noble Truth is intended to explain (describe) the existence of human nature as unsatisfactory and painful. How can one fall in love amid the uncertainty of life and in the midst of suffering? The love that we engage in and enjoy together in this world is only momentary pleasure and is unreal. The reality of life is not (always) satirical and logical; (in this sense,) love is meaningless. Since we have no power to demand that our lives be perfect or that we live together happily for the rest of our lives, and since love can be transformed into suffering—indeed, love *is* a sign of suffering because love is one of the desires (*kāma-tanhā*)—then one loves another and only becomes selfish, in the sense that "this person is mine," "I am hers or his," and so forth. If love works out well, one will be happy momentarily. But it is not real; it is only artificial and delusional. Love has to consist of sympathy and be beyond desire. One must understand that there is no way of satisfying our life, whether we love or hate. Love is only another form of suffering. The Buddha says, "*Piyato jāyate soko*" [63]—"From affection, grief is born." Hence, the First Noble Truth describes the nature of life. Basically, life is painful, unsatisfactory, and often-ridden with uncertainty. This life is naturally and logically subject to suffering:

"This is the Noble Truth of *Dukkha*: birth is *Dukkha*; decay and old age is *Dukkha*; disease is *Dukkha*; death is *Dukkha*; association with what is unpleasant is *Dukkha*; separation from what is pleasant is *Dukkha*; failure to obtain what one wants is *Dukkha*. Briefly stated, the five groups of physical and mental processes that make up the individual (which are due to grasping and are the objects of grasping) (are *Dukkha*). These five groups of grasping are known as *Dukkha*." [64]

This teaching aims to help people become aware of their own experiences, so they may give up attachment to the delusions of life—that is, to understand the impermanence of life and its processes as they truly are. Humans should experience and enlighten themselves, rather than ignore their condition, and realize the nature of life, thereby avoiding fear and insecurity. Finally, they will feel free here on earth. The Legend of the Four Signs reveals, in simple form, the Buddha's realization that all beings and things are transitory (*anicca*). All beings are born, must grow, grow old, become ill, and die.

We find that some schools of Buddhism have different ideas regarding the interpretation of the Four Noble Truths. As Th. Stcherbatsky says:

"In any comparative study of them, they should be understood according to the context of their school system. For example, the Theravāda method of *Magga-Sacca* is intended for the Theravāda conception of *Nirodha-Sacca*, which is pertinent to the Theravāda notion of *Samudaya-Sacca*. Similarly, the Sarvāstivāda, Madhyamika, and Yogācāra views of *Marga* (Path) and *Nirodha* (Cessation) relate to their specific views of *Samudaya* (Cause) and *Dukkha* (Suffering)." [65]

The fundamental doctrine of Buddhism falls into three categories: impermanence (*Anicca*), suffering/imperfection (*Dukkha*), and no-self (*Anattā*). This *Dhamma* (doctrine) encompasses both animate and inanimate objects, as already mentioned. However, each school views this doctrine differently:

- **All *Dhamma* is real.** It does not change from one period to another, or from the past and future, but exists momentarily in the present. This is held by the *Sarvāstivādin* School.
- **All *Dhamma* is empty (*Śūnyatā*).** What we perceive is only the relational, natural reality, which is (conventionally) real. This view is held by the *Madhyamaka* school.
- ***Dhamma* is nothing but the creation of our mind (*Vijñaptimātratā*).** This is held by the *Yogācāra* school.

The theory of *Dhamma*, as defined by Th. Stcherbatsky, interests me. Here I will present his definition:

"The conception of *Dhamma* is the central point of the Buddhist doctrine. In the light of this conception, Buddhism discloses itself as a metaphysical theory developed out of a fundamental... principle, viz., the idea that there exists an interplay of a plurality of subtle, ultimate, and not further analyzable elements of matter, mind, and forces... the final result of the world-process is its suppression, absolute calm: all co-operation is extinct and replaced by immutability." [66]

We can see, according to the quotation above, that *Dhamma* is characterized by: a) conventional use, and b) its ultimate, absolute reality (*Nirvana*), which is super-mundane.

Fundamentally, we can compare the Theravādin and *Yogācārin* notion of *Dharma* as being the same, since they both believe in the same textual content and hold the same belief that there is nothing in *Dhamma* but the structure of our mind. In the verse which was considered sufficiently important to be placed at the beginning of the *Dhammapada*, all *dhammas* are said to be dominated, governed, and created by mind.

We should also be aware that most Buddhist scholars describe the *dhammas* as *Saṅkhatadhamma* (relative reality or *Saṅkhāra*) and *Asaṅkhatadhamma* (independent reality or *Nirvana*). [67] Broadly speaking, the common man who holds theories and ignores the practical part might describe *dhammas* as being in three parts to make their theory look quantitatively better; they do not know the quality of Buddhist *Dhamma*. Hence, by *quality* (of the *Dhammic* practitioner), *Dhamma* is divided into the categories previously mentioned. By *quantity*, *Dhamma* is divided into three categories, viz., the five *skandhas*, the 12 sense fields, and the 18 elements. At any rate, these three categories fall into the two main categories. The (apparent) contradiction of this system is that *Saṅkhatadhamma* and *Asaṅkhatadhamma* are measurements of the five *skandhas*, etc., in regard to the degree reached by the *Dhammic* practitioner.

For example, a *Puthujjana* is "still-becoming" *Saṅkhatadhamma*. In the same way, if he works his way up to the path of an *Ariya*, he becomes an *Ariya*; he is then on the *Asaṅkhatadhamma* level. Thus, in *Saṅkhatadhamma* and *Asaṅkhatadhamma*, the five *skandhas* are interrelated. The *Parinibbāna Sutta* describes that the Enlightened One still maintains his life (*khandhas*) on earth; he is both *Saṅkhatadhamma* and *Asaṅkhatadhamma* (*Sopādisesa-Nibbāna*). [68]He who passes away from this world with his enlightenment is *Asaṅkhatadhamma* (*Anupādisesa-Nibbāna*). [69]

Buddhaghosa describes the *Dhamma* of the five *skandhas*. The *skandhas* (heaps or groups) are the five constituents of the personality as it appears. On analysis, all the facts of experience—of ourselves and of objects in relation to us—can be stated in terms of the *skandhas*. The purpose of the analysis is to do away with the nebulous word "I." The *skandhas* "define the limit of the basis of grasping after a self, and what belongs to self." [70] The doctrine of the five *skandhas* is considered the metaphysics of man. Man generally believes that there is a "self" or "ego," as was taught by the Hindus before the Buddha. They grasped, with ignorance, that size, shape, color—i.e., of hair, eyebrows, noses, hands, legs, etc.—are "self" and belong to them. The Buddha taught that one should give up attachment to the five *skandhas* by appealing to the reason that *Anicca*, *Dukkha*, and *Anattā* are inherent in the five *skandhas*. [71] Why are we deluded by this? We use the body while we have life within it. But just as we rent a house or a car, the *skandhas* are not within our power; they come and go as they are. They do not belong to us. The best way for us is to live our lives *with* the five *skandhas* without either affirming or denying them. We must accept that we are here while we are here—there is little we can do except reason. This is why this teaching of the Buddha is called the Middle Path (not affirming or denying life). Our life appears as the momentariness of the five *skandhas*. We should not fall into a state in which we grasp them as the "self" just because they are united. In the philosophical sense, the Buddha, of course, denied the existence of a "soul" or "personal individuality" that survives death. He set up his doctrine to teach man's nature. Man is nothing but an aggregate of the five *skandhas*: form, sensation, perception, predisposition (mental formations), and consciousness.

The five *skandhas* give rise to (the view of) the *Puthujjanas* (common people) as being permanent and real, but to *Arahants* they are impermanent and illusory. It is easy to get the impression that there is form, soul, and self, but our death proves that this is illusory and "no-self." As soon as we discover this by our experience, we find that it is like the candle and the flame: they both are unreal as soon as they go out. To follow what has left us is *karma*, and *karma* causes us to enter the cycle again and again through the process of delusion. Hence, the five *skandhas* fall into the three fundamental principles of truth: *Anicca*, *Dukkha*, and *Anattā*.

It is difficult for the common man to understand the threefold sight (the *Tilakkhaṇa*) of the five *skandhas*. Only the *Arahant* understands. As the Buddha states to his followers:

"Those who are not yet enlightened (have errors) have the delusion of permanence where it is impermanent; (the delusion of) happiness where it is suffering; (the delusion of) self where there is no self; and (the delusion of) wholesomeness (where there is unwholesomeness). They hold false views. Such as these do not reach *Nirvana* but are tied up in the bonds of the devil (*Māra*) and return to the cycle of life full of birth, decay, and death." [72]

According to this *gāthā*, we can see clearly that the world of our existence is full of delusion and suffering; nothing can be controlled, only realized. One must first realize that everything changes—in the beginning, middle, and end—from one form to another, from one time to another, from one space to another. There is no permanence to our existence in all of this phenomenon. You might call it "coming and going," just like the wave of the sea or the foam of the water, which has organized itself through its natural processes without any meaning or purpose. It just appears as the form of foam at the momentary present that we perceive. Soon the sun will come and dissipate it. There is no longer such a thing as the form of foam that we perceived. Coming and going—happening (*uppāda*) and destroying (*nirujjhati*)—are the ways of nature (*Dhammatā*). [73] This is the case with form. It is analogous to the existence of the *skandhas*, which are always characterized by *Anicca*, *Dukkha*, and *Anattā*. There are no exceptions. As long as we realize the way things are (*Dhammatā*), we can reason and experience that they deceive (delude) us. They do not help us. We are in the middle of their way: neither affirming nor denying, just accepting things the way they are and the way they are not. This is called *Dhammatā*.

I would like to quote Th. Stcherbatsky's statement which relates to my description of the *Dhammic* notion:

"These elements are technically called *Dhammas*—a meaning which this word has in this system alone. Buddhism, accordingly, can be characterized as a system of radical pluralism (*Sanghatavāda*): the elements alone are realities. Every combination of them is merely a name covering a plurality of separate elements. The moral teaching... path toward Final Deliverance... is not something additional or extraneous to this ontological doctrine; it is most intimately connected with it and, in fact, is identical with it." [74]

Actually, *Dhamma* means *Dhrong*. *Dhar* (Sanskrit root *Dhṛ*) is the root of this word and means *Dhrong* (pronounced as in "song"), which means "to stay by itself" or "to be supported by itself," that is, to exist independently, to be a substance. Therefore, *Dhamma* means everything without exception: from the finest speck of dust that has no material value and is changeable, to abstract things, meaning spirit, thought, feelings, even acts or *karma*, including the acquisition of *Nirvana*. All these are called *Dhamma*. It can thus be said that *Dhamma* means "everything" if we take *Dharma* in its literal sense. [75]Obviously, "the word" is none other than *Dhamma* in the sense of Natural Laws, or what is known in Buddhism as the Truth (*Sacca-Dhamma*). [76] In Buddhism, what forms the essence of everything is termed *Dhamma*... there is no word better than that. Etymologists might examine the roots of the word "spirit" in Latin and Greek, so that the Thai version can be more accurately produced, both literally and meaningfully. [77]

In brief, one has realized what life is, according to practicing *Sīla*, *Samādhi*, *Paññā*, and *Vimutti* (viz., right view, right speech, etc.). That way of practicing leads one to the Middle Path "which giveth vision, which giveth knowledge, which... leadeth to enlightenment, *Nirvana*." [78] Thus, he is free from attachment to the five *skandhas* through the experience of the three sights (*Tilakkhaṇa*). He is no longer caught up in the power of delusion or the worldly conditions (good, bad, happiness, sadness, etc.). At the same time, he is free from the power of desire and delusion, or co-originating causes; he cuts off his life cycle. He is free both from "he is" and "he is not." He is ready for "he will be" and "he will not be" according to his own experience, rather than being taught.

Religious experience is absolute. It is indisputable. No matter what the world thinks about religious experience, the one who has it possesses the great treasure of that which has provided him with a source of life, meaning, and beauty, and that which has given a new splendor to the world and to mankind. The opening of *Satori* is the remaking of life itself.

*** Jung, C.G., Psychology and Religion, pp. 1,3.**

***"Dr. Suzuki, Essay in Zen Buddhism, I.P. 217**

REFERENCE NOTES

1. *Dhammapada. Bangkok: Mahamakut University, 1962, p. 85.*
2. *Dīgha Nikāya. PTS. Vol. III, p. 219. Cf. the word "Cakkhumant."*
3. *Visuddhimagga. PTS. Vol. XVIII, p. 517.*
4. *Majjhima Nikāya. PTS. 1887-1902. Vol. I, p. 356 and Vol. II, p. 95. Cf. D. II, p. 156 (sādhu hoti saddhati Tathāgatassa bodhiṁ).*
5. *Dhammacakkhu (n.) - "the eyes of wisdom," the eyes (or vision) of the Truth. Skt. Dharma-cakṣus. (From Suadmontra Plakhongkou and Buddhapavati). Vol. I, p. 65. Cf. D. I. 86, 110; Vol. II. 280; S. LV., 48; A. LV., 186; Vin. I, p. 16, 40, etc. Expl. DA. 1, 237.*
6. *Pañca-khandhā (five aggregates), viz: rūpa (form), vedanā (feeling), saññā (perception), saṅkhāra (mental formations), and viññāṇa (consciousness). (Form is the physical or material side of things... Feelings are pleasant, unpleasant, or neutral. Perception: six, corresponding to the six sense organs. Impulses (formations): active dispositions, tendencies, strivings, emotions (love, hate, etc.), both consciously and unconsciously. Consciousness: the most important and elusive category of the five skandhas. Sometimes it is referred to as the "soul" in a Buddhist sense.)*
7. *Sopādisesa-Nibbāna*
8. *Anupādisesa-Nibbāna*
9. *Tisikkhā (Threefold Training), viz: sīla (morality), samādhi (concentration), and paññā (wisdom).*
10. *Synonymous terms for the path are Ekayāna Magga, Visuddhi Magga, Majjhimā Paṭipadā, Ariya Magga, Bodhi, Sambodhi. Generally, it is called the Noble Eightfold Path, a path of Moral Development, viz.: Right View (Sammā Diṭṭhi), Right Aspiration (Sammā Saṅkappa), Right Speech (Sammā Vācā), Right Action (Sammā Kammanta), Right Livelihood (Sammā Ājīva), Right Effort (Sammā Vāyāma), Right Mindfulness (Sammā Sati), Right Concentration (Sammā Samādhi).*

11. *Vaṇṇa (Casteism), viz.: Khattiya (king/warrior), Brāhmaṇa (spiritual leader), Vessa (trader), Sudda (working class or slaves).*
12. *Muller, Max. The Sacred Books of the East. Vol. XL, p. 107.*
13. *Ibid., p. 107.*
14. *All novices and monks in Thailand are given the first Establishment of Mindfulness by the Preceptor (Upajjhāya) directly after ordination (upasampadā). Thai Buddhists call this Taca-Pañcaka-Kammaṭṭhāna—meditation on the five parts of the body (hair, body hair, nails, teeth, skin) to perceive whether they are Anicca, Dukkha, or Anattā. Cf. Rhys Davids, Buddhism, pp. 169-171. Also see Alabaster, Henry, The Wheel of the Law: Buddhism, p. sliv and p. 206.*
15. *Mahāsatipaṭṭhāna Suttanta, p. 327.*
16. *Stcherbatsky, Th. The Conception of Buddhist Nirvana, p. 31, n. 1.*
17. *Abhidharmakośa by Vasubandhu. L. de Lallée-Pousin, L'Abhidharmakośa de Vasubandhu, trd. ed annote LX 221.*
18. *Ibid., p. 253.*
19. *Gāthā Dhammapada (in Thai scripture), verse 96, p. 26.*
20. *My translation.*
21. *Sutta Nipāta Commentary. PTS. 1916-1917, p. 151. Also, cf. Khuddaka-Pāṭha Commentary (KhA). PTS. 1915, p. 209.*
22. *Cf. Alabaster, Henry. The Wheel of the Law: Buddhism, p. 171.*
23. *Āyatana - sense organ and sense-object.*
24. *Adhyatma-Āyatana (Internal Sense Bases), viz: Cakkhu-āyatana (Eye-base), Sota-āyatana (Ear-base), Ghāna-āyatana (Nose-base), Jivhā-āyatana (Tongue-base), Kāya-āyatana (Body-base), Mana-āyatana (Mind-base).*
25. *Bāhya-Āyatana (External Sense Bases). Sometimes called Visaya (Sense Objects), viz: Rūpa-āyatana (Form-base), Sadda-āyatana (Sound-base), Gandha-āyatana (Odor-base), Rasa-āyatana (Taste-base), Phoṭṭhabba-āyatana (Tactile-base), and Dhamma-āyatana (Mental-object-base).*

26. *In "The Wheel of the Law" (Dhammacakkappavattana Sutta), the Buddha taught two absolute laws: the following of the Middle Way and the understanding of the Four Noble Truths. He first taught this after his enlightenment to the Pañcavaggiyā (group of five monks): Kondañña, Vappa, Bhaddiya, Mahānāma, and Assaji. He claimed this Sutta as the highest enlightenment. (Samyutta Nikāya 56.11, Thai Description).*
27. *Dukkha-Ariyasacca (Noble Truth of Suffering), Dukkha-Samudaya-Ariyasacca (Noble Truth of the Origin of Suffering), Dukkha-Nirodha-Ariyasacca (Noble Truth of the Cessation of Suffering), and Dukkha-Nirodhagāminī-Paṭipadā-Ariyasacca (Noble Truth of the Path Leading to the Cessation of Suffering).*
28. *Dhamma Subhasit (Thai Beginner Dhamma in Thai Pali scripture, my translation).*
29. *Nyanasatta, Thera C. Basic Tenets of Buddhism. Rojagiriya, Ceylon: Ananda Semage, 1957, p. 40.*
30. *The main collection of Jātakas includes 550 stories. Many additions have been made by people in Ceylon and the mainland of Southeast Asia, including Thailand. The Jātakas were adopted as custom and folklore. The Thais, for instance, adopted the Vessantara Jātaka, one of the great stories of the Buddha, as their national story and folklore. They call it Mahājati Khamluang.*
31. *Stcherbatsky, Th. "The Central Conception of Buddhism and the Meaning of the Word 'Dhammo'." London: Royal Asiatic Society, pp. 73ff.*
32. *Ibid., p. 73 ff.*
33. *Muller, op. cit., p. 107.*
34. *My translation from the Vipallāsa Sutta in the Aṅguttara Nikāya. This is a Gāthā: Anicce nicca-saññino, dukkhe ca sukha-saññino, Anattani ca atta'ti, asubhe subha-saññino; Micchādiṭṭhigatā sattā, khitta-cittā visaññino. Te yogayuttā mārassa, ayogakkhemino janā; Sattā gacchanti saṁsāraṁ, jāti-maraṇa-gāmino.*
35. *Stcherbatsky, Th., op. cit., pp. 73 ff.*

36. *The Venerable Bhikkhu Buddhadasa Indapanno. Dhamma the World Saviour. Buddhist University Press, pp. 2-3.*

37. *Buddhadasa Bhikkhu. Christianity and Buddhism, p. 108.*

CHAPTER II

The Second Principle Of The Four Noble Truths—The Nature Of Causation (Samudaya-Sacca)

The teaching of Gautama Buddha in the Second Principle of the Four Noble Truths is for man to realize his own nature. This is the rediscovery of the solution to the First Noble Truth: that there must be a cause of suffering, since the existence of nature is, itself, suffering. This is the imperfection of man's natural condition. Hence, the Second Principle of this doctrine raises a more crucial question.

Even in the West, Hume and his followers emphasize the causal relation of the nature of man. Hume, however, never paid attention to *what* was happening, as he found that question obvious and unnecessary. *How* things come to happen was a more interesting question to him. I will address this problem in a later discussion. Here, I am stressing that the teachings of the Buddha and Hume are incidentally similar because the Buddha, like Hume, was a radical empiricist. He attempted to control human nature by understanding what was happening. Merely knowing that the existence of man *is* suffering is not enough for the Buddhist. *What is the cause* of suffering is more important to know, in order to control or master himself and nature, and to find the ultimate goal of his life. Man has to learn how to control events in order to achieve freedom, which is called "freedom to *Nirvana*."

Thus, the Second Principle of this doctrine illustrates how and why suffering arises. All compounded things are threefold: *anicca* (impermanent), *dukkha* (suffering), and *anattā* (no-self). This phenomenon implies that life is imperfect and unsatisfactory, since it is transient and lacking a self.

Buddhism presents the viewpoint that life is a process, continuing as a phenomenon with no discernible beginning and no end. This is called *samsara*. Knowing that *samsara* is the conditioned world, Buddhists try to control it by rediscovering the nature of causation and suffering. In a *gāthā* it is said:

Ye dhammā hetuppabhavā, tesaṁ hetuṁ tathāgato āha;

Tesañca yo nirodho, evaṁvādī mahāsamaṇo.

(The *Tathāgata*, who is peaceful, has always taught that all phenomena arise from a cause. He further taught the cessation of that cause. This is the doctrine of the Great Ascetic.)

According to the above *gāthā*, we can remark that the Buddha always realizes for himself and teaches others that all phenomena must have a cause; nothing is able to happen (exist) without a cause. Thus, the concept of cause (*hetu*) is significant for Buddhist teaching. Buddhists do not believe in chance.

What is the cause of suffering? Buddhism answers that it is co-dependent origination. For example, delusion causes *kamma* (action), which produces in man a different identity (*kammam satte vibhajati*, "action distinguishes beings"). *Kamma* creates mankind. Then the question arises: Why do we have *kamma*? We have *kamma* because we have desire (*tanhā*). Hence, desire is the cause of suffering. Buddhists believe that in order to make life perfect and happy, they have to remove suffering (*nirodha*).

This is why I mentioned earlier that a Buddhist attempts to struggle against the nature of man and tries to control his own events in order to master nature. He controls nature by his ability to destroy suffering according to the Second Principle of the Four Noble Truths. If he can do this, he overcomes the force of nature (*samsara*) and achieves the freedom of life that is *Nirvana*. Life will be meaningful, and he can live beyond fear and suffering, since he has stopped his suffering. Hence, he learns to live and make himself free from all conditions of the world. He no longer separates happiness from suffering. He makes the transitory state of life permanent and imperfection perfect.

We live day by day; the more we live, the more experience we gain. It is not difficult for us to discover the truth of suffering as long as we experience living. What we actually discover is that all beings are born, grow, decay, and die: this is *anicca*. Life is unsatisfactory: this is *dukkha*. Life is *becoming* rather than *being*: this is *anattā* (no-soul, no-self). Life has no self-reliance, no continuity of unchangeable happiness, "I-ness," or "my-ness." How could there be such a term if there is no self? "The 'self' is that which appropriates and owns. This function is simply denied... owning and belonging are dismissed as categories invented by people swayed by craving and ignorance, who superimpose their own imaginations on the real facts as they exist."[1]

"I-ness" and "my-ness" are "becoming" from the purity of their own elements (*mahābhūta-rūpa*—earth, water, air, fire), which are known as the five *skandhas*. Because of this, each man has his own individual *skandhas*. The result gives rise to man's deluding himself that there is such a thing as "I-ness" which exists. What are the five *skandhas*? They are phenomena. Each man is a constantly changing conglomerate—from one moment to the next—of sensations, perceptions, mental formations, and consciousness. Hence, there is no such thing as (permanent) form. There is only momentary gross physical form with sense functions (sight, sound, etc.). This appears to us as momentary phenomena. Nothing is (permanently) real. Things come and go as they truly are. They neither belong to us nor are they (independent) of themselves. And so it is with perception.

If one has the delusion or notion that there is an "I" because of his attachment, he will suffer when he discovers that it is transitory and imperfect. This is why the Buddhist doctrine teaches us the truth of suffering.

Having mentioned earlier that the cause of suffering is desire (*tanhā*), as described in the Second Principle:

This is the Noble Truth of the origin of dukkha:

It is this craving (tanhā) that leads to ever-fresh and repeated rebirth. It is connected with delight and pleasure, finding now here, now there, its objects of enjoyment, namely: 1) craving for sense pleasure (kāma-tanhā), 2) craving for self-continued becoming/existence (bhava-tanhā), and 3) craving for self-annihilation after death (vibhava-tanhā).[2]

It is quite evident, according to the above passage, that *tanhā* is the cause of, or the data of, suffering. Hence, if one wants to be free from *samsara* and reach complete freedom—not only "freedom from" but also "freedom to" (I will discuss freedom later)—one has to cut off *tanhā*. One must have the ability to control oneself over the natural forces of being reborn, decaying, and dying. Immediately upon obtaining *Nirvana*, one goes beyond that state, because one realizes that being born, decaying, and dying are not (ultimately) real, but are only states of mind.

Tanhā literally means "thirst." Thirst for what? For the sensual, material world—namely, the human world and the animal world. Because of desire, man cannot see "I-ness" as "no-ness." Thus, desire is the central "I-creator." The "I-creator" is produced by attachment, and attachment produces a sensual fetter of what one wants and what one does not want. "This is analogous to the thirst of a thoughtless man... he grows like a creeper; he runs from life to life, like a monkey seeking fruit in the forest."[3]

Furthermore, desire causes man to be occupied by a natural fire, which continually burns with its power of sensuality.

"Everything, brethren, is on fire. How, brethren, is everything on fire? The eye, brethren, is on fire; visible objects are on fire; the faculty of the eye is on fire; the sense of the eye is on fire; and also the sensation, whether pleasant or unpleasant or neutral, which arises from the sense of sight, is on fire. With what is it on fire? With the fire of passion (*rāga*), of hate (*dosa*), of illusion (*moha*), is it on fire;

with birth, old age, death, grief, lamentation, suffering, sorrow, and despair, thus I declare. The ear is on fire; sounds are on fire... The nose is on fire; scents are on fire... The faculty of the mind is on fire."[4]

In this passage, the Buddha teaches that life is full of suffering and that suffering is caused by the external and internal senses (*āyatana*). These causes create the burning of mental and physical phenomena. These (fires) are called *rāga* (passion), *dosa* (greed/hate), and *moha* (self-deception/delusion). These three aspects of delusion become the major powerful discharges (*āsava*, outflows) which tie man to the world's never-ending cycle.

The condition of man in *Samsara* is called the "Twelvefold Chain of Causation." Man has to strive for cessation. That is, he has to practice the Eightfold Noble Path until he reaches *Arahantship* (the state of an enlightened being). Otherwise, he continues in the cycle with no beginning and no end.

What is the cycle of life? We should look at the comments that follow.

Saṁyojana, "The Chain of Interdependent Origination" or "Continued Co-production," applies to the rebirth and evolution of man:

Ignorance (Avijjā) $\to$ Kamma Formations (Saṅkhāra) $\to$ Consciousness (Viññāṇa) $\to$ Mind and Body (Name and Form, Nāma-Rūpa) $\to$ Six Sense Fields (Saḷāyatana) $\to$ Impression/ Contact (Phassa) $\to$ Feeling (Sensation, Vedanā) $\to$ Craving (Desire or Thirst, Taṇhā) $\to$ Grasping (Upādāna) $\to$ Existence (Becoming, Bhava) $\to$ Birth (Jāti) $\to$ Old Age and Death (Jarā-maraṇa).

- **Ignorance:** Not knowing; the creation of erroneous knowledge and false views; not seeing things as they are. That is, not knowing in regard to suffering, its origin, its stopping, and the course leading to its stopping.

- **Kamma Formations:** Formations of body, speech, and thought. The result of these three actions determines why we are here right now.
- **Consciousness:** The first moment of the new life (present), and consciousness due to visual, olfactory, auditory, gustatory, tactile, and mental phenomena.
- **Mind and Body:** Material existence (form, body, four elements) and mental existence (feeling, perception, volition, and wise attention).
- **Six Sense Fields (Present life):** The fields of the eye, ear, nose, tongue, body, and mind.
- **Impression (Contact):** Contact due to the eye, ear, nose, tongue, body, and mind.
- **Feeling (Sensation):** Feeling due to the eye, ear, nose, tongue, body, and mind. There are three types: pleasant, unpleasant, and neutral.
- **Craving (Desire or Thirst) / Grasping:** Grasping and attachment; the beginning of new *kamma* formations.
- **Existence (Becoming):** Actions.
- **Birth / Old age / Death (Future life).**

Greed, Hatred, and Delusion

- **Greed:** Human beings kill, steal, become jealous, etc., because of their greed for things or ideas.
- **Hatred:** Human beings kill, become jealous or envious, etc., because of their hatred for things or ideas.
- **Delusion:** Human beings have greed and hatred because of their delusion. In their delusion, they think that they are happy when they are suffering or causing others to suffer.

REFERENCE NOTES

Here is the corrected list of references:

1. *Conze, Edward. Buddhist Thought in India. p. 103.*
2. *Nyanasatta, Thera C. Basic Tenets of Buddhism. Rajagiriya, Ceylon: Ananda Semage, 1957, p. 40.*
3. *Dhammapada. p. 90.*
4. *Thomas, Edward Joseph. Buddhist Scriptures. London: John Murray, 1913, pp. 54-55.*

CHAPTER III

The Gradual Development Of The Second Principle: The Nature Of Causation

The Chain of Interdependent Origination" (*Paṭiccasamuppāda*), or "continued co-production," applies to the rebirth and evolution of man.

Ignorance (*Avijjā*) $\to$ *Kamma* Formations (*Saṅkhāra*) $\to$ Consciousness (*Viññāṇa*) $\to$ Mind and Body (*Nāma-Rūpa*) $\to$ Six Sense Fields (*Saḷāyatana*) $\to$ Contact (*Phassa*) $\to$ Feeling (*Vedanā*) $\to$ Craving (*Taṇhā*) $\to$ Grasping (*Upādāna*) $\to$ Becoming (*Bhava*) $\to$ Birth (*Jāti*) $\to$ Old Age and Death (*Jarā-maraṇa*).

1. **Ignorance (*Avijjā*):** Not knowing; the creation of erroneous knowledge and false views; not seeing things as they really are. That is, not knowing in regard to suffering, its origination, its stopping, and the course leading to its stopping.

2. **Karma Formations (*Saṅkhāra*):** Formations of physical action, verbal action, and mental action. The result of these three actions determines why we are here at this moment.

3. **Consciousness (*Viññāṇa*):** The first moment of the new life (present). Consciousness is also due to visual, olfactory, auditory, gustatory, tactile, and mental phenomena.

4. **Mind and Body (*Nāma-Rūpa*):** Material existence (form, body, four elements) and mental existence (feeling, perception, volition, and wise attention).

5. **Six Sense Fields (*Saḷāyatana*):** The fields of the eye, ear, nose, tongue, body, and mind.

6. **Impression (Contact, *Phassa*):** Contact due to the eye, ear, nose, tongue, body, and mind.

7. **Feeling (*Vedanā*):** Feeling due to the eye, ear, nose, tongue, body, and mind. There are three types: pleasant, unpleasant, and neutral.

8. **Craving (*Taṇhā*):** Desire or thirst.

9. **Grasping (*Upādāna*):** Grasping; attachment; the beginning of new *kamma* formation.

10. **Becoming (*Bhava*):** Existence; action.

11. **Birth (*Jāti*)**

12. **Old Age and Death (*Jarā-maraṇa*)**

The following is a diagram of the Twelvefold Chain of Gautama Buddha, as translated by Rhys Davids. Please compare it with the list provided above.

The Wheel of Becoming (Bhava-Cakka)[2]

Illustrating the Formula of Dependent Origination (Paṭiccasamuppāda)

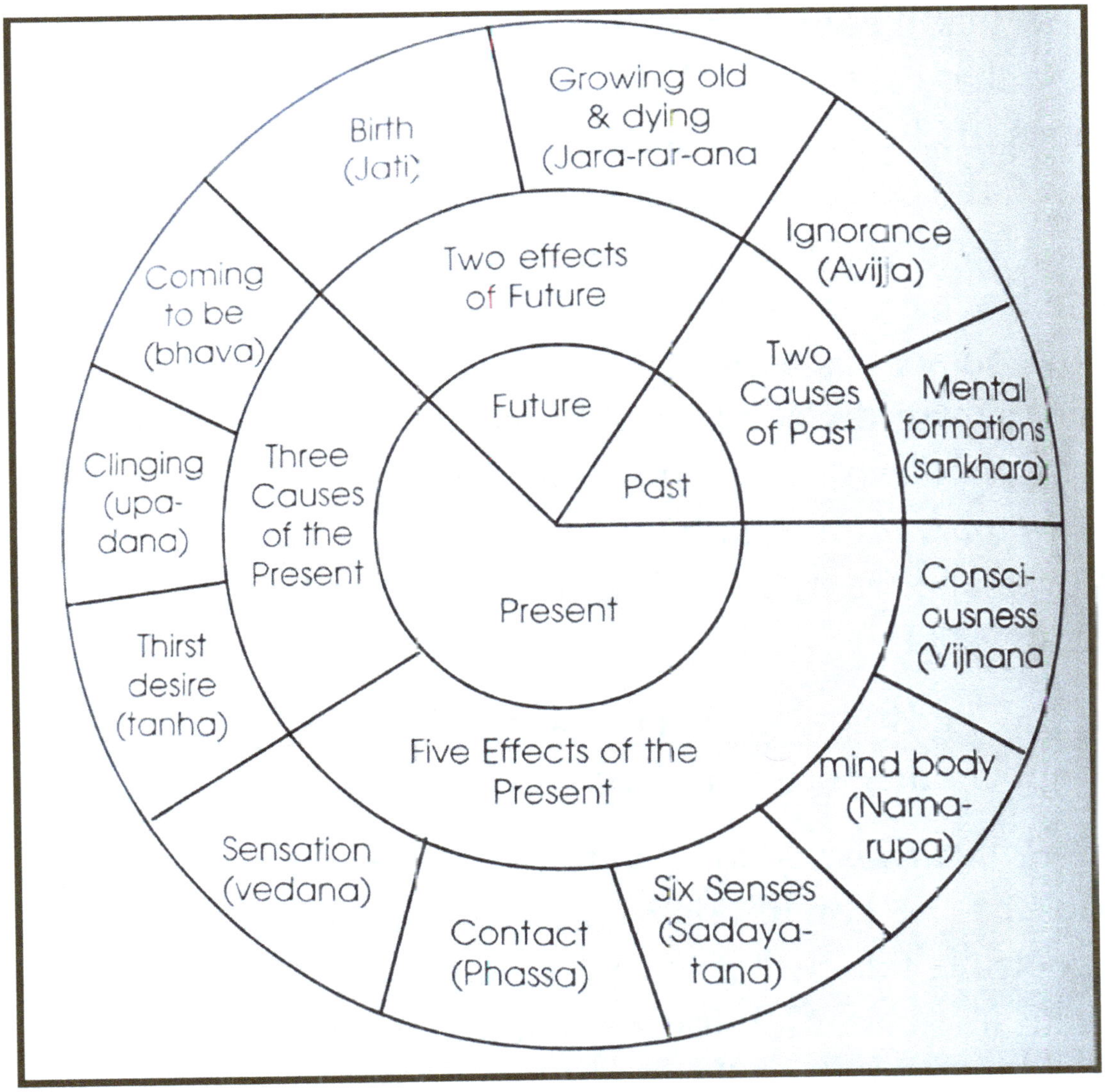

Both diagrams are self-explanatory. Both illustrations of Dependent Origination are the same in content but different in organization, especially in the division of the three consecutive existences: past, present, and future. The illustrations are, I believe, clear and easy to understand.

"In this respect," the Buddha says, "one may rightly say of me: that I teach annihilation, that I propound my doctrine for the purpose of annihilation, and that I herein train my disciples; for certainly, I do teach annihilation—namely, the annihilation of greed, anger, and delusion, as well as of the manifold evil and unwholesome things."[3]

Truly, if one holds the view that the vital principle (*Jīva*, or soul) is identical with this body, a holy life is not possible; and if one holds the view that the vital principle is something quite different from the body, in that case also, a holy life is not possible. Both of these two extremes the Perfect One has avoided, and He has shown the Middle Doctrine: the Dependent Origination (*Paṭiccasamuppāda*), illustrated above. Therefore, one who follows the *Paṭiccasamuppāda* holds the Middle Doctrine as his real Venerable Path (the highest, purest path). (He, of course, has overcome the whole mass of suffering;[4] he goes beyond the worldly condition.) He is then free. Free from what? From suffering (*dukkha*). Since he is free, he also reaches *Nirvana*. This I call *Arahantship*, or Sainthood, or "life in God," or the Noble Truth. Whatever one wants to call it, it means freedom from the origin of suffering.

No god, no Brahman, can be called The maker of this wheel of life: Empty phenomena roll on, Dependent on Conditions all.[5]

The *Paṭiccasamuppāda* (literally, "Dependent Origination") is the doctrine of the conditionality of physical and mental phenomena. This doctrine, together with that of impersonality (*anattā*), forms the indispensable condition for the real understanding and realization of the Buddha's teachings. It shows that the various physical and mental life-processes—conventionally called "personal," "animal," etc.—are not merely a play of blind chance but the outcome of causes and conditions. Above all, the *Paṭiccasamuppāda* explains how the arising of rebirth and suffering is dependent upon conditions; and, in its second part, it shows how, through the removal of these conditions, suffering must disappear. Hence, the *Paṭiccasamuppāda* serves to elucidate the Second and Third Noble Truths by explaining them from their very foundations upward and giving them a fixed philosophical form.[6]

When discussing Buddhist philosophy, one must agree that the *Paṭiccasamuppāda* is a crucial doctrine in solving the problem of life, as Nyanatiloka has mentioned.

Let us now consider "sensuality." What is sensuality? Sensuality is *tanhā* (craving), which is the main ground of craving—"that craving which leads to continuation of rebirth."

According to the Twelvefold Chain, the first and second link members, ignorance (*avijjā*) and *kamma* formations (*saṅkhāra*), are the preconditions of the third link member. Hence, the third link member, consciousness (*viññāṇa*), is the effect of the previous two (see diagram). Thus, the third member is the first locus of perceiving the new life that has emerged momentarily. This third link member has been given different translations (from the terms *Upapatti* or *Jāti*), including "rebirth," "consciousness," and the "I-maker." From a philosophical standpoint, these are (sometimes used as) synonymous terms in the English language, (though) there is also a distinction between "consciousness" and the "I-maker." I would like to express my interpretation of the terms *Upapatti* and *Jāti*. Both relate to consciousness. Consciousness cannot be consciousness *of* itself. Consequently, consciousness is always consciousness *of* something. In this context, it becomes consciousness *of* "I-ness." Therefore, when we have consciousness constantly, an idea arises, and that idea is the idea of "I-ness." The idea of "I-ness" comes to mind *because* of consciousness. Suppose there is no "consciousness." Then there is no "I-ness," no *animus*—nothing which can exist in our mind.

"The qualities (of things) come into existence after the mind (lit. 'the qualities have mind as their precursor'); they are dependent upon mind and are made up (formed) of mind. If a man speaks or acts with an evil thought (mind), sorrow pursues him as the wheel follows the foot of the draught-ox."[7]

Manopubbaṅgamā dhammā, manoseṭṭhā manomayā; Manasā ce paduṭṭhena, bhāsati vā karoti vā; Tato naṁ dukkhamanveti, cakkaṁ 'va vahato padaṁ.

As my teacher explains:

"In *Dhamma* language, the word 'birth' refers to the birth of the idea of 'I' or 'me,' any time it arises in the mind from day to day. In this sense, the ordinary person is born very often, time and time again. A more developed person is born less frequently; a person well advanced in practice (*Ariya-puggala*) is born less frequently still, and ultimately ceases being reborn altogether. Each arising in the mind of the idea of 'I' in one form or another is called a 'birth.' ... When the Buddha was speaking, if he was expounding Higher *Dhamma*, he wasn't talking about physical birth... He was talking about the birth of the obsessive idea of 'me' and 'mine,' 'myself' and 'my own.' ... In *Dhamma* language, the word 'death' refers to the cessation of the idea of 'I' or 'me.'...

There is no birth, and therefore, there is also no death. This state is the unconditioned. It is what we call *Nirvana*, and what, in other religions, is often referred to as the 'life everlasting.'"[8]

Essentially, sensuality arises from delusion. It should be accepted that delusion occupies the mind. In addition, sensuality is a *karmic* act that requires physical action. Nonetheless, the psychological distinction and relationship of physical acts are the outward expression of a thought which seals the commitment of good or bad deeds. The result of these deeds returns to the faculty of the mind. Then the mind will move from its essential and natural being to mix with all *karma*.

What is *kamma* in the sexual context? *Kamma* in the sexual context is described in the *Samyutta Nikāya* and the *Aṅguttara Nikāya*. The third precept of Buddhism, *Kāmesumicchācārā veramaṇī...* ("abstaining from sexual misconduct") is called self-control in regard to the most powerful and delightful of human instincts: sex. The Buddha said, "Of all the lusts and desires, there is none so powerful as sexual inclination." Buddhists regard women in four positions: Is she old? Regard her as your mother. Is she honorable? Regard her as your sister. Is she of small account? Regard her as a younger sister. Is she a child? Treat her reverently with politeness.[9]

The sex of the physical body is a matter of *karmic* result, and sexual desire is a carnal appetite, as natural in its proper sphere as food. Both women and men may attain the highest goal of life. The best example of this is found in a conversation between the Buddha and Ānanda. The Buddha told Ānanda that all mankind has equal rights, i.e., *Bhikkhu* (monk) as well as *Bhikkhunī* (nun), layman as well as laywoman. Buddhism does not say, as does Christianity, that woman is sinful.

One of the objects of Buddhist meditation is the teaching of *anicca* (impermanence) of fresh beauty and focusing attention on the beauty of the informed mind. Buddhists try to realize that all visual attraction is the reaction of the "lower self" from *tanhā*, or the craving of unregenerate desires. They can thereby perceive that sexuality is the delusion of vanity and charm.

Today in the West, especially America, women are often regarded as sexual objects. Westerners often occupy their minds with uncontrolled desires; even when they do manage to control their minds, they do so ineffectively, allowing their minds to descend to the level of the lowest self, expressing themselves in terms of natural desires. Mere physical control with foul thoughts in the mind is a greater defilement than a natural physical outlet with a wholesome, clean mentality. For as a man thinks, so he is. A person retains more sexual energy if they do not let their mind be occupied by desire. Sex is a clean, impersonal, creative force, as natural as water in a river bed, as restless and tremendous as the emotional plane itself. On the physical plane, we call it sex; on the emotional plane, it functions as artistic impulse.

Thus, enthusiasm and emotional power, while in the realm of creativity, manifest as that "creative urge" which is responsible for all that man has ever made, including himself. The third precept of Buddhism may be useful for Western society today. Why? Because it is the mental element that matters, for the precept is primarily aimed at the control and sublimation of desire. Having practiced the third precept, one gradually withdraws the creative force from purely physical, emotional, or mental levels by the exercise of clear vigilance and self-control. Since it is most important for one's life, one should realize self-control and clearly distinguish between control and suppression.

The psychological distinction between male and female is essentially a matter of energy. In the past, it was thought that men had more powerful energy than women; this is no longer the prevailing thought. Man can easily destroy nature—the Himalaya Mountains or the universe—but he often lacks energy in the self-control of his sexuality. It is written: "Man can harness the fiercest mountain stream, but he cannot dam the humblest rivulet without providing an outlet for its energy." Sexuality is a conscious fire which burns more powerfully and destructively than natural fire.

There is nothing wrong with sexual pleasure. The problem is *attachment* to sex. In the *Mahāparinibbāna Sutta*, Ānanda asked the Buddha how we should approach sex. He was told that having no attachment to it is the best way. This is illustrated by the *Haṁsa* (Swan King), who has no attachment to the lotus pool, the lotus flower, or the fish, having realized—after having swum and fed himself—that they do not belong to him. He remains free from attachment. This is how the Noble One should practice and remain free from the (desires related to the) five *skandhas*. Be reminded that there is no permanence in the fresh beauty (of this body), but only *dukkha* and *anattā* (no-self).

Beauty, or the lack of it, is not real; it is only "in the eye of the beholder." What a thing "is" or "is not," or how things "should be," is determined by how our mind receives and refers to it. It is not the "thing in itself," which is a phenomenological point of view.

Thus, giving up attachment to sexuality is the way to solve the problem of sexual infatuation. Sexual pleasure is no different from making a mark in the water; as soon as we finish making the mark, it is gone. Why do we become attached to sex? Basically, it is only two fresh bodies touching one another. There is no meaning without the mind's giving it meaning.

Hence, the problem is how the mind *re-forms* or perceives that action through the power of delusion. Thus, one has to control one's own mind, freeing it from attachment (e.g., "she is mine," "he is mine") by meditating on the impurity of the body. Giving up attachment is destroying the whole mass of suffering. (This is the end of the) rebirth of "I-ness" and "my-ness." Hence, one reaches the free life that is deliverance from conditions—*Nirvana*. Sensuality is (related to) *Samsara*. Therefore, sensuality is a cause of the cycle of life. Thus, one must destroy the idea of beauty as being inherent in the impermanent body—an idea which is re-formed by the mind. The third precept is required for self-control.

REFERENCE NOTES

1. *Selected from my lecture to my Buddhist class at the University of Washington, 1971-1973.*
2. *Sources: Dialogues of the Buddha. Sacred Books of the Buddhist Series. "Mahā Nidāna Suttanta," T.W. Rhys Davids & C. A. F. Rhys Davids, trans., vol. 3, pp. 50-70; Collection of the Middle-Length Sayings, "Sammādiṭṭhi Sutta," Lord Chalmers, trans., vol. I, pp. 3-40; Book of the Kindred Sayings, Translation Series, "Nidāna-vagga," T.W. Rhys Davids, trans., vol. 2, pp. 1-94 passim.*
3. *Aṅguttara Nikāya VIII, 12.*
4. *Samyutta Nikāya XII, 25.*
5. *Quoted in Visuddhimagga XIX.*
6. *Nyanatiloka. The Word of the Buddha. Kandy, Ceylon: Buddhist Publication Society, 1959, p. 45.*
7. *Dhammapada, Text in Devanagari, trans. by Dr. P.L. Vaidya, Second Edition Revised, Poona: The Oriental Book Agency, 1934.*
8. *Buddhadasa Bhikkhu. Two Kinds of Language, trans. by Ariyananda Bhikkhu, pp. 16-18.*
9. *Beal, Samuel. A Catena of Buddhist Scriptures. p. 198.*

CHAPTER IV

A Critique Of The Truths In Mahayana Buddhism

The growth of Buddhism amid changing socio-political events has been defined within three periods, according to *Sprawozdania*, as:

1. The phase of the so-called "pure Hīnayāna."
2. The phase of the formation of Mahāyāna and its rivalry with Hīnayāna.
3. The phase of the final prevalence of Mahāyāna.[10]

In the so-called "pure Hīnayāna" phase, the *Mahāvibhāṣā* (an encyclopedic commentary on the *Jñānaprasthāna*) was the champion text of the Sarvāstivādins. Nagarjuna was the champion of the second phase and the author of the *Mādhyamikaśāstra*. As the authors of the *Yogācārabhūmi* and *Abhidharmakośa*, respectively, the brothers Asanga and Vasubandhu were the champions of the third phase.

Asanga was the founder of the Yogācāra school and the author of the *Yogācārabhūmi* and numerous other works. He converted his younger brother, Vasubandhu, who was initially a Hīnayāna adherent. Vasubandhu was a significant philosopher in relating Hīnayāna and Mahāyāna thought more closely, particularly with his treatise on the *Abhidharmakośa*, which he combined with the doctrine of Yogācāra. Later developers, including Dignāga and Dharmakīrti, produced important literature, such as Dignāga's *Pramāṇasamuccaya* and Dharmakīrti's *Nyāyabindu*.

Before attempting to discuss Mahāyāna philosophy fully and effectively, I will organize my paper according to historical facts, divided into subtitles. I believe this will be helpful for the reader; it will be easier to see how the entire stream of Mahāyāna thought developed. That is to say, we should look at the skeleton of Mahāyāna in its formative stage before its growth into the full body of thought we have today.

Literary History

Generally, Mahāyāna texts developed from Hīnayāna texts intellectually, collectively, and selectively. How do we know this? It is evident that Nagarjuna condemned the Hīnayāna school, specifically the Sthaviravāda (not the *Piṭaka* itself). He was dissatisfied with the way in which the Sthaviravādins accepted the *Anātmavāda* (the doctrine of no-soul). His interest lay in systematizing the *Prajñāpāramitā-sūtras*. The *Prajñāpāramitā* literature, which most interested him, did not originate from Nagarjuna himself. There was much development from one school to another, and the stream of textbook development became the major driver of Buddhism. The Tibetan saying, "Every district its own dialect, every lama his own doctrine,"[11] comes close to this condition. As the *Mahābhārata* puts it:

"The *Vedas* are diverse, and the Traditions (*smṛti*) are diverse. He is not a sage whose doctrine (*mata*) is not individualized. The truth of *Dharma* is hidden in the cave (of the heart). That by which a great man has gone is the path (*panthāḥ* = school)."[12]

Putting together the various suggestions offered by the Abhidharma and then making their own observations, the old teachers worked out the mechanism of the stream of consciousness, the "thought series" (*cittavīthi*), in which mental phenomena occur.[13] The Sthaviravāda differed from Mahāyāna by using the word *artha* in the *Kathāvatthu* and the *Yamaka* to mean "meaning." The word *tarka* (logic) is used synonymously for the word *artha*. The meaning of "logic" for this school refers to phenomena, not to the words of the text. Therefore, logic for them is a logic of meaning, of phenomena, not of words, and it defines reality only as it occurs in the Abhidharma. For example, (2 + 2 = 4) is a logical equation. But the perception of (2 & 2 = X) can be (5) or (simply) a "bracket." The mind can create any phenomenon in the "bracket." A phenomenon is therefore something more than the description of words (*tarka*).

However, a major concern of this school was its affiliation with the Sātavāhana dynasty, which was the longest-reigning dynasty in the history of the Krishna and Godavari region in Southern India. The Mauryan dynasty was overthrown, and a new dynasty established, favoring orthodox beliefs like Brahmanism. Because of these political events, Buddhism in Southern and Northern India developed different ideas, and different schools began to emerge.

One of these schools, the Caitika, originated during this period and was located in the northern part of India, near Magadha and Avanti. The Caitika school rejected the Andhra (Sthavira) point of view in the Abhidharma. The Andhra school held that the most important point in Buddhism is related to the Buddha. It is said by the Andhra school that:

"...the Buddha's discourse (*vyavahāra*) is transcendental; that the power (*ṛddhi*) of the Buddha or his pupils enables them to effect whatever they wish, regardless of the laws of nature; and that a (or the) *Bodhisattva* (future Buddha) was (among his numerous previous lives) sometimes reborn in very unhappy circumstances (ruin, i.e., in purgatory, as an animal, ghost, or a demon) of his own free will (i.e., not as a result of his previous actions)."[14]

This school began to give birth to the Mahāyāna, according to this idea of the *Bodhisattva*. The other schools (i.e., the Śaila, Rājagirika, and Siddhārthika) argue that the *Bodhisattva* was born *certain* of attaining enlightenment, that phenomena were not classifiable under other phenomena (nor contained within other phenomena), and that "mental phenomena" (*caitasikas*, i.e., the mental forces) do not exist.[15]

The latest thinkers in this school modified the Abhidharma by determining previous thought and maintaining that of only the two latest schools, as they believed this seemed to be fundamental and early Abhidharma. These thinkers were much like some monks within this community. This idea gave rise to the late Mahāyāna schools.

We do not know for sure that the Mahāyāna school originated from the Khotan area. Mahāyāna Buddhism may have risen from the Andhra school.[16] The Mahāyāna school developed the idea of the *Bodhisattva* and made a sharp distinction between *Arhatship* and *Bodhisattvahood*. "However, with the growth of Mahāyāna practices, there started a twin tendency to deify the Buddha and to concentrate upon the ideal of the Buddha-to-be (or *Bodhisattva*). This ideal derives mainly from the story of the Buddha himself... Before his enlightenment, he was tempted by *Māra* (the Buddhist equivalent of Satan)... (Rejecting the temptation to) ultimately vanish into final *Nirvana* without communicating his spiritual discoveries to mankind, the Buddha went on to preach and teach for some forty-five years in North India. Thus there arose the notion that the Buddha sacrifices himself on behalf of mankind... (and) displayed heroic activities of self-sacrifice."[17]

Mahāyāna Buddhism originated from the *Mahāsāṃghika* school and included the development of the *Lokottaravāda* (transcendentalist) idea, which held that "the Buddha was a transcendental being whose body was not of this world." This naturally led to increased interest in the story of the Buddha's life, and to some extent in his previous lives leading up to this culmination.[18]

Presumably, the Mahāyāna text *Prajñāpāramitā* revised some parts of the ***Śīla*** text. However, I believe that Paramārtha had in mind the *Prajñāpāramitā* of Nagarjuna.[19] Unfortunately, his works were not effective among the Mahāyāna Buddhists. It is possible that the Pūrvaśailas intended these verses to refer only to the non-origination and non-cessation of "being" and of the "World" in the sense of the totality of "beings" or "persons." In contrast, Candrakīrti makes them refer to all phenomena.[20]

I perceive the historical facts as these: "At sometime... during the founding of the Pūrvaśaila school in the last century B.C., certain monks felt the need not simply to interpret the original *sūtra* (such as the new Abhidharma texts of the schools, or the *Paṭisambhidāmagga* of the Sthaviravāda), but to wholesale restate the doctrine."[21] Hence, Nagarjuna based his work on the *Prajñāpāramitā-sūtras*, which resulted in his *Mūlamadhyamakakārikā*. It is important to note that it refers by name to the *Bodhisattva Piṭaka* for the basic doctrine of the six "perfections" (*pāramitā*), to be fulfilled by the *Bodhisattva* as a prerequisite for becoming a Buddha.[22]

Hence, I will summarize the fundamental content of the *Prajñāpāramitā* literature to see how this text was supported as the basic authority for Nagarjuna. The thousands of lines of the *Prajñāpāramitā* can be condensed into the following two sentences:

1. One should become a *Bodhisattva* (a "Buddha-to-be"), i.e., one who is content with nothing less than "all-knowledge" attained through the perfection of wisdom for the sake of all beings.

2. There is no such thing as a "Bodhisattva," or as "all-knowledge," or as a "being," or as an "attainment." To accept both of these contradictory facts is to be perfect.[23]

Nagarjuna studied other works of the Hīnayāna Sthaviravāda school, including the *Milinda Pañha*, which contributed to the development of his *Mūlamadhyamakakārikā*. Professor Rhys Davids states that "One Greek king, Menandros (Prakrit Menendra), deserves particular mention: (he is the) Sanskrit Milindra (Pali Milinda) (of the text), who reigned, according to the latest authority, around B.C. 155-130."[24] This text was composed as a dialogue between King Milinda and the monk Nāgasena during the period when the Greeks ruled India.

What I am trying to say here is that the idea of the *Bodhisattva* is found not only in Mahāyāna thought but also in Hīnayāna thought. The doctrine of the non-existence of the soul, which was misinterpreted by Brahmins before the Buddha, was also accepted by the Hīnayāna schools.

The "Questions of Milinda" (*Milinda Pañha*) can be summarized like this: "The king said, 'How is your reverence known? What is your name?' Nāgasena replied, 'I am called Nāgasena by my parents, the priests, and others. But "Nāgasena" is not a separate entity.' The king objected to this idea. Nāgasena attempted to explain this to him by breaking down the five *skandhas* into their constituent parts. The king still did not agree with him and only understood that Nāgasena was being negative. 'Then,' said the king, 'I do not see Nāgasena. "Nāgasena" is a sound without meaning. You have spoken an untruth. There is no Nāgasena.' The mendicant asked, 'Did your majesty come here on foot, or in a chariot?' 'In a chariot' was the answer. Nāgasena kept asking, 'What is a "chariot"?' and tried to point out that there is no *reality* of a chariot, only the *name* of it, which exists because of the unity of many parts. We do not see clearly. We deludedly call a 'chariot' a 'chariot.' In the case of humans, we delude ourselves into calling them 'human' because they are a unification of the many parts of the five *skandhas* (viz., body, form, consciousness, existence, etc.)."[25]

As the argument goes, the idea of a "soul" in man as a separate substance is refuted, just like the idea of a separate "chariot-ness" in the chariot. This doctrine was emphasized in the *sūtras* before Mahāyāna, but the problem is that *Avidyā* (ignorance) stops one from seeing ***śūnyatā*** (emptiness). Furthermore, this argument indicates that ***Śūnyatā*** originated from Brahmanism and Jainism rather than from Buddhism. What I mean here is that the concept of ***Śūnyatā*** was held in religions prior to Buddhism. "Brahmanism and Jainism teach that the soul is material or is immaterial or is both, or is neither: that it is finite or infinite, or both, or neither; that it will have one or many modes of consciousness; that its perceptions will be few or boundless; that it will be in a state of joy or misery or of neither."[26] This doctrine was developed into the "mentalist" school of Mahāyāna by the Yogācāra school. "One of the chief agents in this line of development seems to have been Asanga, an influential monk of Peshawar in the Punjab, who lived and wrote the first textbook of this creed—the *Yogācāra-*

bhūmi—about the sixth century of our era."[27] It is my personal opinion that he developed Buddhism from the Hindu faith and also addressed the mystical and fantastic doctrines prevalent in animism. I further believe that his creed is the so-called "newer" Buddhism.

Another account should be added here: Mahāyāna Buddhism has an unclear starting point, and the information is incomplete and inadequate. Many different texts present different historical literature. For example, in the *Dhammapada* commentary (in the first book, *Paṭhamo Bhāgo*, or "First Volume"), it is said that there were two groups of monks. There was a dispute between the disciples of a *Dhammadhara* (Dhamma-expert) and the disciples of a *Vinayadhara* (Vinaya-expert) regarding water being left in a bathroom, and whether this was right or wrong according to either *Vinaya* or *Dhamma* doctrine. The argument continued for three months (one *vassa*, or rains retreat), and reaching an agreement seemed impossible.

The Lord Buddha came to judge the dispute. They still disagreed. The Buddha left for the Pārileyyaka forest and lived among elephants and monkeys. The monkeys offered honey to the Buddha, which contained baby bees. The Buddha did not accept it. Finally, the monkeys removed the baby bees and offered him the honey. The Buddha accepted it. The elephants gathered wood and lit a fire to keep the Buddha warm. The monkeys boiled water, lit a fire to keep the Buddha warm, and also used the water for his bathing and drinking. Both the animals carried out these duties for the Buddha for one *vassa*.

Finally, the monks assembled, went to visit and apologize to him, and invited him back to Sāvatthī. They thought the Buddha had no one taking care of him and felt terrible, since they had left him suffering. Hence, they agreed not to have the argument anymore. The Buddha taught them the lesson of *Eka cariyā* (living alone): when one lives with another who does not listen, it is better to live alone. In the end, they understood that all phenomena are empty. That is to say, emptiness, or ***śūnyatā***, is the result of attaining *Arhantship* or *Bodhisattvahood*. However, this account is still confusing to us.

I believe that the concept was misinterpreted by Mahāyāna. Indeed, Mahāyāna (concepts) were fully established in the Buddha's time, as an agreement on the above quarrel was later reached. This argument was set forth in the South of India. Secondly, the term "Mahāyāna" first appears in the *Aṣṭasāhasrikā-prajñāpāramitā* and, according to Lamotte, it originates from Khotan. Thirdly, the *Mahāparinirvāṇa Sūtra*[28] mentions that Mahāyāna was established in the South after the *Parinirvāṇa* and later spread into the East and North due to various factors that led to the adoption of a new doctrine for interpreting the *Tripiṭaka*. One of these was Nagarjuna, who became the most important master of Mahāyāna. Lastly, other major *sūtras* that show new phases in Mahāyāna also had connections with the South. For instance, the detailed itinerary of the *Gaṇḍavyūha* and

Patty Kay Dumdeang and grand child KYRA Dumdeand
on the Trip visit GSM in Thailand January - 2003

the locations of the Bodhisattva Maitreya are there, while the *Laṅkāvatāra Sūtra* is connected with Ceylon.

Personal History of Nagarjuna

Nagarjuna was born in the Vidarbha country in Maharashtra.[29] There is some confusion about him. I believe that he became a monk at Nālandā and was a ***śiṣya*** (disciple) of Rāhulabhadra. He has a legendary personal history.

He went to the Dragon-world (a city in a heavenly realm) by invitation of the Dragon King. He returned to earth as soon as possible with a "hundred thousand perceptions of understanding," culminating in the Mahāyāna *sūtras* which he found in the Dragon-world. He taught his doctrine for numerous centuries and built and improved many pagodas and *vihāras*. His biography can be found in Tāranātha's work and other sources from the period of the Sātavāhana kings.

There were many figures named Nagarjuna, but the founder of the Madhyamaka school was the author of the *Mūlamadhyamakakārikā* (the foundational doctrine of this school). Other works believed to be his include the *Vigrahavyāvartanī*, ***Śūnyatāsaptati***, *Yuktiṣaṣṭikā*, *Vaidalyasūtra* (and *Prakaraṇa*), and *Suhṛllekha*, and perhaps the *Ratnāvalī* and some "hymns" (*stotra*) in praise of the Buddha.

Literally speaking, Nagarjuna borrowed terminology from the *Piṭaka* without referencing the text. I mean to say that (the concepts in the) *Mūlamadhyamakakārikā* were found in the Pali and Sanskrit canons of the early schools of Buddhism. Furthermore, the *Mūlamadhyamakakārikā* nowhere mentions "Mahāyāna," nor does it appear to make reference to any Mahāyāna *sūtra* (canonical text), either by name or by quotation.[30]

Warder presumes that Nagarjuna here quotes from key *suttas*, saying that the Master (the Buddha) avoids both the extremes of "It exists" (*asti*) and "It does not exist" (*nāsti*). (Writing in verse *kārikās*, Nagarjuna cannot reproduce the exact wording of the original prose *sūtras in extenso*.)[31]

Furthermore, Professor Warder maintains that Nagarjuna quotes similarly (from other *suttas*), such as the *Acelakassapa Sutta*.[32] We can, however, see a distinction in the notions between the *Piṭaka* and Nagarjuna's work. In the *Tipiṭaka*, there are no "souls" or "beings," but there *are* phenomena (*dhammā*). For Nagarjuna, there seem to be no phenomena either, at least from the standpoint of ultimate truth. Of course, this possible contrast depends on the meaning of "are" and whether it should be assimilated to "exist" (eternally).[33]

It can be seen that in the commentary, he denied the doctrine of the "own-nature" (*svabhāva*) of phenomena found in the *Tripiṭaka*, denying both "it is" and "it is not." That is the viewpoint I have tried to use to distinguish between the *Piṭaka* and Nagarjuna's works.

We shall now examine the idea held by the early school itself and try to determine how and in what way Nagarjuna responded to that school.

The Sarvāstivādins believe that every element (*dharma*) that appears in consciousness is a function of a corresponding transcendent "bearer," which is a separate, real entity. Nagarjuna rejects that idea and holds that this real entity is "empty" (***śūnya***)—having no real attributes and being indescribable.[34]

Having discussed Nagarjuna's philosophy, we should remember the later school of Yogācāra, which gives a monistic solution: from the standpoint of absolute truth, there is no underlying plurality corresponding to the elements of empirical individuality. All the diversity given by immediate experience reduces itself to one 'storehouse consciousness" (***ālayavijñāna***).[35]

Professor Shotaro Iida gives an account of the Mādhyamika *Svātantrika* school, saying that "Mādhyamika-Svātantrika, Śāntarakṣita denies *svabhāva* (own-being) in ultimate reality. However, as a *Svātantrika*, he retains the notion of *svabhāva* as far as *tathya-saṁvṛti-satya* (conventional truth) is concerned. Lastly, as a Yogācārin, he denies the absolute reality of the external world which is taken as independent of our experiencing it."[36]

Professors Iida and Warder agree that Nagarjuna denied both external reality and the soul. For instance, it is said in the *Rāṣṭrapālaparipṛcchā* (dealing with the way of a Bodhisattva) and also in the *Amitābhavyūha*... that in the *Mūlamadhyamakakārikā* (which was adopted originally from Sthiramati) and in the Heart Sūtra (*Prajñāpāramitā-hṛdaya-sūtra*), ***śūnyatā*** is *neither* the five *skandhas*, *nor* the twelve ***āyatanas***, *nor* the eighteen *dhātus*, *nor* the Twelvefold Chain of Origination, *nor* the Four Noble Truths. "Such a negation of all things expresses the conception that emptiness must be the basis which brings everything into existence, a non-being free of all restrictions."[37]

(Therefore,) there is no distinction between extinction (*Nirvana*) and transmigration (*samsara*).[38]

Philosophy of the Mādhyamika School

According to Professor Yensho Kanakura in his *A History of Hindu-Buddhist Thought*, the notion of ***Śūnyatā*** is an ancient concept that was one of the ***Āgamas*** (collections) in the *Madhyamāgama*. There are two *suttas*: the *Mahāsuññata-sutta* and the *Cūḷasuññata-sutta*. The *Mahāsuññata-sutta* (and other texts like the) ***Śāriputra-Abhidharma-Śāstra*** contain six kinds of ***Śūnyatā***; the Hīnayāna *Abhidharma Mahāvibhāṣā Śāstra* contains ten kinds of ***Śūnyatā***.

Professor Kanakura tells us that the ***Śūnyatā*** doctrine was surely Hīnayāna before. There is nothing new for the Mahāyāna doctrine *except* that it denies the existence of the ego-self on one hand, but asserts the existence of *dharma* (phenomena) on the other. Mahāyāna developed the theory of knowledge and delusion, presupposing that if *dharma* is ***Śūnyatā***, then ***Ātman*** is also ***Śūnyatā***. Ultimately, Mahāyāna ***Śūnyatā*** means that there is no apprehension whatsoever.[39]

In the *Prajñāpāramitā*, all *Dharma* is empty; hence, it is ***Śūnyatā*** and free from all being. It appears that Mahāyāna views *Dharma* as a negative concept rather than an affirmative one. But that is not true. Mahāyāna denies the reality of "self" (or *anattā*, no-soul) in the lower degree (the empirical and conventional realm) and accepts the existence of "Self" in the higher degree (the ultimate reality). The *Dhammic* analysis of this school is common to all Buddhist schools. As the *gāthā* in Pali may be applied to the whole notion of *paṭiccasamuppāda*, it is said:

Yo paṭiccasamuppādaṁ passati, So dhammaṁ passati.

Which I translate to mean: "The person who sees Dependent Co-origination, he (at the same time) sees *Dhamma...*"

Stanisław Schayer also states that:

"This (*Dharma*) term possesses such importance in Buddhist philosophy that the whole of this system might be named 'theory of *Dharma*': Just as we call the philosophy of Plato a 'theory of Ideas' and the philosophy of Leibniz a 'theory of Monads'."[40]

Hence, Nagarjuna developed his theory and called it the "theory of new causality underlying the *Dharma* argument."

In the mind of the Mahāyāna Buddhist, all *Dharma* falls into three categories:

1. ***Sandiṭṭhiko***: well-established
2. ***Akāliko***: timeless (neither past nor present nor future)
3. ***Ehipassiko***: "come and see" (under the sense of feeling or seeing)[41]

A.K. Warder states that:

"Comparing M.K. (Mūlamadhyamakakārikā) I and XXIV, we see that it can be said that *dharmas* 'occur,' 'originate,' 'cease,' provided that this is understood only of 'empty' *dharmas*, not (self-)existing *dharmas*... i.e., what are called *bhāvas*, 'existings,' 'existent things.' This last term derives from a late phase of Abhidharma discussion, as in the Sthaviravāda commentary *Atthasālinī*."[42]

According to the above statement, there is nothing new that Mahāyāna Buddhism developed. What bothers me is that Nagarjuna is credited not only with the *Prajñāpāramitā-sūtra* but also with the term *prajñā* itself. I believe the term *prajñā* originated from the three learned principles of early Buddhism: *Sīla* (the principle or law of morality), *Samādhi* (meditation), and *Paññā* (wisdom). These fundamental principles are found in all Buddhist *Tipiṭakas*, not just in Mahāyāna Buddhism. If Mahāyāna Buddhism does not draw on the original source of the three learned principles from Hīnayāna, from where do they derive the doctrine in the first place? Of course, some Buddhists agree that Nagarjuna's fundamental doctrine came from the six *pāramitās*.

"To follow the definition of Vasubandhu, *Abhidharma* is the pure knowledge and the concomitant *dharmas*. 'Knowledge' consists in processes of cognition, the subjects of which are 1) *Nirvana* as *Dharma* 'par excellence' and 2) the analysis of the *santāna* (mind-stream) into its components. The concomitant *dharmas* are all (psycho-)physical states connected with the evolution towards ultimate deliverance."[43]

I believe that when Nagarjuna talks about *Dharma* as being empty, he means that it is the ultimate deliverance and is not strictly for one or some beings, but for all beings. For example, in chapter 2 of the *Suvikrāntavikrāmi-paripṛcchā Prajñāpāramitā-sūtra*, it is said that all good *dharmas* are born of transcendental insight; and the chapter "On the Mother of the Buddhas" in the *Pañcaviṃśatisāhasrikā-Prajñāpāramitā-sūtra* explains that *prajñā* gives rise to works that praise the positive function of *Prajñā*.[44]

Nagarjuna's thought was broad, as follows: his monism states that all phenomena co-arise from non-existence, and behind it lies the only real existence.[45] Nagarjuna's notion of ***Śūnyatā*** also emphasizes the problem of *being* (viewing the real nature of all *dharmas* as empty) but takes little interest in the problem of *becoming* (of how phenomena can come into existence).[46] It is under this subject that we find a verse (verse 21) practically identical with one in the *Ratnagotravibhāga* to the effect that "there is nothing to be removed, nothing to be obtained, but simply reality has to be seen."[47] The phenomenal and transcendental universes are identical—with separateness of phenomena on the surface but perfect harmony and unity within.[48]

According to the *Aṣṭasāhasrikā-prajñāpāramitā*, "the *Dharmakāya* (Dharma-bodies) are the Buddhas, the Lords; but monks, do not think that this individual body is my body. Monks, you should see me from the accomplishment of the *Dharmakāya*."[49]

Here we can see that Mahāyāna not only disagrees with Hīnayāna but also with Jainism. Jainism accepts only an individual god but not a universal god. So there is room for argument for Mahāyāna.

Nagarjuna's viewpoint of ***Śūnyatā*** is that it does not mean merely negativity or nihilism. He terms ***Śūnyatā*** as always having a double meaning: that *Māyā* (illusion) *is*, as well as *Brahman*. In the same vein is the Upanishadic tradition, as "we know that there are two standpoints of meaning: empirical and ultimate/absolute." When I say that Nagarjuna had a double meaning, I am referring to what has been well-expressed by Kanakura: "Such a negation of all things expresses the conception that emptiness must be the basis which brings everything into existence, a non-being free of all restrictions."[50] For Nagarjuna, *Samsara* is *Nirvana*, as the Buddha taught. However, Hīnayānists (specifically Sthaviravādins) misunderstood the meaning and purpose of the Buddha's *anattā* theory.

What Nagarjuna developed was likely present in early (primitive) Buddhism: his concept of a Middle Path, which the Buddha understood as being neither body nor mind, but spirit. The Buddha believed the spirit persists here as well as hereafter, so "it is wrong to say, as is often done, that Buddha denied the self... (or) identified it with the body and mind." Hīnayāna continues to say that "early Buddhism is thus a gospel of happiness and not a gospel of despair, as it is commonly represented to be."[51] Secondly, Nagarjuna adopted *Buddhi* (intellect) according to K.M. Sen, in the same sense in which Hindus did. "Buddha is still accepted by the Hindus as one of the *Avatāras* spreading enlightenment to all creatures, and the fact that Buddhism had so much in common with the *Upaniṣads* of course made his assimilation easier."[52]

The Hīnayānist's misunderstanding of the doctrine of "no-soul" became a serious problem for the Mahāyānist, who believes everything is (conventionally) real *or* (ultimately) unreal.

Nagarjuna treated the notion of *Avidyā* as "unseeable knowledge" and ***Ātman*** as "emptiness," wherein he believed *Avidyā* to be *Māyā* and ***Ātman*** to be *Anattā* (no-self). Likewise, he has a better theory for removing ignorance and emptiness together than other early schools of thought have. Hence, we are wrong to claim that his ***Śūnyatā*** is (purely) metaphysical. He treated ***Śūnyatā*** as both epistemological and metaphysical simultaneously.

Hīnayāna's idea of *Eka cariyā* (living alone) is wrong, according to Mahāyāna. Mahāyānists hold that our world is not "alone" (*eka*). To escape from this world means to be free from *Samsara*. That is to say, to obtain *Nirvana*, which is *in* the world and at the same time not *of* the world. Hence, Mahāyānists involve themselves in an apparent contradiction. To put it another way, Hīnayānists believe in terms of a two-value system: *Samsara* on one hand and *Nirvana* on the other. To become free from *Samsara* meant to be *out* of this world. Mahāyāna argues that there is no two-value system but a dynamic system. Hence, they held that mundane reality is, as well as ultimate reality. I have found that Nagarjuna held the *Satyadvaya* (Two Truths) point of view: that "everything is both real and unreal," which I find incomprehensible.

Furthermore, Nagarjuna emphasizes as most important the last of the three categories (of the *Tilakkhaṇa*): *Anattā* (no-self). As it is said in the Pali text:

Sabbe saṅkhārā aniccā'ti yadā paññāya passati, Atha nibbindati dukkhe, esa maggo visuddhiyā. Sabbe saṅkhārā dukkhā'ti yadā paññāya passati, Atha nibbindati dukkhe, esa maggo visuddhiyā. Sabbe dhammā anattā'ti yadā paññāya passati, Atha nibbindati dukkhe, esa maggo visuddhiyā.

My translation is:

When one perceives with wisdom (*paññāya*) that "all conditioned things are impermanent" (*sabbe saṅkhārā aniccā*), one turns away from suffering (*dukkha*). This is the path of purity. When one perceives with wisdom that "all conditioned things are suffering" (*sabbe saṅkhārā dukkhā*), one turns away from suffering. This is the path of purity. When one perceives with wisdom that "all *dhammas* are no-self" (*sabbe dhammā anattā*), one turns away from suffering. This is the path of purity.

According to the above *gāthās*, it can be seen clearly that the phrase *Sabbe dhammā* was a favorite of Nagarjuna. He means (all *dhammas* are) empty of the five *skandhas*, etc.; hence, free from all "being." He draws the conclusion that all *dhammas* lack their own-being by criticizing the notion of *svabhāva* (own-being).

In addition to this, he greatly emphasized the *pratītyasamutpāda*, or the so-called "Twelve Chains" of Gautama. Thus, the basic alternatives are: permanent events or states, etc. But clearly, it is absurd to speak of change in regard to what is permanent.[53]

Professor Iida, in his "The Nature of Samvrti," quotes from the *Prajñāpradīpa*:

"All the *dharmas* (are neither born nor do they perish)... (This is) *Nirvana*. However, this (view) is considered from the ultimate point of view. Many virtuous acts (like giving) are able to be held and followed. In social convention, also, these (virtues) have real (value). Therefore, everybody knows that these internal and external entities (such as the sense organs and their objects) are real. (On the other hand, a flower in the sky, a turtle's hair, etc.) are regarded as unreal by everybody. According to the social conventional truth, Nagarjuna says: everything is (conventionally) real or unreal."[54]

For this reason, ***Śūnyatā*** is called "void," which means that:

1. It correlates with the voidness of inner states, which is one of the marks of Buddhist contemplation.
2. The apprehension of the void becomes equivalent to the attainment of *Nirvana*. In the "greater vehicle" (Mahāyāna), the quest for *Nirvana* is seen as the quest for the Lord Buddha.
3. The Buddha's essential nature is the void. In brief, the Buddha becomes a manifestation of the Absolute. The Absolute equals *Nirvana*, which equals Buddhahood.

4. The Absolute, equated with the "Truth Body" (*Dharmakāya*) of the Buddha, phenomenalizes itself as the celestial Lord and, on earth, as the historical Buddha.[55]

Some translations regarding the perfection of *Dhyāna*, which became a major Buddhist practice in the northern part of China around the third or fourth century, say, as Professor Arthur E. Link points out, that "as regards making wisdom (*prajñā*) the conveyance for entering meditation (*dhyāna*). Indeed, there are three classes of beings: *Arhats*, *Pratyekabuddhas*, and *Bodhisattvas*. *Arhats* denied the soul and tried to leave this world... But Mahāyāna Buddhism accepts the 'soul' and tries to be *in* the world."[56]

Nagarjuna denied, as Warder states, that (in the *Vedanā-samyutta*) *all* feelings (*vedanā*) are unhappiness (*dukkha*). Nagarjuna's *Kārikā* extends this to all forces (*saṁskāras*); Candrakīrti also mentions it as if it were part of the *sūtra*.[57] It seems as if Nagarjuna followed this *sūtra*.

Nagarjuna himself, as well as other Buddhist masters whose words he accepts, admits that all of the Buddha's teachings are nothing more than the Four Noble Truths and Dependent Origination.[58] If that statement is true, then what Nagarjuna rejects, what he attacks, is not Abhidharma as such, but the systems and methods of certain schools, some of which are known to us from texts still available.

Furthermore, Nagarjuna denied that the six perfections of the *Prajñāpāramitā* are not from early Buddhism. Nagarjuna follows the Buddha in the sense of realizing what man is, what he is and is not; man is only a superimposition.

Hence, he draws the conclusion of his ***Śūnyatā*** theory. It is ***Śūnyatā*** because of:

1. ***Samāropa***: superimposition, namely, adding something that is not there (i.e., memory, imagination, or a dream).

2. ***Apavāda***: depreciation, to subtract something which *is* there (e.g., (denying that the) *Dharmakāya* body is universal, not individual).

There is nothing to attain and nothing to remove; nothing to be escaped. Likewise, Nagarjuna developed the theory of dynamic reality rather than static reality. His work is essentially a theory of metaphysics. "The works on metaphysics demonstrate the (5) groups of elements, the (18) component elements of an individual, the (12) bases of cognition, the difference between them and their special characteristics—from the standpoint of empirical reality. Such is the Abhidharma literature, the *Mahāyāna-lakṣaṇa-samuccaya*, etc."[59]

As to the interpretation of special divisions of scripture (that of the early, the intermediate, and the late period), the works containing them are (respectively) of three kinds:

1. Treatises interpreting Hīnayāna Scripture.
2. Those elucidating the theoretical part.
3. Those referring to religious practice.

In some ways, the Mahāyāna doctrine is self-contradictory. Firstly, they accept the cause-effect principle in the doctrine of *pratītyasamutpāda*. The doctrine of cause and effect is the major principle for them. Yet they deny the relationship of time, accepting only the present and future while denying the past. How can perfection exist with only the present and future? How can two things be true, while only one thing (the past) is untrue? Why is it untrue at all? The past is the origin of both the present and the future. If there is truth for both the present and future, there is also truth for the past. The notion of *Nirvana* is timeless for Hīnayāna (not only true for past, present, and future, but also objectless—no *skandhas*, no soul, only a name; no space, no definite cosmology). If the Hīnayāna notion of time is incorrect, what can be correct?

The Mahāyānist "void" uses multiple negations as a slogan to justify their intention to show that all views about reality are contradictory. But (they) hold that this did not involve *them* in contradiction since they (allegedly) do not affirm any views. Hence, the doctrine of ***Śūnyatā*** of Nagarjuna is beyond the problem of metaphysics and beyond the question of "Is he a Mahāyānist?" It is said to be the state of perfect freedom, joy, and bliss.[60]

Mahāyānists admit a degree of reality, and the levels of insight into reality depend on spiritual maturity and the degree of *Samādhi*.[61]

For me, the Madhyamaka argument is too loose, and Nagarjuna seems to be setting up his system for the sake of argument rather than to articulate a specific point of view.

Hīnayāna and Mahāyāna Buddhism share a common tenet: it is said in canonical Buddhism that all things must be conceived as impermanent. Hence, this doctrine of Hīnayāna and Mahāyāna is the doctrine of momentariness (*kṣaṇika-bhaṅgavāda*).

In Hīnayāna doctrine and elsewhere, *Nirvana* is a transcendent state. This means that it is distinct from the empirical world. And does not *Nirvana* consist in release from the cycle of existence and from the process of rebirth? "It therefore must seem an extraordinary paradox to affirm that after all *Nirvana* and the empirical world are identical."[62]

Note: See bibligraphy at end of Chapter V.

REFERENCE NOTES

1. *Rocznik Orientalistyczny* 1-2. Krakow. p. 293.
2. Bell, C.A. *Grammar of Colloquial Tibetan*. Alipore: 1939, p. v.
3. Mādhava Āchārya. *The Sarva-Darśana-Saṁgraha*. Translated by E.B. Cowell. 6th edition. London: Kegan Paul; Varanasi (Banaras): Chowkhamba Sanskrit Series, 1961, p. x.
4. Warder, A.K. *Indian Buddhism*. New Delhi: Motilal Banarsidass, 1970, p. 325.
5. Warder, A.K. *Indian Buddhism*. New Delhi: Motilal Banarsidass, 1970, p. 327.
6. Ibid., p. 328.
7. Cf. Conze, Edward. *Prajnaparamita-Literature*. pp. 10-11.
8. Smart, Ninian. *Doctrine and Argument in Indian Philosophy*. p. 29.
9. Warder, A.K., op. cit., p. 328.
10. Ibid., p. 365.
11. Ibid., p. 353.
12. Warder, A.K. *Indian Buddhism*. p. 354.
13. Ibid., p. 357.
14. Conze, Edward. *The Prajnaparamita Literature*. Calcutta: The Asiatic Society, 1958, p. 15.
15. Narain, A.K. *The Indo-Greeks*. p. 330.
16. Rhys Davids, T.W. *Buddhism*. New York: The Macmillan Co., 1877, pp. 96-97.
17. Ibid., p. 98.
18. Rhys Davids, T.W. *Buddhism: Its History and Literature*. New York and London: The Knickerbocker Press, 1901, p. 43.
19. Cf. Warder, A.K. *Indian Buddhism*. pp. 354-357.
20. Cf. Robinson, Richard H. *Early Mādhyamika in India and China*.
21. Warder, A.K. *The Problem of Two Truths in Buddhism and Vedanta*. Dordrecht, Holland / Boston, U.S.A.: D. Reidel Publishing Co., p. 79.
22. Ibid., p. 79.
23. Ibid., p. 79.

24. Warder, A.K. *Indian Buddhism*. p. 377.
25. *Sprawozdania, Rocznik Orientalistyczny*, I-II. Krakow, 1916, p. 288.
26. Ibid., p. 299.
27. Iida, Shotaro. "The Nature of Samvrti and the Relationship of Paramartha to it in Svātantrika-Mādhyamika." In *The Problem of Two Truths in Buddhism and Vedanta*, edited by Mervyn Sprung. Dordrecht, Holland / Boston, U.S.A.: D. Reidel Publishing Co., 1973, p. 66.
28. Kanakura, Yensho. *A History of Hindu-Buddhist Thought*. Translated by Neal Donner and Shotaro Iida, p. 109.
29. Ibid., p. 109.
30. Ibid., p. 109.
31. Schayer, Stanisław. *Rocznik Orientalistyczny* 1-2. Krakow, p. 300.
32. Cf. p. 111.
33. Warder, A.K. "Is Nagarjuna a Mahayanist?" In *The Problem of Two Truths in Buddhism and Vedanta*, edited by Mervyn Sprung. D. Reidel Publishing Co., 1973, p. 82.
34. Schayer, Stanisław, op. cit., p. 301.
35. Kanakura, op. cit., p. 109. (Also) Niwano, Nikkyo. *The Lotus Sutra: Life and Soul of Buddhism*. Tokyo, 1970, p. 157.
36. (Citation missing in original text)
37. Kanakura, op. cit., p. 121.
38. Warder, A.K., op. cit., p. 412.
39. Ibid., p. 427.
40. Conze, Edward. *The Prajnaparamita Literature*. p. 35.
41. Kanakura, Yensho, op. cit., p. 109.
42. Hiriyanna, M. *The Essentials of Indian Philosophy*. London: George Allen & Unwin, 1949, p. 73.
43. Sen, K.M. *Hinduism*. Baltimore: Penguin Press, 1961, p. (page number missing).
44. Iida, Shotaro, op. cit., p. 68.

45. Smart, Ninian. *Doctrine and Argument in Indian Philosophy*. London: George Allen & Unwin, 1964, p. 183.
46. Smart, op. cit., p. 55.
47. Link, Arthur E. "Evidence for Doctrinal Continuity of Han Buddhism from the 2nd Through the 4th Centuries." p. 29.
48. Warder, op. cit., p. 80.
49. Warder, op. cit., p. 80.
50. Bu-ston. *History of Buddhism*. Translated from Tibetan by Dr. E. Obermiller. Heidelberg, 1931, p. 49.
51. Matilal, B.K., op. cit., p. 73.
52. Ibid., p. 73.
53. Smart, op. cit., p. 55.

CHAPTER V

The Yogācāra School

Let us now turn to the Yogācāra school in order to re-examine its major synthetic problem, which stems from the Mādhyamika school. However, there is no need for me to go into detail, as I established earlier that my emphasis would be on the Mādhyamika school. At any rate, I feel I cannot be adequately informed about the Mādhyamika school without (understanding its) connection to the Yogācāra school. The Mādhyamika school emphasizes the ultimate reality (*paramārtha*) more than the empirical world (*saṁvṛti*), whereas the Yogācāra school emphasizes both.

One of the chief agents in this line of development appears to have been Asanga, an influential monk from Peshawar in the Punjab, who lived and wrote the first textbook of the creed—the *Yogācārabhūmi-śāstra*—around the sixth century of our era.[1] Professor Yensho Kanakura states that just as Nagarjuna, Āryadeva, and Rāhula are regarded as the founders of the Mādhyamika school, so are Maitreya, Asanga, and Vasubandhu venerated as the founders of the *Yogācāra-Vijñānavāda*.[2] *Vijñānavāda* theories are mentioned in the *Viniścaya-saṁgraha* section (of the *Yogācārabhūmi*), in which it is explained that the ***ālaya-vijñāna*** (storehouse consciousness) is the cause of the arising of both the sense-world and the physical world.[3] The rest of the arguments are similar to those of the Mādhyamika school and are therefore unnecessary to repeat.

(The contents of the *Prajñāpāramitā* text) can be briefly discussed as follows:

- a. The first two chapters expound the elusiveness of perfect wisdom and contain the essentials of the book.

- b. Chapters 3-5 are devoted to the advantages derived from the practice of perfect wisdom.
- c. Chapter 6 concerns metaphysical problems and the process of dedicating all merit to the full enlightenment of all beings.
- d. Chapters 7-10 cover a variety of topics, including the attributes of the *pāramitās* (perfections) and their relations to each other. The reason? Some believe in it, others do not. Its depth and purity in the realm of reality and illusion, and its effect on the believer.
- e. Chapter 11: ...one cannot achieve the study of *Prajñāpāramitā* because of the obstacles created by *Māra*.
- f. Chapter 12 gives the explanation of the kind of knowledge which the *Tathāgata* has of the world.
- g. Chapter 13 describes the attributes of the absolute.
- h. Chapter 14: one cannot compare the *Bodhisattva* favorably with ***śrāvaka*** disciples and *pratyekabuddhas*.
- i. Chapter 15: the help that the *Bodhisattva* gives to others and the description of perfect wisdom.
- j. Chapter 16: Suchness (*tathatā*) ... the *Tathāgata's* helping ...
- k. Chapter 17: Irreversibility.
- l. Chapter 18: The ontology of perfect wisdom, i.e., emptiness (***śūnyatā***).
- m. Chapter 19: The six perfections; practice in relation to other beings; a description of the prediction of Buddhahood for the Ganges Goddess.
- n. Chapter 20: Skill in means; delusion; back to irreversibility...
- o. Chapters 22-28: Varieties of topics such as good friends, the meaning of emptiness, the value of perfect wisdom, the influence of *Māra*, the marks of perfect training, the nature of illusion,

the praise of the life of a *Bodhisattva*, and the perfection to Buddhahood by many thousands of monks.

- p. Chapter 29: Litany.
- q. Chapters 30-32: The story about the Bodhisattva Sadāprarudita and his search for perfection.
- r. Chapter 32: Once more, the transmission of the *sūtra* to Ānanda.[4]

One of the similarities between Hīnayāna and Yogācāra is the belief that in about 5,000 years, the universe will be burned by natural fire and human fire (the fires of passion, *rāga*; anger, *dosa*; and delusion, *moha*). Man will be full of confusion; there will be no love among humans. Man will have no appreciation of morality whatsoever (i.e., children will not know their parents and will kill them, etc.). The universe will burn and destroy the entire human race. Right afterward, the Bodhisattva Maitreya will come to earth and bless mankind, who will be newly created in their next life cycle. "All beings there would have 'compassion' (*pratisaṁvid*) when studying. The world will be full of radiance, jewels, incense, fragrance, jewel-flowers, and musical clouds."[5] All beings will be completely happy (in) complete freedom, by the blessings of the Bodhisattva who now dwells in the *Sukhāvatī* heaven. I would like to quote the description of *Sukhāvatī* heaven from A.K. Warder's work:

"Sukhāvatī is then described by the Buddha in more detail, with, for example, its enormous jewel-lotuses, its absence of mountains, its fragrant rivers bearing jewel-flowers and making sweet sounds, its heavenly music whose soft and lovely sounds produce happiness by suggesting 'impermanence, calm and non-soul.' The beings there spend their time in pleasure, play, and enjoy whatever they wish... those who wish to hear (the music) do hear it, and hear whatever music they would like to hear, including, of course, the chanting of the doctrine if they so wish: the doctrine of emptiness, signlessness, uncommittedness, non-synthesizing, not-being-born, non-occurrence, non-existence, cessation, etc. There is no difference between gods and men there."[6]

Maitreya says, "the world is endowed with 60 distinctive features of transcendental nature." Asaṅga, Vimuktasena, Vasubandhu, and others (profoundly versed in scripture) state that this very *sūtra* (the *Tathāgata-guhya*) mentions 60 different features.[7]

It may be stated that there is evidence to show that the Yogācāra school also admitted an absolute consciousness or universal Self, in addition to the particular egos and subjective ideas referred to in the account given above.[8]

According to the *Tipiṭaka*, both Mahāyāna and Hīnayāna are the same, in that merging with the absolute is the same as annihilation. But Mahāyāna claims that Hīnayāna's ideal of the *Arahat* is selfish and individualistic, escaping the world and not assisting the welfare of others. The person who helps others is called a *Bodhisattva* (wisdom-being). They took the position that the Buddha *was* a *Bodhisattva* in many former lifetimes.

The Lord Buddha is not an individual body, but a *Dharmakāya* (Dharma-Body); the Buddha is ***Śūnyatā*** (Emptiness). Gautama Buddha is also a reflective phenomenon, not (ultimately) real. As it occurs in one of the passages of the *Lotus Sūtra*: "the Buddha is originally the equivalent of existence to all people, so each of them can become a Buddha." Some heretics ridicule this with malicious intent and address the believers of this *sūtra* with the words, "All of you are Buddhas! Aren't you?"[9]

Yogācāra, according to the *Yogācārabhūmi-śāstra* and *Mahāyāna-sūtrālaṁkāra*, believes that "the fundamental argument of this ***Śāstra*** is to show how mind manifests itself as both subject and object." All *dharmas* are divided into five categories: mind, matter, mental (factors), non-mental/non-material, and unconditioned. This concept developed into the three theories of knowledge (the "Three Natures" or *Trisvabhāva*):

1. The first principle is called the conceptually constructed (*parikalpita*), e.g., "the jar is in front of me," as well as "another jar that is not there."
2. The second principle is "the relative" (*paratantra*), e.g., "I see the rope as a snake."
3. The third principle is the "ideally absolute" or "perfected" (*parinișpanna*) and is said to rest on "the relative" in the sense that the former is a corrective of the latter, e.g., "I see the rope as the rope and the snake as a snake."[11]

This school is also known as *Vijñānavāda* (Consciousness School) and was founded by Asanga and his brother. Herbert Guenther calls this school "mentalist." As he said, "I used the term 'mentalist' for the adherents of those views which are referred to by such terms as Yogācāra and Vijñānavāda and Cittamātra."[12] The *Sandhinirmocana-sūtra* explains that even the dependent nature (*paratantra*) is only a partial truth: the fundamental reality is *tathatā*, the "suchness" that underlies all things equally. Thus, the originality of this school can be seen in its tripartite division of the metaphysical foundation of phenomena into the purely mentally constructed nature (*parikalpita*), the relative nature (*paratantra*), and the perfect reality (*parinișpanna*).[13]

Parinișpanna refers to *Nirvana* and means the cessation of *being* (as falsely constructed), but not (total) extinction; it is the absence of the three fires of passion: *rāga*, *dosa*, and *moha*.

According to the *Prajñāpāramitā*, "the *Dharmakāyas* are the Lords; but monks, you should not think that this individual body is me. Monks, you should see me from the accomplishment of the *Dharmakāya*."[5]

Mentalists (*Cittamātrins*) hold that nothing exists but mind. This definitely developed from the Hīnayāna school and appears in the *Dhammapada*: Mind is the forerunner of all things.

As it is said in the first verse of the *Dhammapada*: *Manopubbaṅgamā dhammā, manoseṭṭhā manomayā; Manasā ce paduṭṭhena, bhāsati vā karoti vā; Tato naṁ dukkhamanveti, cakkaṁ'va vahato padaṁ.*

This is translated to mean: All man's (states) are the child of thought, the creative process of the mind, even as the forms of nature are the product of Universal Mind. The essence of the mind is intrinsically pure. All things, good or evil, are only its manifestations; good deeds and evil deeds are only the result of good thoughts and evil thoughts, respectively.[15]

Professor Max Müller pointed out that "if we look in the *Dhammapada* at every passage where *Nirvana* is mentioned, there is not one which would require that its meaning should be annihilation, while most, if not all, would become perfectly unintelligible if we assigned to the word "Nirvana" that signification."[16] The Buddha has pointed out the way of salvation, which consists in the attainment of *Nirvana*. *Nirvana* can be attained in this life by abandoning all attachment to the transitory and finding a resting place in the eternal.[17]

Nirvana is neither born nor originated; it is neither *within* the five *skandhas* nor *without* the five *skandhas*. Mentalist philosophers believe that the transmigratory state (*samsara*) and the ultimate absolute (*Nirvana*) are identical. In sum, all *Dhammas* are nothing but projections of consciousness—all is pure consciousness.[18]

Vasubandhu supports this doctrine synthetically wherever it occurs in the *Viṁśatikā* (Twenty Verses). His theory is "consciousness-only" (*vijñaptimātra*) and "no-external-world." The *Triṁśikā* (Thirty Verses) explains the transformations of the ***ālaya-vijñāna***.[19]

He developed his brother Asanga's Three-Nature (*Trisvabhāva*) doctrine, holding that "the triple-world-show (i.e., the worlds of desire, form, and formlessness) is nothing but a transformation of consciousness, because these phenomena have no objective reality and are merely subjective ideas."[20]

It may be pointed out again that phenomena are nothing but the object of the mind. Accordingly, Vasubandhu set forth the possible objections of critics, arguing that the greater part of them can be refuted. He believes in the reality of existence in the dream state as well as in the waking state. He goes on to (refute) several objections with his arguments that the "external" is nothing more than the imaginal (discriminated) nature, which appears as both subject and object over and above the constant flow of consciousness.[21]

He maintains that ***ālaya-vijñāna*** is the "seed of all things," but we do not realize it as the "way things are" (*tathatā*). We cannot see the relationship. These relationships are indicated briefly by the formula: "seeds produce manifestations; manifestations perfume (influence) seeds; seeds produce seeds."[22] Hence, this fundamental principle of co-existing in the process of nature made Vasubandhu believe that "all is a product of false discrimination" and that "all *Dhammas* are nothing but transformations of consciousness."[23]

CONCLUSION

Mentalists do not distinguish clearly between the reality of existence in dreams and reality in the waking state. Realities are not literally part of the perceived object, although they resemble physical objects as ordinarily conceived. They are more like mental states in their privacy and dependence upon the mind of the observer.[24]

Mentalists hold reality in the ultimate sense rather than the conventional sense. They emphasize the epistemological question rather than the metaphysical question. Hence, Mahāyāna, especially Yogācāra, denied not only external objects but also the "soul." It made the Buddha a god, due to the influence of Hindu thought, whereas Hīnayāna made the Buddha the greatest of men. Their doctrine tends to be idealistic rather than practical. Its concern is the esoteric truth about phenomena and how we know them. To this extent, it seems far from the words of the Buddha, whose preaching was practical, whose goal was the extinction of suffering for every man. "I have preached the truth without making any distinction between exoteric and esoteric doctrine: for in respect of the truths, Ānanda, the Tathāgata has no such thing as the ‘closed fist’ of a teacher who keeps something back.”[25]

REFERENCE NOTES

1. *Davids, T.W. Rhys, op. cit., p. 207.*
2. *Kanakura, Yensho, op. cit., p. 123.*
3. *Ibid., p. 123.*
4. *Conze, Edward. "The Composition of the Aṣṭasāhasrikā Prajñāpāramitā." BSOAS (Bulletin of the School of Oriental and African Studies), XLV, 1952, pp. 251-262.*
5. *Warder, A.K., op. cit., p. 360.*
6. *Ibid., p. 361.*
7. *Bu-ston, op. cit., p. 29.*
8. *Hiriyanna, M., op. cit., p. 83.*
9. *Niwano, Nikkyo, op. cit., p. (page number missing).*
10. *Kanakura, Yensho, op. cit., p. 124.*
11. *Sprung, Mervyn (ed.), op. cit., pp. 92-96.*
12. *Ibid., p. 92.*
13. *Kanakura, Yensho, op. cit., p. 122.*
14. *Davids, op. cit., p. 115*
15. *Christmas. Humphries. Studles in the Middle way Beirg Taught on Buddhism: London. Allen and Urwin Limited Ruskin House, p. 226*
16. *Davids, op. cot., p. 115*
17. *Carus paul, Nirvana, Chicago : 1913, p. 92*
18. *Kanakura, op. cit., p. 126*
19. *Ibid., p. 127*
20. *Ibid., p. 127*
21. *Kanakura, op. cit., p. 127*
22. *Ibid., p. 128*
23. *Ibid., p. 128*

24. Sprung, (ed.), op.cit., p.91

25. Davids, op. cit., p. 211

The Author visited GSM Orphan Children in India

The Author meets the GSM Board Members, Kakinada, India (Left to Right) Rev. Dr. P. Yesu Ratnam, The Author, Mr. Jatla Venkateswara Rao, Mr. Kallakuri Satyanarayana Rao

CHAPTER VI

The Third Principle

ABSOLUTE FREEDOM IN PERFECT EXISTENCE

In the second and third chapters, we treated the First and Second Principles of the Four Noble Truths, along with some related aspects of the Third Principle. In this chapter, I would like to further consider the Third Noble Truth. Let us begin with four illustrations and their interpretations.

1) The Truth of the Origination of Suffering (*Samudaya Sacca*)

"That craving which leads to continued rebirth, seeking its pleasure now here, now there."

One finds momentary pleasure in one of the six inward-outward sense fields. One then wishes to perpetuate this momentary pleasure, believing it to be the source of one's happiness. In this delusion, one continually seeks and craves impermanent things, which only cause struggle and continued rebirth.

From our "not knowing" (ignorance, *avijjā*), we act by body, speech, or mind. From the result of these actions, sensual defilements (*kilesa*) arise (greed, hate, delusion), and in these defilements we find momentary happiness or pleasure, which again leads us into ignorance. Thus, we act again, because we seek pleasure here and now.

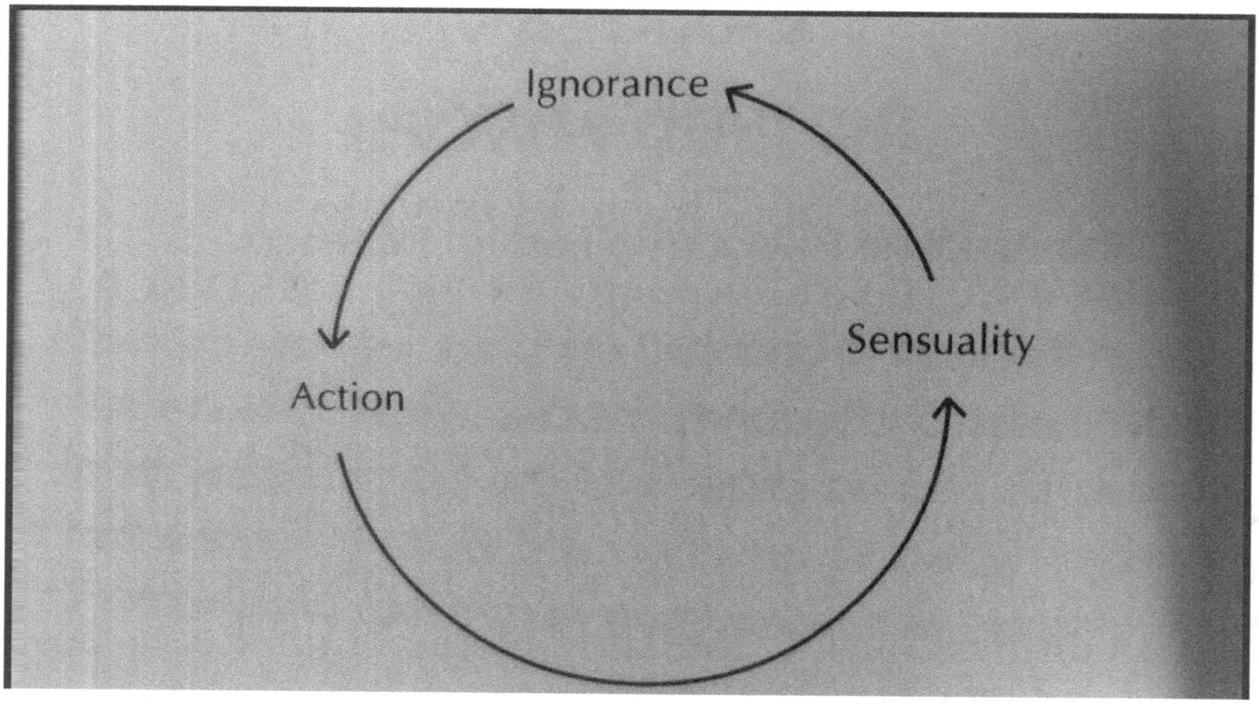

2) Origination and Cessation of Suffering

- **Origination of Suffering (*Samudaya*):** This is craving (*tanhā*) which leads to rebirth; one seeking delight "now here, now there."
- **Cessation of Suffering (*Nirodha*):** This is the complete stopping of that craving; withdrawal from it, liberation from it, and non-attachment to it.
- This requires the stopping of the three main types of craving: a) Craving for sense pleasure (*kāma-tanhā*) b) Craving for existence (*bhava-tanhā*) c) Craving for non-existence (*vibhava-tanhā*)

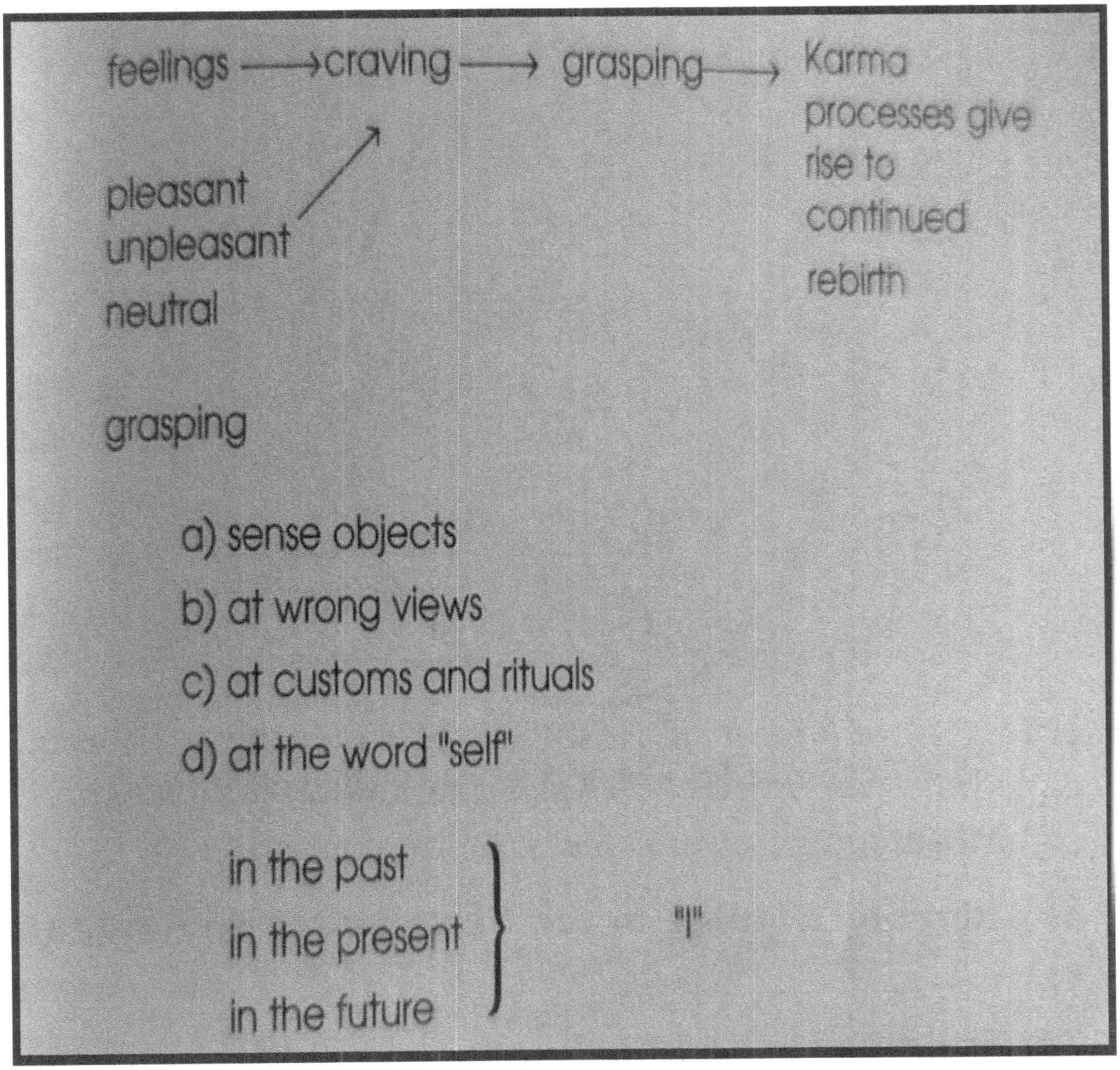

- **Cessation of Craving leads to:**
    - **Nirvana** (like the eye of a hurricane). In *Nirvana*, the five *skandhas* become extinct.
    - **Peace and Calmness:** Occurs because the three defilements (greed, hatred, and delusion) are overcome.
    - **Escape:** In *Nirvana*, you are free from anything which may cause suffering.

3) The Cause of Suffering (*Samudaya*)

1. Sensuality (Defilement, *Kilesa*)

2. Action (*Kamma*) -- *Samsara* (the cycle of life, the wandering of lives).

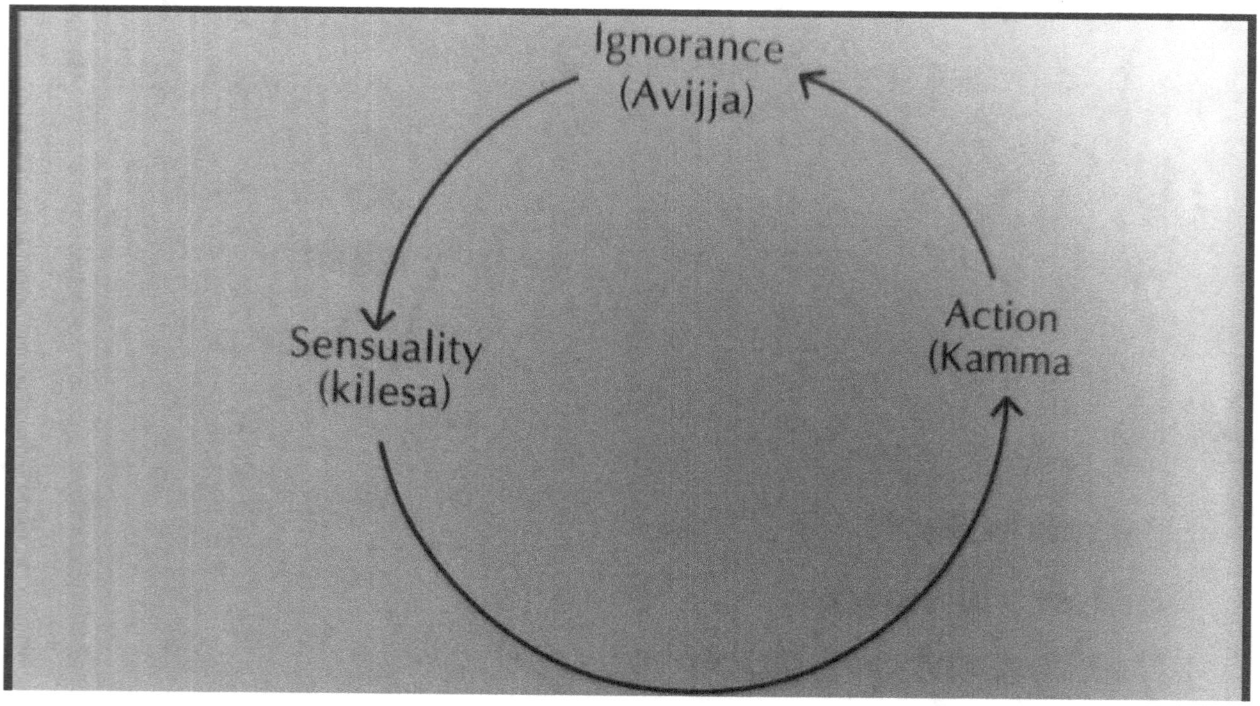

3. **Effect (*Vipāka-citta*):** Resultant consciousness. If good, it is called *kusala-citta*; if bad, *akusala-citta*. This produces *paṭisandhi* (rebirth-linking consciousness, or "new mind").

4) The Path Leading to the Cessation of Suffering (*Magga Sacca*)

- This is the **Noble Eightfold Path**.
- It includes: Right View, Right Intention, Right Speech, Right Conduct, Right Livelihood, Right Effort, Right Mindfulness, and Right Concentration.
- **Right View (*Sammā Diṭṭhi*):** Understanding the Four Noble Truths (this is suffering, this is the origination of suffering, this is the cessation of suffering, this is the path leading to the cessation of suffering).
- **Right Intention (*Sammā Saṅkappa*):** The desire to attain *Nirvana*; the intention of renunciation, absence of ill will, and non-harming (inoffensiveness).
- **Right Effort (*Sammā Vāyāma*):** Abandoning unwholesome *dhammas* and developing wholesome *dhammas* which lead to enlightenment.

- The Eightfold Path must be followed if one wants liberation from suffering.

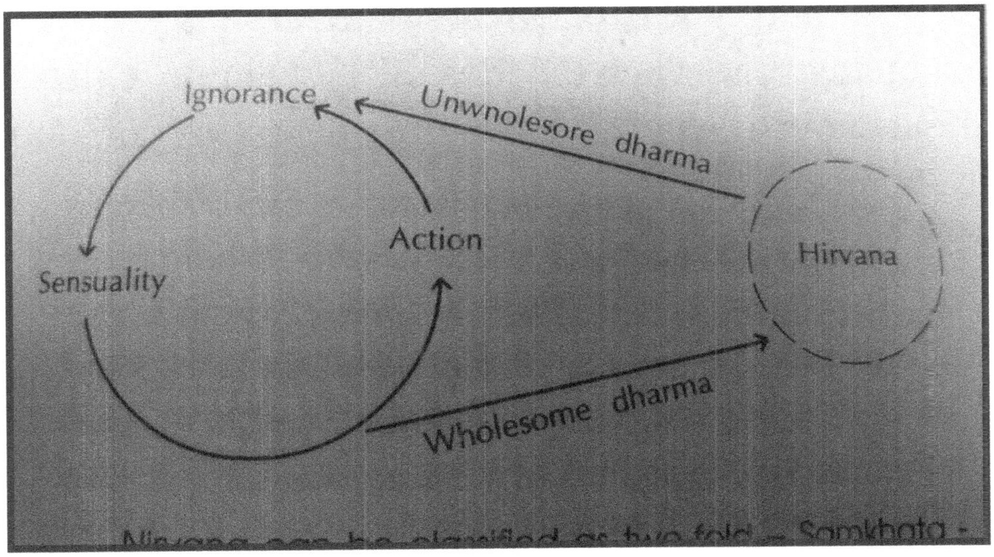

Nirvana (Nibbāna) can be classified as twofold—*Saṅkhata-nibbāna* (Conditioned) and *Asaṅkhata-nibbāna* (Unconditioned)—or as threefold: *Tadaṅga-nibbāna* (momentary freedom), *Vikkhambhana-nibbāna* (freedom by suppression), and *Samuccheda-nibbāna* (complete freedom by eradication). The twofold classification has been clearly discussed in a previous chapter; the threefold will be confirmed here. Nonetheless, I will emphasize only *Tadaṅga-nibbāna*, which occurs in the *Aṅguttara Nikāya*. Once again, I will render a preference given by my teacher, Buddhadasa, in a lecture he gave in the Pattalung province in southern Thailand on July 16, 1969.

"In *dhamma* language, 'nirvana' refers to the kind of coolness that results from eliminating mental defilements. At any time when there is freedom from mental defilements, at that time there is coolness, momentary *nirvana*... when no such idea arises, there is no birth, and this freedom from birth is a state of coolness... and whenever there is freedom from defects of these kinds, there is *nirvana*, *nirvana* of the type referred to as *tadaṅga-nibbāna* or *vikkhambhana-nibbāna*... *Tadaṅga-nibbāna* is the momentary cessation of the idea 'I' and 'mine' due to favorable external circumstances. At a higher level than this, if we develop some form of *Dhamma* practice, particularly if we develop concentration so that the idea of 'I' and 'mine' cannot arise, that extinction of 'I' and 'mine' is called *vikkhambhana-nibbāna*. And finally, when we succeed in bringing about the complete elimination of all defilements, that is full *nirvana*, total *nirvana*... It must be understood that at any time when the idea of 'I' or 'mine' exists, birth, suffering, and the cycle of *samsara* also exist. The 'I' is born, endures for a moment, then ceases; is born again, endures for a moment, and again ceases—which is why the process is referred to as the cycle of *samsara*. It is suffering... (but) at any moment conditions happen to be favorable, so that the 'I' idea does not arise. There is peace—what's called *tadaṅga-nibbāna*, peace, coolness... How can a human being become 'cool'? This question is complicated by the fact that man's present knowledge and understanding of life has not been suddenly acquired; it has evolved gradually over a long period... The *Jhānas* are states of genuine mental coolness, and this was the kind of *nirvana* people were connected with in the period immediately before the Buddha's enlightenment. Gurus taught that *nirvana* was identical to the most refined state of mental concentration. The Buddha's last guru, Udaka Rāmaputta, taught him that to attain the 'jhāna of neither-perception-nor-non-perception' (*nevasaññānāsaññāyatana*) was to attain complete cessation of suffering. But the Buddha did not accept this teaching; he did not consider this to be genuine *nirvana*. He went off and delved into the matter on his own account until he realized the *nirvana* which is the total elimination of every kind of craving and clinging. As he later taught: 'True happiness consists in eradicating the false idea "I".' When defilements have been totally eliminated, this is *nirvana*. If the defilements are only momentarily absent, it is momentary *nirvana*. Hence, the teachings of *Tadaṅga-nibbāna* and *Vikkhambhana-nibbāna*, as already discussed. These terms refer to a condition of freedom from defilements... There are times when we are asleep, and there are times when the mind is clear, cool, and at ease. A person who can manage to do as Nature intended can avoid nervous and psychological disorders; one who cannot is bound to have more and more nervous disorders until he becomes mentally ill or even dies. Let us be thankful for momentary *nirvana*, the transient type of *nirvana* that comes when conditions are favorable. For a brief moment there is freedom from craving, conceit, and false views, in particular freedom from the idea of 'I' and 'mine.' The mind is empty, free, just long enough to have a rest or to sleep, and so it remains healthy."[1]

At this point, I would like to further discuss the illustrations and their meanings. The simple illustration (A) clearly shows that where there is ignorance, there is action; consequently, there is sensuality. Illustration (C) also shows that where there is ignorance, there is sensuality. Ignorance is the most basic of defilements. It gives rise to the defilements of sensuality (i.e., *rāga*, *dosa*, *moha*, etc.). This sensuality results in action, or *kamma*; therefore, *kamma* arises.

If *Avijjā* (ignorance) is a *kamma* process, and sensuality is caused by *Avijjā*, then sensuality is also a *kamma* process.

What is sensuality? Sensuality is *tanhā* (craving). *Tanhā* is the flower of all man's defilements, which results in the present and future, returning to repeat itself again and again in the same phenomena (birth, death, etc.) from the past. This is why the Buddha taught that *Tanhā* is fire. In the Fire Sermon (***Ādittapariyāya Sutta***), the Exalted One said to the brethren:

"'Brethren, the All is on fire.' 'What All, brethren, is on fire?' 'The eye, brethren, is on fire, visible objects are on fire, eye-consciousness... eye-contact... that pleasant or painful or neutral feeling which arises owing to eye-contact, that also is on fire.'... 'The tongue is on fire, tastes are on fire, tongue-consciousness... tongue-contact... that pleasant or painful or neutral feeling which arises owing to tongue-contact, that also is on fire.'... 'On fire with the blaze of lust... '

'So seeing, brethren, the well-taught Ariyan disciple is repelled by the eye, is repelled by visible objects, by eye-consciousness... by that pleasant or painful feeling... by mind, by mind-consciousness... Being repelled by it, he conceives disgust. Being disgusted, he is set free. In this freedom comes the insight that he is free. Thus he realizes:

"Rebirth is destroyed, lived is the righteous life, done is the task. For life in these conditions, there is no hereafter.""[2]

Thus, *Tanhā* is the craving that leads to continued rebirth.

On the other hand, if there is no sensuality or action, there is no delusion. Delusion and *kamma* are extensions. Both give rise to sensuality, while (mind and matter) act as the momentary bases for the present existence. Consequently, there is no end:

"Thus, through the entire fading away and extinction of this 'Delusion' (*avijjā*), the *kamma*-formations (*saṅkhāra*) are extinguished. Through the extinction of the *kamma*-formations, 'Consciousness' (*viññāṇa*) is extinguished. Through the extinction of consciousness, 'Mental and Physical Existence' (*nāma-rūpa*) is extinguished. Through the extinction of mental and physical existence, the six 'Sense-Bases' (*saḷāyatana*) are extinguished. Through the extinction of the six sense bases, 'Contact' (*phassa*) is extinguished. Through the extinction of contact, 'Feeling' (*vedanā*) is extinguished. Through the extinction of feeling, 'Craving' (*tanhā*) is extinguished. Through the extinction of craving, 'Clinging' (*upādāna*) is extinguished. Through the extinction of clinging, the process of 'Becoming' (*bhava*) is extinguished. Through the extinction of 'Rebirth' (*jāti*), 'Decay and Death, Sorrow, Lamentation, Pain, and Despair' are extinguished. Thus takes place the extinction of this whole mass of suffering. This is called the Noble Truth of the Extinction of Suffering."[3]

In speaking about the extinction of suffering, I would like to further mention the Twelvefold Chain. The 12 links of the chain can be categorized by the three elements of conditions: delusion, *kamma*, and sensuality. Thus, I find it wise to speak of the 12 chains rearranged as follows:

- Links 1 and 2 result from links 1, 2, 8, 9, & 10.
- Links 6 and 12 result from links 3, 4, 5, 6, & 7.
- Link 11 results from itself or from link 1.

One might wonder why I say that Link 1 and Link 11 are equivalent. I say this because rebirth (*jāti*) results from delusion (*avijjā*). Suppose that there is no delusion; then there is no rebirth. Therefore, there is no *dukkha*, which is *Nirvana*.

REFERENCE NOTES

1. *Buddhadasa Bhikkhu, op. cit., Another Kind of Birth, p. 10.*
2. *Phra Daksinganadhikorn. "Adittapariyaya Sutta" (The Buddha's Sermon of Fire). In Buddhism. Bangkok, Thailand: Thai Watana Panich Press Co., Ltd., 1973, p. 65.*
3. *Samyutta Nikāya XII, 1.*

CHAPTER VII

The Principle Of Nirvana

Regarding the concept of *Nirvana*, one should bear in mind that the doctrine of release is the individual's capacity for release—that is, the capacity for the overthrowing of the self (*atta*, "I-ness," "ego"). Thus, the concept of *Nirvana* arises out of thought, which it ultimately transcends. It is free from worldly conditions (*samsara*). Hence, *Nirvana* is neither of empirical quality nor datumless. In Buddhism, this realization is related to the practice of concentration, or *Samadhi*. *Nirvana* is inconceivable on the one hand, though it is conceivable as an internal idea (object) that is identical with the experience of simultaneous apprehension (*sahopalambhaniyama*). On the other hand, *Nirvana* is conceivable by the individual (*paccattaṁ*) who has purified his mind. As it is said, *Nirvana* can be perceived as the experience of an *Arahant*, a *Paccekabuddha*, or a Buddha who has completed the practice of the Four Noble Truths. *Nirvana* is, to some degree, like a dream or a wish, which cannot be (fully) described or predicted.

Nirvana appears as... an inconceivable phenomenon between delusion and *Nirvana*. This phenomenon, at that moment, is neither identical to, nor different from, delusion. The renunciation or complete freedom of man is attained when his mind is beyond the defilements of delusion and reaches *Nirvana*. How do I know that I have reached *Nirvana*? By the instrument of the Middle Path, of which the crucial element is meditation. The mind calms down, becomes enlightened and peaceful, and no longer moves forward, driven by the power of desire. This phenomenon of the mind lies between delusion and *Nirvana*. This is called the one way of the Middle Path... This phenomenon is almost impossible to prove except by a purified mind—(the mind of) a saint or a Buddha. Hence, *Nirvana* is understood not merely in the metaphysical sense, but also as the expression of something given to the saint or Buddha in their experiences.

The problem with the explanation of the concept of *Nirvana* is that *Nirvana* itself is self-descriptive. In most cases, *Nirvana* is within consciousness (whether or not it corresponds with consciousness) and can be perceived.[4] The fact is that *Nirvana* involves knowledge (*bodhi*) on the one hand and does not involve (conceptual) knowledge on the other. Consequently, knowing that one is attaining *Nirvana* or not depends upon believing or disbelieving. Believing and disbelieving are simultaneous and both exist in the consciousness of the person (no matter who). My own view is that "when I know 'P' while believing 'not-P,' I am aware on two different levels. I would like to call the first level 'pure awareness' or 'awareness involving intentionality of feeling (knowing 'P' or 'not P')."

Suppose I raise the question, "Why do I not know that I am attaining *Nirvana*?" In that case, this comes about because I may be distracted by something else, or because I may deliberately ignore it, or because my mind is in an empty state already, or because I may not wish (or care) to think about it, or for whatever reason my mind corresponds with at the moment. In any case, one cannot make the claim, "I am not attaining *Nirvana*." If one claims, "I knew all along I was attaining *Nirvana*," this does not mean he has attained *Nirvana*. His claiming a knowledge of *Nirvana* could create a false mental state (*bhāvanā-maya*... "something more 'ideal' in the 'intermediary world,' springing from meditation, truer to what is really there than that found in the sensory world"),[5] which is not the virtue of *Nirvana* that is real within his consciousness. He is "carrying" a claim of *Nirvana*, which mentally functions as the recognition of something revealing his past apprehensions, hopes, or fears that result from social habits, not from himself. By the same token, when a person says, "I am no good, because I am not practicing *samadhi*, or performing good *kamma*," examining the failure of his life, he does not mean that he is not attaining (anything). What he says is giving a description of his mental state at that moment, which does not correspond to what exists in his mind. But even if this is what is existing with his momentary and sensory consciousness, we have not established that the man knew (*Nirvana*) while he believed "not-P" (not-*Nirvana*) or that he intended to believe "not-P" (not-*Nirvana*).

In other words, the *Nirvana* of Buddhism is relevant to Kant's transcendental wisdom and intellectual wisdom, which functions freely as it is understood as phenomena or noumena. Buddhist *Nirvana* is concerned with one true reality—*Dhamma*. Kant's purpose of transcendental wisdom is a spiritual discipline, that is to say, the will of God. *Nirvana* has a teleological function, transforming "objective lure" into subjective efficiency. What is transformed into what is here, and why and how this is, remains obscure. To such questions, "there are answers and the *Tathāgata* knows them. Still, he does not reveal them because they are of no use to us."[6]

One fundamental defect of contemporary religion is that it is concerned with speaking and arguing about philosophical, moral, and psychological matters, but is not concerned with practice. For the Buddhist, there is first of all the pure path of moral law, the *Visuddhi Magga Paṭipadā* (Path of Purification).[7] Second is the beauty of the Middle Way: practicing calmness of mind and joining its peacefulness with the purest state of mind for all beings, which is called practicing meditation or *samadhi*. Third and last is the beauty of allowing the mind to be filled with complete wisdom, namely, having immediate comprehension of what is and what is not... knowing and perceiving that there is no birth of *dukkha* occurring within phenomena. This is called renunciation by wisdom, or enlightenment. Whoever lives with this beauty is said to live life with the beauty of life.

Religious believers, by and large, reduce religion to the concepts of skeptical science, accepting immediate notions of practice and ignoring all they cannot observe and measure. This is mistaken behavior. From another point of view, metaphysical reflection about the world arises from the confused notion of religious experience:

war, economic depression, racism, cultural and educational problems, and tribal, group, national, and international conflict.

I know that I have digressed from the central discussion. Nevertheless, I would like to make a few more remarks about Western religions. Westerners should not overlook that some problems arising in faith come from the belief in a God or Gods, to whom are often ascribed a variety of conflicting characteristics. Such beliefs conflict with the Oriental faith. Theravādins, especially, do not believe in a personal God. Thus, intelligent Westerners like Kant and Hume were unsatisfied with Christian theologians who conceptualized God with an exclusive, limited interpretation.

Adolf Hitler saw the leading Buddhist viewpoints as only an ethical system and nothing else; but Buddhism is more than a formal ethical system. Those who see Buddhism as merely mystical, with its cognates, give no room for Buddhism to be evaluated in any other sense. But something beyond our knowledge and consciousness about Buddhism should be observed.

Elder Buddhism regards God as quite peripheral to its main spiritual interests. The elder Buddhists are interested in 'spirit,' not 'religion.' Religion, (in this view,) has to do with this world. Indeed, by and large, they teach that real Buddhism is the clarity of agnosticism about a creator. Thus, Buddhism in this sense is unlike other philosophical beliefs, such as humanism, the atheism of Nietzsche, or the existentialism of Sartre, Camus, and so forth.

In my opinion, however, Buddhism is better described by the term 'spiritual' rather than 'religious,' or even 'spiritual' rather than 'God-centered.' Elder Buddhist doctrine involves a certain kind of "spiritual practice." An example is the contemplative life, which I will discuss later in the treatment of meditation.

We then have two choices in which to talk about Buddhism: 1) Use the word 'religion' to refer to the simplest Buddhist sense, or 2) create a new term which is not limited to 'God' or 'God-believers,' a term to cover both 'religion' (as God-oriented) and Buddhism. The first is the more plausible and radical choice, since Buddhism, mysticism, and the contemplative life are found both at the heart of agnostic Buddhism and in some phases of the "Oriental God" concept of various other branches of Buddhism. What I mean by "Oriental God" is that (these) Buddhists show either devotion to a personal God, a contemplative life, or both.

We may then connect this concept of Buddhism with Western points of view, like Wittgenstein's "Doctrine of Family Resemblance," which is reflected in the thought of Paul Tillich, or the humanism of Marx, seen as a "quasi-religion."[8] Buddhism is, therefore, unlike other religions, since it can be mystical without a god.

My aim here is not to explain mystical Buddhism as such. I merely wish to emphasize the contemplative life, in the particular sense that while life is surely marked by suffering, there are ways in which Buddhism helps us to alleviate that suffering—the foremost being the path that leads to ultimate freedom. We can find this freedom in a transcendental state, which reframes the world's process-cycle of existence (of life and rebirth). The contemplative life is related to Buddhist concentration, in which the mind itself is withdrawn from the conceptual mental images of the socially conditioned world. Thus, past, present, and future life are (seen as phenomena) in the mind of man.

Therefore, *Nirvana* is simply without empirical qualities—it is datumless. In Buddhism, the form of concentration is known as *samadhi* or *vipassanā*. I will not explain this here, as I will explore it in full detail in a later chapter. Thus, *Nirvana* is not inconceivable for the saint who has attained a mystical state through various forms of meditation. I believe it is nonsense and false to say that *Nirvana* is inconceivable, since enlightened people have indeed perceived it. *Nirvana* is able to be perceived not merely in a metaphysical sense but also as something *given* in the experience of all saints. When one is enlightened, having the 'inner eye,' one easily perceives *Nirvana* through interior experiences.[7] Hence, *Nirvana* is supreme tranquility, that bliss reported by mystics in other traditions. It is equal to Immortality or (what others call) God.

Conclusion

The conclusion of this chapter can be drawn as follows: Life is to be lived. But merely living is not the question; the question is *how* to live. The technique of living is often referred to as the 'art of living.' The art of living is avoiding bondage and gaining deliverance from the continuity of the life cycle. How? By practicing and experiencing the (contemplations related to the) Third Precept, regarding meditation on the impurity of life, and by destroying the delusion of the fresh beauty and permanence of the body. This is an improvement in the life process. If one does not do so, the continuity of life becomes a form of bondage.

Life is transitory. This transitory condition is caused by the members of *Samsara*.

Delusion is the (root cause) of life itself and the first member of *Samsara*.

Sensuality is a subsequent member of *Samsara*.

Therefore, sensuality is a cause of the cycle of life.

REFERENCE NOTES

1. *This is the conclusion answering the various questions raised in the first chapter, pp. 1 ff.*
2. *Conze, Edward. Buddhist Thought in India. p. 254.*
3. *This is certainly and perfectly clear from Majjhima Nikāya No. 63 and the fuller account of Nāgārjuna in Étienne Lamotte, translator, Le Traité de la Grande Vertu de Sagesse (Louvain: Bureau du Muséon, 1944), Vol. I, pp. 155-8.*
4. *Visuddhimagga means "most pure" and Paṭipadā means "path" or "practice."*
5. *Tillich, Paul. Christianity and the Encounter of the World Religions. pp. 5 ff., on the treatment of the definition of religion, especially the relation to Theravāda Buddhism. See also "Noumena, Nirvana and the Definition of Religions," Church Quarterly Review, January-March 1958, p. 216 ff., by Ninian Smart.*
6. *Cf. the first chapter.*

CHAPTER VIII

The Notion Of Freedom

Let me clarify the concepts of human morality and the betterment of man. These are not the *being* of man but the *quality* of man. What is the quality of man? The quality of a man can be classified into two states, generally known as mundane and super-mundane. The Ven. Chao Khun Phra Tepsiddhimuni Mahathera describes these states more clearly than other philosophers. I am quoting him below, adding my own divisions of mundane and super-mundane.

"In Buddhist tradition the term 'Path' has two (meanings), one being '*Pakati Maggo*' or an ordinary path, i.e., a way for men and animals, and another being '*Paṭipadā Magga*' or the path of good or bad behavior for men alone, traversed through deeds, words, and thoughts.

Paṭipadā Magga is divided into five kinds:

1. The Descending Path, brought about by offences against the normal Code and based on Greed, Hatred and Delusion.
2. The Human Path, the path of five moralities or the 10-fold wholesome course of action (*kusala-kamma-patha*).
3. The path to the six classes of Heaven, which comprises eight classes of moral consciousness, culminating in moral shame (*Hiri*) and Moral Dread (*Ottappa*), resulting in alms-giving, attending sermons, building chapels, temples, ecclesiastical schools, hospitals and ordinary schools.
4. The path to the Abode of Brahma, which is the development of tranquility of mind (*Samatha Bhāvanā*) by means of meditation upon any of the forty traditional subjects; very briefly, these are classified technically as the ten '*kasiṇa*' (Contemplation devices), ten '*Asubhas*' (impurities), ten '*Anussatis*' (Reflections), four

'*Brahma-Vihāras*' (Sublime States), one '***Āhārepaṭikūlasaññā***' (Reflection on the loathsomeness of food), one '*Catudhātu-vavatthāna*' (Analysis of the four elements), and four '*Arūpa-kammaṭṭhāna*' (Stages of *arūpa-jhāna*).

5. The path of Nirvana (Pali: *Nibbāna*; Sanskrit: *Nirvana*) which is the development of Insight (*Vipassanā Bhāvanā*), having *Nāma-rūpa* (mental and physical states) as the objects of meditation."[10]

Buddhism can be described simply not as a religion but as a science which allows all beings to realize who they are, thus breaking the transitory state (*samsara*). As soon as *samsara* has been destroyed, one no longer has delusion. Complete freedom (*Nirvana*) can be accomplished and attained; it is the outcome of clarity which caused him to follow and practice human morals and human goodness correctly and perfectly, according to the ideal of the Eightfold Noble Path. Hence, he attains the *Caturāriyasacca* (the Four Noble Truths), the victory over the life cycle. All defilements are weakened and finally, rebirth is exhausted (destroyed). This is the complete freedom of mankind.

Let us begin with the question, "What is freedom?" In my sense (not in formal terms), freedom means 'the condition of being able to choose and to carry out purposes created by man in his socio-political realm; purposes compatible with individual and universal choice as well as the purposes of nature.' The term freedom means 'freedom from' and 'freedom to'—freedom from one state of being to another.

The word "freedom" in the broad sense employs three meanings: 1) the primary dictionary meaning—the absence of external constraints; 2) practical purpose, or actual capability (having available means); 3) a power of conscious choice between significant, known alternatives. This encompasses the fundamental concepts of "freedom from," "freedom to," and "freedom of." Therefore, my purpose is to attempt to explain the meaning of freedom in the third category and open the common question for the self to answer: "freedom *from* what, freedom *to* what, and freedom *of* what." Basically, I mean that man is free in the dialectical sense. By dialectical sense, I mean the positive and negative sense, insofar as man can do something and also choose not to do it; that man can make up his mind, can freely say "yes" or "no" when he wants to, to any given question or command. Furthermore, he can decide for himself the crucial questions (matters) of duty, such as "what," "to what," and "of what." If there is will, there is freedom of action. In short, I mean freedom of thought, speech, and action from physical-psychological production, individually as well as socially.

Since we are discussing freedom, one may have the question in mind: "What is *not* free?" Man is not free insofar as he is virtually inhibited by others from his will to do something, being obligated from action X to action Y, and so forth. This binds him, whether through direct coercion or by fear of conscious consequences, even though it might be better for him than his heart's willing, attention, or desire. In any case, this causes man to be unfree, since he is socially obligated. Man is naturally and in essence free. The Zen masters aptly expressed that we are born free and equal.

Nevertheless, we live in political and economic societies controlled by tyrannical people. Hence, though freedom is theoretically possible, it has little meaning in the social, conventional world. Freedom exists in the spiritual ground of Zen; all fetters and manacles we seem to be carrying about us are put on later through ignorance, (obscuring) the true condition of existence. This is one of the senses of freedom in Zen Buddhism.

As I mentioned earlier, freedom is related to ethical concerns—good, bad, sinful, and so forth. The Buddha teaches that good or bad is independent of academic or socio-political force. He allows man to re-examine and continue acting according to his freedom of thought. Evidence of this can be found in his conversation with the Kālāmas in the *Aṅguttara Nikāya*:

"Yes, Kālāmas, it is proper that you have doubt, that you have perplexity, for doubt has arisen in a matter which is doubtful. Now look, Kālāmas, do not be led by reports, or tradition, or hearsay. Be not led by the authority of religious texts, or by mere logic or by inference, or by considering appearances, or by the delight in speculative opinions, or by seeming possibilities, or by the idea: 'this is our teacher.' But, O Kālāmas, when you know for yourselves that certain things are unwholesome (*akusala*), wrong, or bad, then give them up... and when you know for yourselves that certain things are wholesome (*kusala*) and good, then accept them and follow them."[11]

What is good or bad has to be decided by oneself, not otherwise. This is the idea of freedom of thought in Buddhism. In the *Vīmaṁsaka Sutta*, the Buddha allows monks and laymen to examine the Buddha himself. As it is said, the disciple should "examine even the Tathāgata himself." He told the *bhikkhus* that the disciple must be fully convinced of the true value of the teacher whom he followed.[12]

Indeed, the Buddhist notion of freedom is practical. Buddhism makes more sense to me than other concepts. I believe I am able to choose *why* I was born; thus I find ridiculous some expressions and opinions that "man is not free according to his ability, therefore he is not able to choose why he was born here." The Buddha taught that freedom exists for all his disciples as well as for himself; freedom existed for him before he discovered it. In the *Mahāparinibbāna Sutta*, the Buddha taught that he never thought of controlling the *Saṅgha* (monk community), nor did he want the *Saṅgha* to depend on him. He stressed that there was no esoteric doctrine in his teaching, nothing hidden in the "closed fist of a teacher" (***ācariya-muṭṭhi***). Or, to put it in other words, there was never anything "up his sleeve."[13]

The Buddha gave the freedom of thought: he taught that he is not the *ruler* of the world (of man) and that the world does not depend on what he knows, which is already "out there." Man must go beyond what he *knows* to what he *needs* to understand: the world *as* the Buddha understands it. Hence, man obligates himself to the world, regardless of the kind of connection he makes. That is the freedom of choice for each person. Even though the world is called the "conditioned world," man can be free through his freedom of choice, which I call momentary *Nirvana*. Man lives in a richly conditioned, or *samsaric*, existence, but in his own mind—as the *Dhammapada* teaches—everything includes freedom and essentially depends upon what we think and nothing more.

Hence, the freedom of thought allowed by the Buddha is not similar to that of other philosophies. Freedom of thought is a necessary part of man's nature, since the emancipation of man depends upon his own realization of his truth and not upon something external to himself, either someone else or some God.

Theories of freedom in Western thought are rooted in academic traditions from diverse sources. It is basically from European thought that Western freedom is defined as individuality, namely, from one man to another. Now, we should examine Indian thought, particularly the Buddhist concept of freedom, in order to return to our original discussion.

The fundamental belief of Buddhism is that man is free and primordial before he is born. He is born here, according to choice, as male, female, etc., before the five *skandhas* have formed. As such, man is completely free in his own will and nature.

Buddhism does not believe in sin, as some religions do. Why do I say that? Because man is originally ignorant (*avijjā*). To be free and clarify his understanding, he must destroy this delusion. Thus, man is free when he destroys delusion with his enlightenment. Here he has real, absolute freedom (*Nirvana*). Freedom in Buddhism comes from the will of man in attempting to destroy the members of the causal chain (the Twelvefold Chain of human nature). As we know, to the Buddhist, man is not "sinful." He does not enlighten himself simply because he does not *know* good or bad. This is caused by ignorance (*avijjā*) and is driven by desire (*tanhā*). Hence, *avijjā* and *tanhā* are the fundamental conditions that he has to overcome. *Avijjā* is man's original nature, and *tanhā* is the attribute of *avijjā*'s agency. This process Buddhists call rebirth, which is synonymous with the Hindu concept of reincarnation.

Hence, for man to achieve absolute freedom, he has to produce the sufficient conditions for the absence of ignorance and the absence of desire. To ascertain that his effort will succeed, he must be able to eliminate the necessary conditions of ignorance and desire. This is the most significant and fundamental basis for humanity to achieve its ultimate freedom. Otherwise, freedom will not be attained. Attaining freedom means to break the "chain of suffering" (the *Four Noble Truths*). There is no accidental way to achieve freedom.

Ethical Science

By "ethical science," I mean morality. Morality is the compatible living with one's own freedom and the freedom of others. In the (Noble Eightfold Path), this is known as "Right Livelihood" (and other moral factors). Later I will further discuss "Right Livelihood."

Why is morality required in all religions? Because all of us are (at times) selfish animal-beings who have desires, commit harmful acts, etc., against one another. This action is due to natural human selfishness, which is "free" for one's own action: one commits this free act under desire, but it is an "unfree" action to others. Why do we do it? To confirm our own good and happiness in a selfish way.

Therefore, morality (Pali: *Sīla*) is required so that man may know himself in his own actions. Every religion has (a concept of) morality. The Buddhist moral doctrine is most significant in the Eightfold Noble Path, which embodies the first step of the practice of morality (*Sīla*), meditation (*Samādhi*), and wisdom (*Paññā*). The practice of morality does not only belong to monks or ministers, but to all society. For instance, Mahatma Gandhi was influenced by Hinduism and Buddhism in the first law of morality—non-violence (*ahiṁsā*). When Great Britain was oppressing the Indian people, under the guidance of Gandhi, they responded with non-violence. Their reward was victory and the return of freedom. There are many good examples that demonstrate the obvious need for morality in human society, although they are unnecessary to describe here. Morality is essential for a social and political system to promote peace and freedom for individuals and society.

In early India, many religious leaders ignored ethical science even though they were aware of it. Among themselves, Brahmins, kings, merchants, workers, slaves, and untouchables treated each other cruelly, like animals. Most religious leaders pronounced that religion tries to rid (the world of) unfreedom and prejudice, providing happiness for all mankind. Obviously, the caste system still flourished. How, then, could all men be happy? Religious leaders had tried to teach their followers to reach super-mundane rather than mundane freedom. Hence, this typical doctrine was invalid and useless, and it dissatisfied Gautama Buddha. He became a revolutionary against the system.

Samādhi is known as the supreme mundane state, as it is the state that allows the practitioner's faculty of mind to reach the ultimate human goal: *Nirvana*. It is necessary to understand morality before I explain the theory of *Samādhi*.

REFERENCE NOTES

1. *The Ven. Chao Khun Phra Tepsiddhimuni Mahathera. The Path to Nirvana. Bangkok, Thailand: Prachandra Printing Press, 1971, pp. 1-2.*
2. *Aṅguttara Nikāya. Colombo, 1929, p. 115.*
3. *Vīmaṁsaka Sutta, no. 47 of Majjhima Nikāya (PTS edition).*
4. *Dīgha Nikāya II. Colombo, 1929, p. 62.*

CHAPTER IX

The Theory Of Samadhi

As space and time are limited, it is most important to discuss the crucial question of meditation (*Samādhi*) and to stress insight (*Vipassanā*) where it is needed. *Samādhi* is known to the West as "meditation." When I speak of meditation, I am also referring to insight. I will not, however, discuss *Samādhi* in complete detail, since it is not the essential aspect of my thesis.

I would like to divide the discussion of *Samādhi* into two subdivisions: A) The Subjects and Methods of *Samādhi*, which deal with the literal sources from the text. B) The Practice of *Samādhi*. This is intended to benefit both Westerners and Thais. If one wants to reach *Nirvana*, of course, one must spend a great deal of time practicing alone—either in a temple with a teacher or in the forest—since *Samādhi* is not something one can learn *only* by intensive study. It is a practical way of life.

A) The Subjects and Methods of Samādhi

I would like to further divide the subjects and methods into two parts:

1. The Literal Sources of *Samādhi*
2. The Connotations and Definitions of *Samādhi*

I) The Literal Sources of Samādhi

Samādhi can be found in numerous canonical texts. If we study carefully, *Samādhi* can be found in almost every collection of the *Tipiṭaka* under the systems of *Samādhi* and *Vipassanā*. In order to recognize it easily, we should use the following order: a) *Samādhi* found in the *Nikāyas* b) *Samādhi* found in the *Abhidhamma* c) *Samādhi* found in the Commentaries

Samādhi is general mental training. *Vipassanā* is physical and mental training. Both may be practiced individually or in conjunction with other forms of training, which are related to the *Jhānas* (absorptions). There are four *Jhānas*. The four *Jhānas* are discussed in the *Aṅguttara Nikāya*. The "Jhānavagga" of the *Aṅguttara Nikāya*[1] provides a comprehensive list of all types of *Samādhi*.

a) Samādhi Found in the Nikāyas

According to my observation of textual references, these methods of meditation have numerous sources; we will not discuss all of them here. However, we will look briefly at these sources.

1. Samādhi and Vipassanā (The Four Jhānas) The *Jhānavagga* of the *Aṅguttara Nikāya* has the fullest information about the Four *Jhānas*. "Detached from sensual objects, detached from evil things, the disciple enters into the first Absorption, which is accompanied by Thought-Conception (*vitakka*) and Discursive Thinking (*vicāra*), is born of detachment, and is filled with Rapture (*pīti*) and Happiness (*sukha*)."[2] ... "This first absorption is free from five things, and five are present: when the disciple enters the absorption, the five hindrances have vanished (lust, ill will, torpor and sloth, restlessness and mental worry, and doubts), and there are present: Thought-Conception (*vitakka*), Discursive Thinking (*vicāra*), Rapture (*pīti*), Happiness (*sukha*), and One-pointedness of Mind (citt'ekaggatā or *samādhi*)."[3]

Let's examine the literal meaning. In the *Visuddhimagga*, *vitakka* is compared to grasping a pot, and *vicāra* is likened to wiping it. In the first absorption, *vitakka* and *vicāra* are present. They are absent in the subsequent absorptions. "In the second Absorption, there are three Factors: Rapture, Happiness, and Concentration... In the third Absorption, there are two Factors: Equanimous Happiness (*upekkhā-sukha*) and Concentration (*citt'ekaggatā*). Right after practicing the third Absorption, he enters the state beyond pleasure and pain... into the fourth absorption, which is purified by equanimity (*upekkhā*) and mindfulness." Except for the first *jhāna*, the practitioner of *samādhi* enters a state free from thought-conception and discursive thinking. The second absorption is born of concentration (*samādhi*) and filled with rapture (*pīti*) and happiness (*sukha*). The fourth absorption contains two factors: concentration and equanimity (*upekkhā*).

Further textual reference should be considered. In the *Visuddhimagga*, forty subjects of meditation (*kammaṭṭhāna*) are enumerated and treated in detail. One should also study *Visuddhimagga*, IX, 1-3, and A. I, pp. 38-43. In conclusion, all Four Absorptions can be obtained through Mindfulness of Breathing (cf. *Vis. M.*, VIII, 3), the ten *Kasiṇa*-exercises (cf. *Vis. M.*, IV, V), the contemplation of Equanimity (*upekkhā*), and the practice of the fourth *Brahma-vihāra* (cf. *Vis. M.*, IX, 4).

2. The Four Excellent States (*Brahma-Vihāras*: Mettā, Karuṇā, Muditā, and Upekkhā) Perhaps the best topics of study to enrich one's understanding of Buddhism are the *Jhānas* and the Four Exalted States. If one wants to be an expert in Buddhist meditation, I highly recommend that he (or she) become a monk (or nun). Study alone is, of course, only academic and intellectual grounding, leaving practical matters unattended.

The *Brahma-Vihāras* are inter-related with the absorptions: The first three absorptions are attained through the development of Loving-Kindness (*mettā*), Compassion (*karuṇā*), and Sympathetic Joy (*muditā*), which is the practice of the first three *Brahma-Vihāras* (cf. *Vis. M.*, IX, 1-3). The first absorption is attained through the ten concentrations on Impurity (*asubha-bhāvanā*, i.e., the Cemetery Contemplations, which are ten according to the enumeration in *Vis. M.*, VI) and the contemplation of the Body (i.e., the 32 parts of the body, *Vis. M.*, VIII, 2). This is merely an example. The absorptions are related to the *Brahma-Vihāras* and other concentration/contemplation practices treated in *Vis. M.*, III-XIII. Again, the absorptions and *Brahma-Vihāras* are one of the noble paths for reaching the end of suffering. "This is the Middle Path which the perfect one has discovered, which makes one both to see and to know, and which leads to peace, to discernment, to enlightenment, to Nirvana."[4] Therefore, "following upon this path, you will put an end to suffering."[5]

3. The Four Applications of Mindfulness (*Satipaṭṭhāna*) This is the same as the seventh step of the Eightfold Noble Path (Right Mindfulness). "Now being equipped with this lofty 'Morality' (*Sīla*), equipped with this noble 'Control of the Senses' (*Indriyasaṁvara*), and filled with this noble 'Mindfulness and Clear Comprehension' (*Sati-Sampajañña*), one has attained the Four Applications of Mindfulness." This method is used for both *Samādhi* and *Vipassanā*.

4. The Four Right Efforts (*Sammappadhāna*) (See my discussion on the concept of Right Effort.)

5. The Four Bases of Psychic Power (*Iddhipāda*) This method aligns with the Eightfold Noble Path and the Four Absorptions, yet places more emphasis on concentration (*Samādhi*) practiced respectively with will (*chanda*), energy (*viriya*), mind (*citta*), and investigation (*vīmaṁsā-iddhipāda*). This system is practiced in *Samādhi* as well as in the last state of *Vipassanā*. *Samādhi* and *Vipassanā* are inter-related. One should bear in mind that *Samādhi* is (sometimes) preceded by *Vipassanā*, although some authorities believe *Vipassanā* is preceded by *Samādhi*.

6. The Five Faculties (*Indriya*) The five faculties include faith (*saddhā*), energy (*viriya*), mindfulness (*sati*), concentration (*samādhi*), and wisdom (*paññā*). (In Pali: *Saddhindriya*, *Viriyindriya*, *Satindriya*, *Samādhindriya*, and *Paññindriya*, respectively). This system is related to the Bases of Psychic Power and the Eightfold Noble Path.

7. The Five Powers (*Bala*) The five powers include the power of faith (*saddhā*), energy (*viriya*), mindfulness (*sati*), concentration (*samādhi*), and wisdom (*paññā*). (In Pali: *Saddhā-bala*, *Viriya-bala*, *Sati-bala*, *Samādhi-bala*, and *Paññā-bala*, respectively). These correspond to the five faculties. Thus, it can be said that they cause and effect each other in an interrelated practice.

8. The Seven Factors of Enlightenment (*Bojjhaṅga*) This section relates to the Four Applications of Mindfulness, the Five Faculties, and the Five Powers. It is said that "The disciple dwells in contemplation of mind-objects (*dhammā*), namely the seven 'Factors of Enlightenment' (*Bojjhaṅga*). He knows when there is in him 'Mindfulness' (*Sati*), 'Investigation of the Law' (*Dhammavicaya*), 'Energy' (*Viriya*), 'Enthusiasm' (*Pīti*), 'Tranquility' (*Passaddhi*), 'Concentration' (*Samādhi*), and 'Equanimity' (*Upekkhā*). He knows when (a factor) is not within him, knows how it arises, and how it is fully developed."

9. The Noble Eightfold Path (*Ariya Aṭṭhaṅgika Magga*) This system is commonly known. It is an extremely significant method for both *Samādhi* and *Vipassanā*. The practice of the Eightfold Noble Path overlaps all other systems. Some authorities say that the Eightfold Noble Path is presented in the context of the *Bodhipakkhiyādhammā* (37 Factors of Enlightenment).

10. The Eight States of Release (*Vimokkha*) It can be said that this system is related to the Four Absorptions and the Eightfold Noble Path. Particularly, it relates to the attainment of *Nirodha-samāpatti* ("Entirely transcending the sphere of neither-perception-nor-non-perception, he enters and abides in the complete cessation (*Nirodha*) of perception (*Saññā*) and feeling (*Vedanā*)"). This system is known in the practice of *Samādhi*. The highest conception of this system is known as *Saññā-vedayita-nirodha*, wherein perceptions and feelings cease.

11. The Eight Spheres of Mastery (*Abhibhāyatana*) This system is related to the Eightfold Noble Path and maintains knowledge of distinct objects of the mind through perception. For example, "Possessing internal form-perception, one sees external forms as limited, beautiful or ugly... Having mastered this... one perceives, thinking, 'I know, I see'." This system, practiced in *Samādhi*, is an effect of *Kasiṇa* meditation.

12. The Ten Devices (*Kasiṇa*) The Ten Devices are: the Four Elements (earth, water, fire, air), the Four Major Colors (blue, yellow, red, white), Space, and Consciousness. The four major colors are identical to the color *kasiṇas*. Space is interrelated with the Four Elements, and consciousness is joined with the *Arūpa* (formless) absorptions. I would like to clearly describe the four elements, as they have the most significant function in our psycho-physical system. The disciple contemplates this body, however it may stand or move, with regard to the elements: "This body consists of the solid element, the liquid element, the heating element, and the vibrating element." This state of being consists of nothing but the elements. The Buddha advised getting rid of attachment. We can see the separateness of the body; that the body can be divided into elements or the five *skandhas*. There is no (permanent essence) in man... This is the best treatment that Buddhist psychotherapy offers: that man is unique on one hand and, on the other, inseparable—"I am not separate from you and you are not different from me." This counters the "Heresy of Separateness." With no attachment to this body, the high state of consciousness is attained (the *Jhānas*). The result is that the meditator perceives the emptiness of the body in regard to the four elements (see details of this in *Visuddhimagga* XII, 2). (The Pali terms for earth, water, fire, air, blue, yellow, red, white, space, and consciousness are: *pathavī, āpo, tejo, vāyo, nīla, pīta, lohita, odāta, ākāsa,* and *viññāṇa kasiṇa*.)

13. Twenty Subjects Known as *Saññā* The term *saññā* (perception) means "contemplation" on one hand and "insight" on the other.[6] (See the discussion on the three aspects of being.) This system is related to both *Samādhi* and *Vipassanā*. One should realize that not all twenty subjects known as *saññā* come from a single source. For example, some are found in the *Aṅguttara Nikāya*. (One should research further in: 1) A.N. III, p. 227; 2) S.N. V, p. 345; 3) M.N. I, pp. 269 & 275; III, p. 3 ff.)

14. The Ten *Anussati* (Recollections/Mindfulnesses)

1. *Buddhānussati* (Recollection of the Buddha)
2. *Dhammānussati* (Recollection of the Dhamma)
3. *Saṅghānussati* (Recollection of the Sangha)
4. *Sīlānussati* (Recollection of Morality)
5. *Cāgānussati* (Recollection of Charity/Generosity)
6. *Devatānussati* (Recollection of the Devas)
7. ***Ānāpānasati*** (Mindfulness of Breathing)
8. *Maranassati* (Mindfulness of Death)
9. *Kāyagatāsati* (Mindfulness of the Physical Body)
10. *Upasamānussati* (Mindfulness of Peace/Calmness)

According to the *Visuddhimagga*, these ten subjects are included in both *Samādhi* and *Vipassanā* meditation. The *Abhidhammatthasaṅgaha* has mentioned the following systems as the *Vipassanā-Kammaṭṭhāna*.[7] The practice of these systems will lead to freedom, or the complete extinction of bondage to the conditional world (*Anupādisesa-parinibbāna*):

1. ***Sīla-visuddhi*** (Purity of Moral Conduct)
2. ***Citta-visuddhi*** (Purity of Mind)
3. ***Diṭṭhi-visuddhi*** (Purity of Views)

4. ***Kaṅkhāvitaraṇa-visuddhi*** (Purity of Overcoming Doubts)

5. ***Maggāmagga-ñāṇadassana-visuddhi*** (Purity of Knowledge and Insight into the Right and Wrong Paths)

6. ***Paṭipadā-ñāṇadassana-visuddhi*** (Purity of Knowledge and Insight into the Path of Progress)

7. **Ñāṇadassana-visuddhi** (Purity of Knowledge and Insight (into the Noble Path))

These systems clearly demonstrate that meditation is a prerequisite for insight, as they proceed from and develop out of one another. By practicing these systems, any person, even one in the social, mundane world, may directly enter *Nirvana*. According to the *Visuddhimagga*, these systems of practice are the successive steps of purification.[8] *Visuddhi* (purification) is concerned entirely with the development of full knowledge (*paññā-bhāvanā*).

Finally, and most importantly, all meditation systems described above are found in the *Nikāyas*.

b) Samādhi Found in the Abhidhamma

One of the passages in the *Visuddhimagga* describes all methods (systems) of *Samādhi* and *Vipassanā* as interrelated with their psychological characteristics. One significant thing to bear in mind is that both *Samādhi* and *Vipassanā* are psychological aspects (related to what is) known to the West as E.S.P.

Samādhi and *Vipassanā* are often practiced in conjunction with the Four *Jhānas*, acknowledging that this system is, to some degree, primarily concerned with insight alone. Why? Because practice of the Four *Jhānas* leads to the highest state of mental training.[9] The rest of the systems in the *Nikāyas* are normally *a priori* and *a posteriori* related.

Generally, the Four *Jhānas* are considered the spiritual goal for all Indian thinkers, including Gautama. The *Jhānas* are the scheme of all states of consciousness. One can become a god or man and perform miracles, depending upon the level of the *Jhānas* attained. This regards both *Samādhi* and *Vipassanā*. Thus the *Jhāyin* (one who has attained the Four *Jhānas*) is the mediator between man and god, *māyā* and enlightenment (knowledge), self and no-self (*Rūpa-Brahma* and *Arūpa-Brahma*), the social mundane and the super-mundane, ordinary men and saints, freedom and bondage, etc.

All of these states of consciousness come from mental phenomena which are controlled by the *Jhānas*. What is in our minds is nothing but thought directed to an object. I would like to call this "sentimental essence"—the *action* of the mind rather than the mind itself. As it is said in the *Dhammapada*, "All that we are is the result of our thought."

Thus, all meditation and insight are accompanied by the *Jhānas*, since the *Jhānas* are the crucial states of consciousness wherein saints ascertain final mental training before becoming aware of reaching *Nirvana*.

The following accompany the *Jhānas*:

1. The Eight *Kasiṇas* (Devices) (The text lists ten previously, eight here refers to all except ākāsa and viññāṇa).
2. The Eight Objects of Mastery (*Abhibhāyatana*)
3. The first three Stages of Release (*Vimokkha*)
4. The four *Brahma-Vihāras*
5. The ten Impurities (*Asubha*), which are:
    1. *Uddhumātaka* (A Swollen Corpse)
    2. *Vinīlaka* (A Discolored Corpse)
    3. *Vipubbaka* (A Festering Corpse)
    4. *Vicchiddaka* (A Mangled Corpse)
    5. *Vikkhāyitaka* (A Gnawed Corpse)
    6. *Vikkhittaka* (A Dismembered Corpse)

7. *Hatavikkhittaka* (A Cut and Dismembered Corpse)

8. *Lohitaka* (A Blood-Stained Corpse)

9. *Puḷavaka* (A Worm-Infested Corpse)

10. *Aṭṭhika* (A Skeleton)

6. The four *Arūpa-Jhānas* (Formless Absorptions), corresponding to the fourth, fifth, sixth, and seventh *Vimokkhas*.

If we compare the above systems to those found in the *Nikāyas*, we see that two *Kasiṇas*, *Viññāṇa-kasiṇa* (consciousness) and ***Ākāsa-kasiṇa*** (space), are missing. Why? Because some authorities think these *Kasiṇas* are connected with the *Arūpas* (formless states). As it is said: "In the *Mahāsakuludāyi Sutta*, ten devices (*Kasiṇas*) are mentioned. Of them, *Viññāṇa-kasiṇa* and ***Ākāsa-kasiṇa*** are infinite consciousness produced by the *Arūpa-Jhānas*... ***Ākāsa*** and *Viññāṇa kasiṇa* relate to the attainment of the formless state."[10]

Therefore, according to the *Abhidhamma*, we can conclude that there are thirty-seven subtypes of *Jhāna* meditation—thirty-three of *Rūpa-Jhānas* (Form Absorptions) and four of *Arūpa-Jhānas* (Formless Absorptions)—which are concerned more with *Samādhi* than *Vipassanā*.

c) Samādhi Found in the Commentaries

The most well-known commentator of the *Visuddhimagga* is Buddhaghosa Thera. He is known as a Hīnayānist commentator. Mainly, he emphasizes the forty subjects known as *kammaṭṭhāna* (exercises of meditation), which appear under the seven following divisions:

1. The ten *Kasiṇas*

2. The ten *Asubhas* (Impurities)

3. The ten *Anussati* (Recollections)

4. The four *Brahma-Vihāras*

5. The four *Arūpas* (Formless Absorptions): A. ***Ākāsānañcāyatana*** (The sphere of infinite space) B. *Viññāṇañcāyatana* (The sphere of infinite consciousness) C. ***Ākiñcaññāyatana*** (The sphere of nothingness) D. *Nevasaññānāsaññāyatana* (The sphere of neither-perception-nor-non-perception)

6. ***Āhāre Paṭikūlasaññā*** (The contemplation of loathsomeness of food)

7. *Catudhātu-vavatthāna* (Analysis of the four physical elements)[11]

In short, Buddhaghosa has gradually developed the *Visuddhis* (Purifications) (in relation to) the *Tisikkhā* (Threefold Training). The first two *Visuddhis*, revealing Moral Conduct (*Sīla*) and Concentration (*Samādhi*), signify *Samādhi* practice. The last five *Visuddhis*, revealing *Paññā-bhāvanā* (meditation on knowledge), signify *Vipassanā*.

He has specifically cited the sixth, *Paṭipadā-ñāṇadassana-visuddhi* (Purity of Knowledge and Insight into the Path of Progress), which signifies *Nibbāna*, in regard to the ninefold *Paññā* (knowledge) of insight:

1. ***Udayabbayānupassanā-ñāṇa***: Knowledge which reflects on the rise and fall of composite things.

2. ***Bhaṅgānupassanā-ñāṇa***: Knowledge which reflects on the breaking up (dissolution) of the perishable nature of composite things.

3. ***Bhayaṭṭhāna-ñāṇa***: Knowledge of the appearance of composite things as fearful.

4. **Ādīnavānupassanā-ñāṇa**: Knowledge which reflects on the dangers of composite things.

5. ***Nibbidānupassanā-ñāṇa***: Knowledge that reflects on the feelings of disgust aroused by composite things that are dangerous.

6. ***Muñcitukamyatā-ñāṇa***: Knowledge of the desire for release from composite things which arouse feelings of disgust.

7. ***Paṭisaṅkhānupassanā-ñāṇa***: Knowledge which reflects on analyzing composite things in order to be released from them.

8. ***Saṅkhārupekkhā-ñāṇa***: Knowledge of indifference toward composite things.

9. ***Anuloma-ñāṇa***: Adaptive knowledge which rises in connection with the Four Noble Truths.

One should bear in mind that normally there are ten kinds of knowledge of insight, but the tenth (*Gotrabhū-ñāṇa*) (functions as a bridge to the tenth *visuddhi*). My personal experience is that as long as the meditator practices all of the first ninefold *paññā*, the final ***Ñāṇadassana-visuddhi*** (Purity of Knowledge and Insight) is attained.

Some authorities argue that (a specific "tenth knowledge"), not being found in the earlier work of Buddhaghosa, is thus peculiar to the *Visuddhimagga*, but *should* be found in the seventh system of purity, the *Paṭisambhidāmagga*, as mentioned by Sāriputta the Great. One should freely criticize this.

It is useful to note that even in the Commentary, Buddhaghosa emphasizes the forty subjects (*kammaṭṭhāna*). He mentions *kammaṭṭhāna* as being thirty-eight in number in the Pali Text.[12] At any rate, detailed information cannot be found. In textual comparative studies, it appears that the last two of the ten *Kasiṇas* (space and consciousness) have been omitted in the *Dhammasaṅgaṇī*. I am almost certain, because of this, that the (related) knowledge should be maintained. The forty subjects have been practiced as the fundamental *samādhi* method of the Theravāda school.

Besides this work, which I have mentioned, one should further study the works of the followers of Buddhaghosa, such as the *Abhidhammatthasaṅgaha* of Anuruddha Thera and the *Compendium of Philosophy* of Mr. S.Z. Aung and Dr. Rhys Davids; the *Vimuttimagga* of Upatissa, translated by Rev. N.R.M. Ehara; and *The Path of Freedom*, from the Chinese source, by Thera Soma and Kheminda Thera. All of these modern works have consequently developed from the works of Buddhaghosa. As Edward Conze says, "This (*Vimuttimagga*) is a treatise very much on the lines of the *Visuddhimagga*, but written from the standpoint of the Abhayagirivāsin sect, whereas Buddhaghosa follows the Mahāvihāra."[13]

It should be noted that when the Buddhist commentaries discuss *Samādhi*, it is connected to certain kinds of *Jhānas*, which in turn are connected to (mastery over) the senses. This is *Jhānic Samādhi*.

Furthermore, *Samādhi* is classified into four kinds in accordance with the Four Stages of *Jhāna* as follows:

1. That which is associated with five mental factors—namely *Vitakka* (Thought-Conception), *Vicāra* (Discursive Thinking), *Pīti* (Rapture), *Sukha* (Happiness), and *Ekaggatā* (One-pointedness)—with the suppression of the five Hindrances, is called "Samādhi of the first Jhāna" (*pathamajjhānaṅga*).
2. That which is associated with the three factors—viz. *Pīti*, *Sukha*, and *Ekaggatā*—is called "Samādhi of the second Jhāna" (*dutiyajjhānaṅga*).
3. That which is associated with two factors—*Sukha* and *Ekaggatā*—is known as "Samādhi of the third Jhāna" (*tatiyajjhānaṅga*).
4. That which is associated with *Ekaggatā*, together with equanimity (*upekkhā*), is called "Samādhi of the fourth Jhāna" (*catutthajjhānaṅga*).[14]

Thus, these systems of *Samādhi* are associated with *Nirvana*. When a *samādhin* (meditator) reaches a certain level, he then penetrates with his mind into the true nature of things in themselves (noumena). When and how knowledge arrives in his mind appears according to the above-mentioned fourfold categories.

What do I mean by knowing the true nature of things, or noumena? The ontological and metaphysical setting falls under the *samādhin's* epistemology. There are two types of *samādhins*: the *Vipassanā-yānika* (who uses *vipassanā* as his vehicle) and the *Sukkha-vipassaka* (“dry-visioned” meditator, who attains *arahantship* without *jhāna*). In any case, it is possible for *samādhins* to know the true nature through their meditation, which is known as the attainment of the Noble Paths and Fruition by pure insight (*Vipassanā*). As it is said:

“Formations are all impermanent” When he sees thus with understanding And turns away from what is ill That is the path of purity.[15]

II) The Connotations and Definitions of Samādhi

“Samādhi” is a Pali word. *Samādhi* and *Vipassanā* are inter-related and depend upon the Threefold Training (*Tisikkhā*), viz., *Sīla* (morality), *Samādhi* (concentration), and *Paññā* (wisdom):

1. ***Sīla-magga*** (The Path of Morality): This may be divided into the *Pañca-sīla* (Five Precepts), *Dasa-sīla* (Ten Precepts), and *Pātimokkha-sīla*, which are further categorized as mundane or super-mundane. The *Pañca-sīla* and *Dasa-sīla* are considered ordinary mundane *sīlas*, while the *Pātimokkha-sīla* (the monastic code) is considered super-mundane. The latter, held seriously by Theravāda Buddhists, is found in the *Vinaya Piṭaka*.

2. ***Samādhi-magga*** (The Path of Concentration): This is the Path of Meditative Concentration and consists of mindfulness (*sati*), concentrative absorption (*samādhi*), and meditative development (*bhāvanā*). It is sometimes called insight. This leads to transcendent comprehension and understanding (*Paññā*; Skt. *Prajñā*), which is enlightenment (*Bodhi*). This path is practiced actively in the Theravāda schools, especially in Thailand and Burma. The Mahāyāna school describes this as the notion of the *Sukhāvatī* (Pure Land) Movement, and the Vajrayāna school has practiced it in the Tibetan culture. The Mahāyāna school in China translated this path as *Ch'an*, which later gave rise to *Zen* in Japan and is maintained similarly in Korea and Vietnam.

3. ***Paññā-magga*** (The Path of Wisdom; Skt. *Prajñā-mārga*): This is the Path of Transcendent Comprehension and Understanding for

Enlightenment (*Bodhi*). (Cf. *Adhipaññā-sikkhā*; Skt. *Adhiprajñā*). There are three kinds of *paññā*: a. ***Sutamaya-paññā***: Wisdom gained from oral tradition (lit. "hearing"), e.g., Ānanda listening to the Buddha. b. ***Cintāmaya-paññā***: Wisdom gained from pure thought or reflection. c. ***Bhāvanāmaya-paññā***: Wisdom gained from meditative development (cultural training). This path is held seriously by the Theravādin school. They have especially used this as a study of the analysis of existence (*atthāna*) in the *Abhidhamma*.

In addition to this Threefold Training are the *Bhatti-magga* (the Path of Devotional Practice relating spiritual aid—the art of committing actions of merit, *Puñña*) and the *Buddhānusmṛti-magga* (the path of complete reliance upon the efficacy of *Karuṇā* (compassion) as manifested and offered by the Amitābha Buddha, who is revealed to the Bodhisattva Avalokiteśvara). We should pay attention to both of these paths, although my aim here is not to elaborate on them.

The Threefold Training (*Tisikkhā*) is held by all schools. It was seriously practiced in early Mahāyāna schools and has become their crucial standpoint even today. This Threefold Training is referred to as the "Only Path" (*Ekayāna Magga*) and is found in texts containing the special theory of the *magga* (path) to the attainment of *Nirvana*, according to all Buddhist faiths. When one practices the Threefold Training, one has virtuous conduct.

What is "path," or understanding-as-path? The path is the way in which man brings himself to liberation from the bonds of phenomenal existence; it is the process of the cognition of the way things are—Truth as *Nirvana*.

The five principal paths noted by E. Obermiller are:

1. The path of accumulating merit (*Sambhāra-mārga*).

2. The path of Training (*Prayoga-mārga*).

3. The path of Illumination (*Darśana-mārga*).

4. The path of Concentration (*Bhāvanā-mārga*).

5. The final path, where one is no longer subject to training (*Aśaikṣa-mārga*).[16] The last three represent "the path of the Saint" (***Ārya-mārga***), whereas the first two are regarded as subservient degrees.

Obermiller further describes the path as having two chief factors of realization: "...the perfect quiescence of the mind (***śamatha***) and transcendental analysis (*vipaśyanā*)... Therefore all the yogins, all the meditators, *eo ipso* all the Saints of their paths, must at all times take recourse to mental quiescence and transcendental analysis."[17]

Buddhaghosa, in his exposition in the *Visuddhimagga*, embodies all Buddhist doctrines in the Threefold Training as:

1. Adhi-Sīla (The higher virtue of moral conduct)

2. Adhi-Citta (The higher mindfulness/consciousness)

3. Adhi-Paññā (The higher wisdom)

Thus, the Threefold Training is the *Sampadā* (accomplishment) in the progress of life toward complete freedom. That accomplishment requires the "aggregates" (*khandha*) which all Buddhists have observed:

1. ***Sīla-khandha***: The principle dealing with the practice of morality.

2. ***Samādhi-khandha***: The principle dealing with the development of concentration.

3. ***Paññā-khandha***: The principle dealing with the development of true wisdom. These three principles are completed by:

4. ***Vimutti-khandha***: The principle dealing with the attainment of emancipation.

5. ***Vimutti-ñāṇadassana-khandha***: The principle dealing with the realization (knowledge and vision) of that emancipation.[18]

The Threefold Training, as it appears in the Theravāda Pali tradition, reads:

"Thus have I heard... (and the Exalted One said): 'Monks, there are these three forms of training. What three? The training in the higher morality (*Adhisīla-sikkhā*), the training in the higher thought (*Adhicitta-sikkhā*), and the training in the higher insight (*Adhipaññā-sikkhā*).... 'And what, monks, is the training in the higher insight? Herein a monk understands, as it really is, the meaning of "This is *Dukkha*"...' These are the three forms of training."[19]

One should bear in mind that the Threefold Training consists of both *Samādhi* and *Vipassanā*. Both moral conduct (*sīla*) and concentration (*samādhi*) are essential, but it is insight (*vipassanā*), or wisdom (*paññā*), that enables one to see things as they truly are.

The Threefold Training is a cardinal training, an integral part of the path, not an isolated reaction. This is clear when the Enlightened One says:

"Concentration perfected by Virtue brings much fruit, brings great advantage; wisdom perfected by concentration brings much fruit, brings great advantage; the mind perfected by wisdom is wholly and entirely freed from the 'intoxications' (***āsava***): (namely,) from the intoxication of sense-desires, the intoxication of becoming, and the intoxication of ignorance."[20]

The Buddha teaches *Samādhi* and *Vipassanā*, at times emphasizing one over the other. *Samādhi* is usually preceded by *Vipassanā* (in some contexts), yet at other times, *Vipassanā* precedes *Samādhi*, as in the *Paṭisambhidāmagga*: "...*Samathapubbaṅgamaṁ vipassanaṁ bhāveti* – One cultivates the path of *Vipassanā* preceded by *Samatha* (calm)."[21]

Why do I say that the Buddha repeatedly emphasized *Samādhi*? Because *Samādhi* and *Vipassanā* share common functions concerning the following: objects (***ārammaṇa***), sense spheres (*gocara*), eradication (*pahāna*), abandoning (*pariccāga*), emerging (*vuṭṭhāna*), peace (*santa*), subtlety (*paṇīta*), liberation (*vimutta*), non-existence of ***āsava*** (*anāsava*), passing beyond (*taraṇa*), the signless state (*animitta*), the desireless state (*appaṇihita*), voidness (*suññatā*), united function (*ekarasa*), and irreversibility (*anivattana*). This is why I am able to guarantee that the Buddha repeatedly emphasized *Samādhi* and *Vipassanā* together.

It is proper for me to say that both *Samādhi* and *Vipassanā*, at the lowest level, are to some degree different, but at the highest level, they are identical, since their aim is to attain the highest purity. Purity is nothing but knowledge, and pure knowledge is *Nirvana*. Most of the time, the root and body of *Vipassanā* and *Samādhi* share the same objects of meditation. The *Vipassanā* system as a whole, as well as the *Samādhi* system, is based on the seven stages of purity and mental exercises. When a meditator wants to put their mind into *Samādhi*, they need to be well-equipped with moral qualities and concentration first. Finally, his mind is pure and delivered from all things.

The seven stages of *Visuddhi* (Purity) can be simply stated as:[22]

1. ***Sīla-visuddhi*** (Purity of Moral Conduct)
2. ***Citta-visuddhi*** (Purity of Mind)
3. ***Diṭṭhi-visuddhi*** (Purity of View)
4. ***Kaṅkhāvitaraṇa-visuddhi*** (Purity of Overcoming Doubt)
5. ***Maggāmagga-ñāṇadassana-visuddhi*** (Purity of Knowledge and Vision of What is Path and Not-Path)
6. ***Paṭipadā-ñāṇadassana-visuddhi*** (Purity of Knowledge and Vision of the Course of Practice)
7. **Ñāṇadassana-visuddhi** (Purity of Knowledge and Vision)

Sīla-visuddhi and *Citta-visuddhi* are the roots of *Vipassanā*; the subsequent *visuddhis* (starting with *Diṭṭhi-visuddhi*) are the body of both *Vipassanā* and *Samādhi*. As the *Visuddhimagga* states, purity of morality and purity of mind are the roots of the full knowledge that should be attained by the disciple who possesses a thorough understanding of the fundamental doctrines, described as the ground of full knowledge (*Vipassanā*).[23]

Another object shared by both *Samādhi* and *Vipassanā* is the Doctrine of Dependent Origination (*Paṭiccasamuppāda*). The meditator recognizes his previous existences (*pubbenivāsānussati-ñāṇa*) through the attainment of the *jhānic* state. That knowledge appears like this:

"With his mind thus concentrated... he applies and directs his mind to the knowledge of recollecting his previous existences. He recollects various kinds of former existences, such as one birth, two, three, four, five, ten, twenty, thirty, forty, fifty, one hundred, a thousand, and many cycles of the evolution and dissolution of the universe. 'In that one I had such a name, clan, caste, such sustenance, such experience of pleasure and pain, and such an end of life. Passing away thence, I was reborn in such a place. There too I had such a name, clan... and such an end of life. Passing away thence, I was reborn here.' Thus he remembers various kinds of his former lives with their modes and details."[24]

The purpose of practicing the Threefold Training is the attainment of *Nirvana*. When one has practiced the Threefold Training, one gradually and eventually attains *Nirodha-samāpatti* (the Attainment of Cessation). Right after attaining this, he perceives the Noble Fruit (*Phala-samādhi*), which refers to *Nirvana*. *Nirvana* is said to be experienced upon attaining *Phala-samādhi*. *Nirodha-samāpatti* (also known as *Saññā-vedayita-nirodha*, "the cessation of feeling and perception") is (an attainment) for one who reaches the stage of *Anāgāmī* (Non-returner) or *Arahat*. This, I believe, is the degree of those attaining *Nirvana* in the present time.

The *Anāgāmīs* and the *Arahats* who have reached the paths by practicing the eight attainments (the four *rūpa-jhānas* and the four *arūpa-jhānas*) can enter into this state in their present lifetime and remain for up to seven days. As it is said in the *Visuddhimagga*:

"Wise men, when they have brought to pass This insight of the Ariyans, attain This trance-calm, practiced by the Ariyans, And called Nirvana, in this very life. Therefore ability to pass into This trance is said to be a good result of Understanding in the Ariyan Paths."[25]

Those who enter the Noble Paths with pure insight, without practicing the *jhānic* state, are known as *Sukkha-vipassaka* ("dry-visioned"). They do not enjoy the attainment of *Nirodha-samāpatti*. At any rate, they enjoy the happiness of *Nirvana* by realizing whatever fruit they have attained. Furthermore, whoever has practiced the Threefold Training automatically attains the fruit of *Nirvana*, since the Threefold Training *is* the state of *Samāpatti*, as well as the path of the entire system of disciple training.

The state of realization is *Nirvana* (*Mokkha* or *Vimokkha*). The commentaries have given two meanings to the word *Vimokkha*: 1) Release (*vimuccana*) from opposite conditions (*paccanīkadhamma*), and 2) absorption into the object in the sense of free confidence (*adhimuccana*).

Thus, the result of practicing *Samādhi* and *Vipassanā* is that the *yogin* or *Arahat* enters into the eight stages of release (*Vimokkha*). (One seeking further information on these states should see: D.N. Vol. II; A.N.; M.N. Vol. II; *Patisambhidāmagga*; Com. on M.N., Vol. II.) The eight states of release, which are relevant to *Ubhatobhāga-vimutta* (one released in both ways), are conclusively described in the following passages:

"When the *bhikkhu* attains these eight states of release in direct order, and can also attain them in reverse order, and in both orders consecutively, so that he is able to enter them as well as to emerge from them, whenever he wishes and remain as long as he wishes; (and) by uprooting the ***āsavas*** (cankers) he attains the final emancipation through *Samādhi* and wisdom, and remains comprehending and realizing it by himself—then he is said to be released from both sides (material and immaterial existence) in two ways (by the formless attainment and by the knowledge of the Noble Path). There is no other release higher or greater than this."[26]

It will be seen from my ordering of the theory of *Samādhi* and *Vipassanā* that the Eight Spheres of Mastery (*Abhibhāyatana*) are regarded as an advanced state of mind development and are acquired through the path of *Samādhi*. It is quite significant to enter this knowledge and overcome terrors and hallucinations, before finally entering *Nirvana*. If saints do not practice this *jhānic* stage, they may be reborn in the form world. As Rhys Davids writes: "Its purpose is to get rid of the delusion that what one sees and feels is real and permanent."[27]

Buddhists hold that the *Abhibhāyatana* is the skillfulness of the training. He who reaches this state lives without the fear of death. He enjoys this *jhāna* in the process of that "namelessness" which is compatible with existence, as when a person, for the first time, experiences or realizes the nature of an element that they had not known before. This *jhāna* might exist as an imageless thought, but it is maintained that no thought even arises without an object. *Arahats* know all things before the object is given a name; they even know their future and past lives before the "name and meaning" grasping processes occur. Their knowing comes from every case of a composite picture (viz., tastes, senses, or physical contents). They have practiced the scheme of the skillfulness of *kasiṇa*, especially sound, or the process for the group of sounds and colors, etc. This is parallel, in some ways, to the teaching of Gestalt psychology, where there is a grasping of "wholes." But unlike that, the Buddha mentioned that the mind does not see (perceive) a whole at once; i.e., I see the "rose" *after* I come to the conclusion that it is accompanied by imagination, memory, association of sensation, discrimination, judgment, etc. But the saint who attains *Abhibhāyatana* is able to perceive a whole at once.

REFERENCE *NOTES*

1. *Aṅguttara Nikāya I, pp. 38-43.*
2. *Dīgha Nikāya 22.*
3. *Majjhima Nikāya 43.*
4. *Samyutta Nikāya LVI, 11.*
5. *Dhammapada, v. 275.*
6. *Saññā is Pali meaning "perception" and has been used synonymously with "contemplation," "meditation," and "insight." Nanamoli Thera, Mindfulness of Breathing (Kandy, Ceylon: Buddhist Publication Society, 1964), p. 5, n. 3.*
7. *Abhidhammatthasaṅgaha, p. 43.*
8. *Visuddhimagga, pp. 436-697.*
9. *Cf. Dhammasaṅgaṇī, pp. 166-264.*
10. *Cf. 1. Atthasālinī, I, p. 186; 2. Majjhima Nikāya I, p. 186; 3. Ibid, p. 423; 4. Majjhima Nikāya III, p. 243; 5. Atthasālinī, I, p. 19.*
11. *Cf. 1. Majjhima Nikāya II, p. 14; 2. Atthasālinī I, p. 186; 3. The Expositor I, pp. 249-250; 4. Dhammasaṅgaṇī, pp. 265 ff.*
12. *Atthasālinī, I, p. 186; Dhammapada Commentary, p. 421.*
13. *Conze, Edward. Buddhism. London: Allen and Unwin, p. 25.*
14. *Visuddhimagga, Vol. I, p. 85; Dīgha Nikāya II, 313.*
15. *Dhammapada, Verse 277.*
16. *Obermiller, E. "The Doctrine of Prajñā-pāramitā as Exposed in the Abhisamayālaṁkāra of Maitreya," Acta Orientalia (Leiden), XI (1933), p. 1.*
17. *Ibid., pp. 14-17.*
18. *Bhikkhu Sangharakshita. "Ordination and Initiation in the Three Yanas," The Middle Way (London) XXXIV, No. 3 (Nov., 1959), pp. 4-5.*
19. *Ibid., XL, p. 1.*
20. *Sīlaparibhāvito samādhi mahapphalo hoti mahānisaṁso, samādhiparibhāvitā paññā mahapphalā hoti mahānisaṁsā, paññāparibhāvitaṁ cittaṁ sammad-eva āsavehi vimuccati,*

seyyathidaṁ: kāmāsavā, bhavāsavā, diṭṭhāsavā, avijjāsavā ti. (D.N. II).

21. *Cf. Paṭisambhidāmagga (Siamese ed.), pp. 433-438, 440-445.*
22. *Visuddhimagga, pp. 1-58 (in the "Sīla-Nidesa") (my condensation).*
23. *Visuddhimagga, p. 443.*
24. *Dīgha Nikāya I, p. 81.*
25. *Visuddhimagga, p. 709; trans. from The Path of Purity, p. 873.*
26. *Dīgha Nikāya Vol. II, p. 71.*
27. *Dialogues of the Buddha, II, p. 118.*

CHAPTER X

The Practice Of Samādhi And Vipassanā

To some extent, I have already explained this clearly in the first chapter on mindfulness. At any rate, I will present the exercises for some of the insights of *Vipassanā* as described by the same author.

EXERCISE 1

1. While sitting, meditate on the abdomen, which rises on inhalation and falls on exhalation. Acknowledge the rising and falling in your mind, noting: "Rising, Falling," according to whether it is a rise or a fall.
2. While reclining, do the same and acknowledge similarly.
3. While standing, acknowledge the posture: "Standing, standing."
4. While performing mindful walking, acknowledge the movement in stages as follows: When the right foot advances, acknowledge the movement by saying, "Right goes thus." Keep your eyes fixed on the tip of the right foot as the left foot advances. Acknowledge every step in this way. Having traversed the space allowed for the mindful walk and wishing to turn back, stand still first. Acknowledge the posture, "Standing, standing." Then turn back slowly and composedly and acknowledge the movement, "Turning, turning." Having turned completely around, stand still first, acknowledging "Standing, standing," then continue to walk mindfully, acknowledging movements as before. Practice each exercise until you are well-experienced in it and can achieve good concentration, then proceed to the next one.

EXERCISE 4

1. While sitting, acknowledge the rising and falling of the abdomen in four stages: "Rising, falling, sitting, touching," acknowledging "touching" several times (until the end of the out-going breath); i.e., "Rising, falling, sitting, touching, touching, etc." (The Ven. Chao Khun Phra Tepsiddhimuni Mahathera, op. cit., pp. 18, 19-22).

2. While reclining, acknowledge awareness in four stages: "Rising, falling, reclining, touching, touching, etc."

3. While standing, acknowledge your posture by saying, "Standing, standing."

4. While performing mindful walking, do as in exercises 1, 2, and 3 for about 10 to 20 minutes each, and then change the acknowledgement. I.e., while advancing with your right or left foot, acknowledge the movement in four stages: "Heel up, lifting, going, treading," for about 10 to 20 minutes. That is: a. Acknowledge the movement of your feet: "Right goes thus, left goes thus," for about 10 to 20 minutes. b. Acknowledge: "Lifting, treading," for about 10 to 20 minutes. c. Acknowledge: "Heel up, lifting, going, treading," for about 10 to 20 minutes.

EXERCISE 2

1. If the mind is contented in sight, sound, smell, or touch, try to realize that this is sensual contentment (*kāmaguṇa*). Acknowledge your feeling: "Contented."

2. When aversion arises, try to realize that it is hatred or a wish for revenge. Acknowledge it: "Hating," or "Revengeful."

3. When the mind is jaded or apathetic, try to realize that this feeling is Torpor and Languor (*Thīna-middha*). Acknowledge it, i.e., "Sleepy."

4. If the mind is distracted, worried, or depressed, try to realize that distraction and worry (*Uddhacca-kukkucca*) have arisen,

and acknowledge your feelings: "Distracted," "Worrying," or "Depressed."

5. When doubts in respect of mental and physical states (*nāma-rūpa*), Ultimate Reality, and concepts (*paññatti*) arise, try to realize that this is Skeptical Doubt (*vicikicchā*). Acknowledge it: "Doubting."[1]

Before going on further, we should bear in mind that morality is the nature of man, which is not alienated from or outside of him. I define nature as nature itself, regarding man's observation through the senses—namely, sense perception. I perceive, am aware of, something which is not thought and which is self-contained for thought. What I mean is that we can think of nature without thinking of thought... "(He) cultivates that part of the higher wisdom called Equanimity—dependent upon seclusion, dependent upon passionlessness, dependent on cessation, resulting in the passing off of thoughtlessness."[2]

It is undeniable that man is by nature physically unequal; for example, one has power over another by birth. Let us say that I am smaller than other men. It is easy for them to hurt me physically if they have no morality. Princess Poon Pismai Diskul addresses her fellow Buddhists, saying:

"Religion... gives man the sense of shame, guilt and other developed qualities collectively called conscience. It is a fact that a religion, by whatever name it goes, is essentially the same as the rest with regard to its fundamental purpose: to make a human being of a man... It may be said that the Buddha taught us the truths of our lives, from the cradle to the grave—how we are enslaved and how we can be free. By the Buddha's teaching, we have come to know how we have been tyrannized by our own passion (collectively called *Kilesa* in Buddhist terms), being driven to spasmodic joys and sorrows imposed upon us by circumstances... That Buddhism has survived all upheavals for nearly 3,000 years should be a fact worthy of reasoning based on the law of cause and effect. It can be said that the teachers of old recognized the three fundamental truths and therefore realized the wonder and excellence of the Buddha's Dhamma. The Three Fundamental Truths, or the Three Signs of Being, are: *Anicca*, *Dukkha*, and *Anattā*."[3]

In short, morality is required by human society in order to attain peace and the complete freedom of man.

Generally, Buddhist scholars do not practice the necessary steps to attain peace and complete freedom. There are monks and laymen in Thailand who have devoted themselves only to theory (*Pariyatti*), excluding practice (*Paṭipatti*) and realization (*Paṭivedha*). Monks in Thailand and elsewhere should be advised that the *Tisikkhā* (the Threefold Training) should be carried out completely and respectively—namely, *Pariyatti*, *Paṭipatti*, and *Paṭivedha*—without exclusion. As I mentioned in my introduction, Thai and Ceylonese monks are (often) divided into two (functional) schools: (the study-oriented school and) the *Vipassanā* school. Today, there are more *Samādhi* monks than *Vipassanā* monks. I am afraid that if Thai monks do not return to study *and* practice, Buddhism will decline as it did in earlier times. The Buddha taught that one who learns but does not practice is "empty-headed," just like the cowboy who takes care of cows for someone else but never gets any benefit from the cows. Hence, Thai monks should develop *Vipassanā* practice. It seems that only 5-7 percent of the monks practice *Vipassanā* as well as *Samādhi*. This is a significant flaw in the Thai monkhood today. According to Sunno Bhikkhu, who conducted research for *A Guide to Meditation Temples of Thailand*, only (certain) temples effectively practice meditation (*Vipassanā*).[4] He practiced at one of these temples, Wat Suan Mokkh. Life in the temple was calm and peaceful. I would like to list the temples he mentioned:

Temples of Bangkok and Central Thailand Wat Plen Wat Pak Nam Wat Maha Tat Wat Bovoranives Wat Cholapratan Wat Asokaram Wat Vivekasrom

Temples of the Northeast Wat Ba Ban Tat Wat Ban Na Hua Chang Wat Ba Pong Wat Nern Panow

Temples of the South Wat Suan Moke Wat Sukontawas Wat Tow Kote

Temples of the North Wat Muang Mang Wat U Mong

Vipassana Temples are Found in Ten Provinces: Chieng Mai Nakhon Sawan Udon Thani Ubon Ratchathani Sakon Nakhon Nong Khai Samut Prakan Chonburi Surat Thani Nakhon Si Thammarat

REFERENCE NOTES

1. *The Ven. Chao Khun Phra Tepsiddhimuni Mahathera, op. cit., pp. 18, 22, 29 & 30.*
2. *Sacred Books of the East. "Sabbasava Sutta," #36, ed. by F. Max Müller, trans. from Pali by T.W. Rhys Davids, p. 306.*
3. *H.S.H. Princess Poon Pismai Diskul. A Human Being. WFB Book Series, No. 45, 1947, pp. 2, 6 & 7.*
4. *For fuller information see A Brief Guide to Meditation Temples of Thailand, especially pp. 46-48.*

CHAPTER XI

The Principle Of The Fourth Noble Truth

In this chapter, I will discuss the path that represents the most important aspect (of the Dhamma), as it is man's final solution. If one has studied the previous chapter and understood it, he may also come to understand this chapter.

Who is Buddha? How can one perceive that the Buddha is free from the bondage of the world? How does one know when he attains enlightenment? What is the goal of the Noble Eightfold Path? All of these philosophical answers can be found in the final principle of the Four Noble Truths. The (Fourth Noble Truth) is the way of removal (the path of cessation).

How do we know that the cessation of *Dukkha* has been attained? The answer lies in consciousness, the integrating factor or "self" which is subject, like all else, to *anicca*, *dukkha*, and *anattā*. This evolving consciousness achieves successive states of spiritual knowledge until the last, (when) our transitory or mortal knowledge is (transcended in) Buddhahood.

The point of all of the Buddha's teachings is that a human being has to struggle and strive for his own freedom. (He must not) only accept (his) natural evolution, (nor) recognize that since (he is) "sinful," something beyond (himself) will help remove (his) "sin." As in one of Aesop's fables, a chariot driver whose chariot had gotten stuck in the mud sat down and cried to the Gods to remove his chariot for him.

A God came and told him that he was foolish and asked why he didn't hit his cow and make it move the chariot. And the God said, "That is all I can do to help you." The chariot driver then hit his cow, and the cow pulled the chariot from the mud. He realized that man has to do all things by himself—no one else can rescue him. How can man do this? In Buddhism, this is known as "release from the last fetters." Human effort without external help is likened to a dewdrop on a lotus leaf.

Aesop's tale represents man as "semi-man." The term "semi-man" means that man is not only man alone, but something more than man himself, and that man is the center of the whole thing, including the properties of the gods. This notion applies to what and where goodness lies. The (Buddhist) way of viewing goodness is that it is within man, within his "fresh bodily state," and is the attainment of happiness while living in the present life on earth. What do I mean by "present life"? The present life is the manifestation of the five *skandhas*, even though we cannot control the imperfections of the self—namely, rebirth, old age, sorrow, death, and the like.[1]

The Buddha, however, gives hope to man that as long as he works through to the attainment of the final path of the Noble Truths—the path of the cessation of *dukkha*—then he is free. Again, "free" or "unfree" to the Buddha is nothing more than the mind-creator, the mind-producer, the mind-maker. In addition to this, knowledge created by the mind extends to the Noble Eightfold Path, which is far more than a code of morality. The final path of Buddhism is practiced by all schools. It is the noblest course of spiritual training yet presented to man.

The first five steps of the path may be classified as ethics, and the last three as the mind's development. "Cease to do evil, learn to do good; cleanse your own mind; this is the teaching of the Buddha." This is, in my opinion, the main key to the cessation of *dukkha*, since there is no such thing as a Saviour in Buddhism. Each person must develop their own mind by cultivating its inner power (*samādhi*, *vipassanā*). The inner power is a significant factor in the mind's understanding that its resources (the external world or ***ārammaṇa***, the mind's object) are infinite. There is no instrument yet invented that is able to do more than the mind of man is able to do while its power is fully developed. This is common to all sense in man.

Logically speaking, this hypothesis can be raised: If only the mind exists, and if real knowledge (not *māyā*, but *bodhi*) is born within the mind, then all things existing in the mind are real. (While the mind is creating these phenomena; hence all things appear to us because of the creating or producing of the mind.)

We can then put it in a different way, like this: If only the mind exists, Then all things exist. Therefore, things exist through the power of the mind's cause. (Mind is the internal cause, things are the external cause; or mind is noumena, all objects of its appearance are phenomena.)

This is knowledge for the common man (*puthujjana*); beyond this is knowledge of the Supreme (*paramattha*).

All power of universal knowledge is *Buddhi* (Skt. *Siddhi*), which is the super-normal faculty (perfection) existing in the mind, because the mind is "made perfect" (at the moment of enlightenment). This perfection of knowledge is (possible) because the five *skandhas* are (ultimately) unlimited. Right after the mind enters the five *skandhas* (at birth), this stage of knowledge is either perfect or imperfect (depending on) the manifestation of the man.

The perfection of knowledge is called the Four Noble Truths. Why is it called the Four Noble Truths? Because only saints like *Arahants*, *Paccekabuddhas*, or *Sammāsambuddhas* can attain that kind of knowledge.

Truth in Buddhism is of two different kinds. The first, *sammuti-sacca* or *pariyāya-sacca*, is conventional truth. This is not the ultimate truth, (which is) called *nippariyāya-sacca*. The second is *paramattha-sacca*—the highest truth or absolute truth, which is the Four Noble

Truths (*Ariyasacca*). The first truth concerns the essentials of elements and unites such things as "man," "woman," "river," "mountain," "building," and so forth. The second truth concerns moral thought or the result of moral thought, and is a mental unit that exists in respect to a higher generalization, or metaphysics. Truth in Buddhism is knowing what is real and unreal in the category of things that follow *anicca*, *dukkha*, and *anattā* in the five-fold mass of a living being. This is described in the *Paṭisambhidāmagga* as the "Mountain of Suffering" on account of four natures. The four natures are: 1) the nature of oppression or causing pain of various sorts (*Pīḷanaṭṭho*); 2) the nature of having to be caused or conditioned (*Saṅkhataṭṭho*); 3) the nature of frequent burning (*Santāpaṭṭho*); and 4) the nature of change on account of breaking up (*Vipariṇāmaṭṭho*).[2] I would like to call these the Four Natures of the Noble Truths. They are present in the five *skandhas*. Realization of this is *Paramattha* or *Ariyasacca*. It is known as the Noble Truth.

These truths share three qualities: 1) they are true in that they always occur as stated (*tathā*); 2) they are not false in that nothing contrary to their statement ever occurs (*avitathā*); 3) there is never a happening in any way other than as stated (*anaññathā*).[3]

The individual self is mortal because it is changing. The existence of the body is ill, and illness, of course, is unsatisfying, as the breaking up and changing of the body occurs in death, and in the change from happiness to unhappiness, from pleasant to unpleasant. This is coming from an internal cause. Friends become enemies, wives and husbands become unfaithful, accidents and assaults occur; children become disobedient; people love and live together, then separate. This is the external cause of the change and is known as *dukkha*, the First Noble Truth.

Everything in existence ought to have a cause. *Dukkha* exists. Therefore, *Dukkha* ought to have a cause.

The cause, the creator or producer of this body (and this) living being, is identified as desire (*tanhā*).[4] Desire is of three different kinds, as I have mentioned before:[5] 1) sensuous desire (*kāma-tanhā*), 2) desire for Eternalism (*bhava-tanhā*), and 3) desire for Nihilism (*vibhava-tanhā*).[6]

The cessation of (this cycle) and the way to cause that cessation is the freedom of man, or freedom from suffering. This freedom I would like to call the *Nirvana*-element.[7] This *Nirvana*-element is significant in freeing man from both the Mundane and the Super-mundane, or the conditioned (*saṅkhata*) and the unconditioned (*asaṅkhata*).[8] Why does man want to be free? Because he has achieved victory in the complete annihilation, the abandoning, and the forsaking of every form of desire.[9] Since he is free, he has no lust, no ill will, and no delusion—*Rāgakkhaya, Dosakkhaya, Mohakkhaya* (the destruction of greed, hatred, and delusion). He then is in a state of complete Purification, peace, security, deliverance, uniqueness, indestructibility, and safety, not having to feel the "old age of the soul," etc.[10]

The path of knowledge and desireless action is the *Dukkha-nirodhagāminī Paṭipadā Ariyasacca*, also known as the *Magga-sacca* (the Truth of the Path). Man has to work through to this state with the highest effort. The well-known Pali phrase, "*Viriyena dukkhamacceti*," states that man can attain complete freedom "because of his highest effort." He is unable to reach this state by simply sitting down and wishing for it.

As we have discussed, life comes and goes because of ignorance and desire. This is the boundary of the *samsara* side. We must strive for the opposite side—that of freedom. Namely, we have to achieve the cessation of life (in *samsara*) through Wisdom and Non-desire. This is the key to destroying all egoism, all attachment such as "I," "Mine," "My," "You," "Yours," "Our," "Ours," "Us," etc.

Living and being on earth is no different from driving an automobile: knowing that an accident may occur, no matter how well we drive; if we do not hit someone, we may be hit by someone. In any case, the existence of accidents is analogous to the *dukkha* of life; striving to get away from all problems, such as accidents and painfulness, is analogous to the cause of *dukkha* (*samudaya*); getting away from accidents, which interfere with our peacefulness of life, is analogous to the cessation of *dukkha* (*nirodha*); knowing how to control all problems which may happen to our car with the skill of experience—keeping the best driving record possible—is analogous to the path of knowledge and desireless action of Life (*magga*).

This Path of life, this *Dhamma*, one has to practice with his own diligent inquiry. This is what the Buddha encourages for all mankind—the extinction of bondage. He can only teach; he cannot *do* (the work) for others. This path is known as the Noble Eightfold Path because it comprises eight distinct parts.[11] This is the major theme to be explored in this chapter. This path is nothing more than reassessing the common characteristics of self through *Nirvana* in practicing the last stage of insight meditation (***Ñāṇadassana-visuddhi***).[12] (See my discourse on the theory and practice of *Samādhi* and *Vipassanā*). The realization of one's own characteristics comes through the Four Noble Truths. The characteristics of Self become immortal.

How does one realize the characteristics of self? By realizing that both life itself and the realization of the goal of life are genuine or unchanged. This kind of realization is the characteristics of self, or the realization of *Nirvana*. This is the essence of the teaching of Buddha which leads to genuine liberation... to freedom from suffering.

In connection with this, Buddhadasa—my teacher—taught the simplest way of realization, which is to perceive non-selfhood (*anattā*) and emptiness (*suññatā*), so that "self" is done away with. He continually says that this is the essence of Buddhism. This expression, as understood in the *Dhamma* language, as the Buddha has put it, is the realization that nothing whatsoever should be grasped at or clung to.

"*Sabbe dhammā nālaṁ abhinivesāya*" "Nothing whatsoever should be grasped at or clung to as 'me' or 'mine.'"[13]

As long as one reaches the Four Noble Truths, then "rebirth" becomes acceptable as "the way things are," namely, the realization of what *is* in itself, rather than its creation or its condition. This is the notion of Wisdom and the Desirelessness of Life. How is knowledge attained by the Self? The Self is split into two parts: 1) the self itself, an unknowable thing or non-perception, or *māyā*, and 2) the knowledge of what the self is, through the destruction of *māyā*. In this knowing, one perceives *dukkha*, the cause of *dukkha*, and the cessation of *dukkha*. The term "stop" means to become the empty self. If there is no "self," what is there to go running about? Why not think about this point? If there is no "I" to go running about, what is the point? Obviously the "I" has stopped. This is a "stop" in the language of the Buddha: "absence of selfhood." I understand this concept clearly and relate this notion of "stop" to ***śūnyatā*** in Mahāyāna Buddhism; a stop is the same as emptiness.

The "rebirth of self" at the lowest level applies to *Anicca*, *Dukkha*, and *Anattā*, which are "unfree." But at the highest level, it applies to the realization of the Four Noble Truths, which is "changeless soul" (in a metaphorical sense), but which involves the *kamma* creator. All characteristics reached by the Buddha-nature are free from attachment.

What happens to one who realizes the Truth? (He who attains) *Nirvana* is the happiest being in the world, free from "complexes" and all human problems.

This happiest being results from practicing the Noble Eightfold Path—i.e., Right View at the beginning and Right Meditation at the end. Thus:

"This, monks, is the Middle Path, the knowledge of which the Tathāgata has gained, which leads to insight, which leads to wisdom, which conduces to calm, to knowledge, to perfect enlightenment, to Nibbāna."[14]

This doctrine is called the Middle Path because it lies between hedonism and asceticism; it is the way of self-discipline towards the cessation of *tanhā* and the acquisition of *Vipassanā*. This includes (actions, or *kamma*) beyond *kamma*—i.e., *kamma* that is neither good nor bad. This also includes the cessation of continued rebirth and re-death.

The Eightfold Path can be summarized as a threefold morality and is practiced through the Path of Mindfulness. (See my discussion on the theory and practice of *samādhi* and *vipassanā*).

(See *Two Kinds of Language* by Buddhadasa Bhikkhu, p. 30. He classified *kamma* into three kinds—good, bad, and neither good nor bad. He felt that most people were interested in the third kind of *kamma* which is neither black nor white, good nor bad, which consists in complete freedom from selfhood and leads to the attainment of *Nirvana*.)

Mindfulness is interrelated with right being and moral conduct. As long as the mind practices mindfulness, it becomes the key instrument for controlling *tanhā* and cultivating insight. *Dukkha*, *samudaya*, *nirodha*, and *magga* must be penetrated and fully realized. This realization comes with the deepest trance of perfect insight. Mindfulness in the classical *Dhamma* is referred to as the *Mahāsatipaṭṭhāna* (see the first chapter and the discussion of *samādhi* and *vipassanā*). Buddhadasa intelligibly explains the notion of Mindfulness: "A person who practices Mindfulness (*satipaṭṭhāna*) consistently is always fully aware. Even if he retires to sleep he is yet immediately fully aware, for the moment he is asleep he is also aware."[15] This is what it is to be "awake" in the *Dhamma* language.

Now we are enlightened by Buddhadasa that although we sleep, as is the nature of man, we are continually "awake" (if we are) practicing Mindfulness. One who does not practice is "not awake," even though he may not sleep all night. One is not "awake" if he is in the bondage of delusion. Likewise, for one who practices mindfulness, even death is not death (immortality); for one who does not practice, even life is death. The "two languages" of Buddhadasa have enlightened his followers in understanding mankind. He has been especially helpful to me while I have been writing this thesis. I almost gave up this work because my life was full of tragedy. My brother was murdered and burned by bandits in the south. Unto his death, he lived his philosophy. This put me out of the road of "good life" and into deepest depression. When I realize that my brother is a Saint (to) Muslims, a *Dhamma* man who committed acts of good merit, I then realize that even though he died, for me he has not died; he is still alive. This Mindfulness is very helpful to me and makes me free from delusion. I sincerely tell you that Mindfulness is the King of *Dhamma* and helps man to be free.

Thus, I have clearly explained that all problems, in all spheres of life—whether individual, social, or political—result from a lack of wisdom.

"To give oneself up to indulgence in Sensual Pleasure, the base, common, vulgar, unholy, unprofitable; or to give oneself up to self-mortification, the painful, unholy, unprofitable: both these two extremes, the Perfect One has avoided and has found out the Middle Path, which makes one both to see and to know, which leads to peace, to discernment, to enlightenment, to Nirvana."[16]

From this thorough discussion of the Path, one should see that it is a way of life that should be followed, practiced, and developed seriously by each individual. It is self-discipline in physical, mental, and verbal action. This action is development and self-purification. It has nothing to do with prayer, worship, or the aid of an external being (God). This is the essence of Buddhism, which leads to the realization of Ultimate Reality and complete freedom. "Freedom from pain and torture is this path; freedom from groaning and suffering: it is the perfect path."[17] This path leads to happiness and peace through moral, spiritual, and intellectual perfection. Thus, our function is to follow and practice, to keep to it (*bhāvetabba*, to be developed) and realize it.[18] "This you will in no long time, in this very life, make known to yourself, realize, and make your own."[19]

REFERENCE NOTES

1. *See the Buddha's Sermon on Non-Self (Anattalakkhaṇa Sutta), Samyutta Nikāya Vol. III, pp. 66-67.*
2. *Rūpupādānakkhandho, Vedanupādānakkhandho, Saññupādānakkhandho, Saṅkhārupādānakkhandho, Viññāṇupādānakkhandho—Idaṁ vuccati, bhikkhave, Dukkhaṁ Ariyasaccaṁ. (The aggregate of grasping to form... feeling... perception... mental formations... consciousness: This, O Monks, is called the Noble Truth of Suffering.)*
3. *Cf. Visuddhimagga (PTS), p. 510.*
4. *Yāyaṁtaṇhāponobhavikānandirāgasahagatātatratatrābhinandinī, seyyathidaṁ: kāma-taṇhā, bhava-taṇhā, vibhava-taṇhā—Idaṁ vuccati, bhikkhave, Dukkha-samudayaṁ Ariyasaccaṁ.*
5. *Cf. K.N. Jayatilleke... (who compares this to) the Freudian concepts of Eros, Libido, and Thanatos.*
6. *Sometimes I translate kāma-tanhā as "sensuality"... vatthu-kāma (sense objects: form, sound, money, etc.)... and kilesa-kāma (defilement-desire)... "Eternalism" (bhava-tanhā) means desire for particular kinds of existence... "Nihilism" (vibhava-tanhā) means the wish for life to cease at death... and the denial that there is a future life and hence rebirth, etc.*
7. *Yo tassyāyeva taṇhāya asesa-virāga-nirodho cāgo paṭinissaggo mutti anālayo—Idaṁ vuccati, bhikkhave, Dukkha-nirodhaṁ Ariyasaccaṁ.*
8. *Kamma-citta-utu-āhārehi saṅkhāriyantī'ti saṅkhārā. The name "conditioned" means that which is fashioned or formed by conditions such as Past Action (kamma), Thoughts (citta), (Temperature) (utu), and Nutriment (**āhāra**).*
9. *Taṇhāya pahānaṁ... ayaṁ vuccati dukkha-nirodho. (The expulsion of Desire... this is called the cessation of suffering.)*
10. *Cf. Dr. C.L.A. de Silva's "Four Essential Doctrines of Buddhism," pp. 89 & 98 (in maintaining these terms).*
11. *Ayameva ariyo aṭṭhaṅgiko maggo, seyyathidaṁ: sammā-diṭṭhi... sammā-samādhi—Idaṁ vuccati, bhikkhave, Dukkha-nirodhagāminī Paṭipadā Ariyasaccaṁ.*
12. *Understanding up to Purity Transcending Doubts (Kaṅkhāvitaraṇa-visuddhi) is called the Full Understanding as the*

*Known (**Ñāta-pariññā**); understanding up to Purity of Knowledge of Progress is called the Full Understanding as Investigation (Tīraṇa-pariññā); understanding thereafter is Understanding as Abandoning (Pahāna-pariññā). I have thoroughly explored this information in the chapter on the theory and practice of Samādhi and Vipassanā.*

13. *Buddhadasa taught me... Please see his teachings in "Human Language" and "Dhamma Language," which were published from his radio program.*
14. *Brewster, E.H. The Life of Gotama the Buddha. E.P. Dutton and Co., 1926, p. 63.*
15. *Ibid, p. 34.*
16. *Samyutta Nikāya LVI, 11.*
17. *Dhammapada, v. 276.*
18. *For further information see Mahāvaṁsa (Alutgama, 1922), p. 10.*
19. *Majjhima Nikāya 26.*

CHAPTER XII

Advaita Vedanta's Doctrine Of Māyā

Practical Indian philosophy is divided into groups. For example, one group accepts the authority of the Vedas (the ***Āstika***), and one does not accept the authority of the Vedas (the *Nāstika*). The classical six *Darśanas*—Sāṅkhya, Yoga, Nyāya, Vaiśeṣika, Mīmāṁsā, and Vedānta—fall into the ***Āstika*** class. The Cārvākas, Buddhists, and Jains are in the *Nāstika* class. This chapter is concerned with the doctrine of *Māyā* in Advaita Vedānta. I am interested in this system because Advaita Vedānta is an outgrowth of the *Upaniṣads* and has given rise to later schools and sub-schools.

Advaita Vedānta arose from the *Brahma Sūtra* (also known as the *Vedānta Sūtra*), the *Upaniṣads*, and the *Bhagavad Gītā*. These three form the foundation (*prasthānatrayī*) of the Vedānta system, founded by Bādarāyaṇa. The most famous exponent of Vedānta was undoubtedly Ādi Śaṅkara, who lived in South India in the eighth century A.D. There are two main subdivisions in the Vedānta school: one is rigidly non-dualistic (*advaita*) in its outlook, and the other tolerates various degrees of dualism (*dvaita*). Ādi Śaṅkara was the champion of the former branch.

Advaita Vedānta is thought to have flourished sometime between the fourth and eighth centuries. It is the non-dualistic system of Vedānta, expounded primarily by Ādi Śaṅkara (ca. 700-750 CE). It has been, and continues to be, the most widely accepted system of thought among philosophers in India, and it is one of the greatest philosophical achievements to be found in the East or West.[2]

The Advaita Vedānta is the result of a synthesis of many philosophical systems. The need for stability and solidarity apparently spawned a system to end systems. Thus, Vedānta is the ultimate science of mankind. Similarly, Hegel's philosophy was founded on a similar need and solidified various works and systems of Kant, Descartes, and (others). Furthermore, Śaṅkara developed Vedānta in response to unresolved problems within the tradition, and indirectly, he also drew on the insights of Buddhist logicians. Again, a similar parallel can be drawn between Freud's theory of mind and Hegel's philosophy, as well as the influence of science.

However, one should bear in mind that Ādi Śaṅkara did not synthesize *all* knowledge as did Hegel or Vasubandhu. He greatly emphasized that the purpose of studying Vedānta was to end *Dukkha* (the suffering) of mankind. He was not satisfied with the *Upaniṣads*, which he considered limited knowledge. Ādi Śaṅkara defines Brahman as "that from which the arising, abiding, and ceasing of the world proceeds." He advised that man should realize that the world and Brahman are one. Śaṅkara further claimed that one should do more than just put faith in the *Upaniṣad* texts, since the person who has seen the truth himself has no reason to rely on those scriptures. As it is put in a *gāthā* of the *Upaniṣad*, "There a father becomes no father; a mother, no mother; the worlds, no worlds; the gods, no gods; the *Vedas*, no *Vedas*..."

The analysis of the word *Advaita* is more than simple non-duality. The Advaitin would use the word to mean a realization of how God (***Īśvara***), *Māyā* (the universe), and transcendence are one within a state of two realities. I prefer to call Advaita an absolute idealism. How Advaita re-examined Buddhism and other systems is relevant to Hegel, who realized that Kant had (created a dichotomy). Consequently, Hegel continued Kant's thought in restoring the universal law (noumena/phenomena). Hegel claimed that Kant did not go far enough to the transcendental or absolute point of view beyond dualism, as Advaita had developed through (its critique of) Buddhism.

Perhaps Kant's subjectivity and objectivity fashioned an *a priori* category relevant to Advaita, in the sense that phenomena are similar to *Brahman* (as Prof. T.R.V. Murti has observed in his *Central Philosophy of Buddhism*).

The absolutism of both Mādhyamika Buddhism and Advaita Vedānta, (like) F.H. Bradley, makes a distinction between an ultimately real realm (the Absolute) and a merely pragmatically real realm (the world of our ordinary experience), thus entailing a doctrine of 'two truths' and a theory of illusion.[1]

Most scholars prefer to address the problem of reality by defining the implied reality of *Brahman* in relation to *Māyā*, rather than focusing on the ultimate accomplishment of humanity. I am inclined to deal with the latter.

Some writers in the East and West treat the *Mokṣa* philosophies as the performance of players in a game with given objectives, resources, and rules. This 'games' approach is a fruitful theoretical one, which has been applied successfully to group dynamics, national defense, and the philosophy of science.[2] Potter shows readers that Indian philosophers play *mokṣa* as a game in different ways. Another writer, Ninian Smart, has judged that religions have had major roles in the metaphysical and philosophical systems of India.[1] Thus, I attempt here to re-examine and find the answer as to why Indian traditions have logical systems such as Advaita, Buddhism, etc. The question is whether they benefit man or repeat philosophical mistakes.

The difference in philosophy between East and West is in theory and practice. Indian philosophy, of both religious and non-religious groups, is concerned with sacred and spiritual matters, whereas in the West, philosophy is (perhaps less) concerned with epistemology, ontology, and physics. As Chandradhar Sharma states:

"Western philosophy has remained more or less true to the etymological meaning of 'philosophy,' being essentially an intellectual quest for truth. Indian philosophy has been, however, intensely spiritual and has always emphasized the need of practical realization of truth."[2]

I agree with him. Indian philosophy can be approached in many different ways, including anthropological, cultural, traditional, religious, ideological, and historical. Each approach emphasizes different aspects according to specific interests. Because each approach has particular interests, it has resulted in a (fragmentation) of philosophy. As Hiriyanna put it:

"The chief argument in support of this realistic position is that... there are differences among men in their views of things; there are certainly points of agreement among them. If there are occasions when each can speak only for himself, there are others when one can speak for all."[3]

I am not interested in how Indian philosophies are similar. It would take far too much time to understand each system. For example, I have been interested in Buddhism for most of my life and feel that there are many things still to be learned. This is only one system. Hence, to me, it is superficial for one to generalize across many systems in order to discover what is really identical. It is foolish to speak of many theories of philosophy while not practicing any one in particular as a way of living. Frankly speaking, the question of which philosophies are identical is not especially interesting to me. It does not mean anything to me other than etymological and epistemological arguments, which have no use in the reality of practical daily life.

Hence, my major concern here is the essence of *Māyā* in Advaita Vedānta. What is knowledge (enlightenment)? Are *Māyā*, *Buddhi*, and *Jñāna* one and the same? If this were the case, how could one remove his *māyā*? Does the Advaita Vedānta system show us anything about the logical relationship between *Māyā* and *Buddhi*, or is there no logical argument at all? Is the world full of *Māyā*? If so, can we live with it, or not? If we know we are *māyā*-makers, can we stop creating *māyā*? "In short, the primary intent of the Advaitic teaching is to lead the mind beyond the level of asking the question to the level of seeing the answer."[1] Ultimately, we would achieve complete freedom, which stems from the Advaita Vedānta heritage. Thus, we would no longer live in the world of delusion or ignorance, fooling ourselves that we are knowledgeable or "enlightenable," but still suffering.

What do enlightenment and *māyā* really mean? Our knowledge does not really give anything to real life. If it does, what does it mean to say that the world is full of *māyā*? *Māyā* is part of the complexity of *Brahman* which is real. The term "real" for the Advaita Vedānta system means "that which is permanent, eternal, infinite... that which is *trikālābādhya* (never subrated at any time by another experience)... and *Brahman* alone fits this meaning." The reality of *Māyā* and *Brahman* is that they are beginning-less and endless. Thus *Māyā* is inseparable from *Brahman*. This Ādi Śaṅkara terms "non-duality." As he writes:

"(One cannot say there is) no experience (of external entities) because external entities are actually perceived... an external entity is invariably perceived in every cognition, such as 'pillar,' 'wall,' 'a pot,' or 'a piece of cloth.' It can never be that what is actually perceived is non-existent."[1]

Advaita Vedānta is a sub-school of the earliest classical *darśanas*. The word *darśana* is derived from *dṛś* (to see) and means "seeing," "a way of seeing," "a vision," or "a viewpoint." It is used to designate philosophical schools, such as Sāṅkhya and Vedānta, as well as sub-schools like Advaita. It is plausible to say that Advaita Vedānta (critiques) the dualistic system (it perceives) in earlier Buddhism. As E.J. Thomas states, (the Buddha addressed) propositions on problems such as whether the world is eternal or whether *Nirvana* consists in the enjoyment of this life.[3] Buddhism, according to Advaita, is then dualistic in the categories of *Samsara* and *Nirvana*. This is the major defect of Buddhism, according to Advaita.

I would like to call Advaita an extension of all systems, since it ties together all of the previous *Upaniṣadic* philosophies. Advaita is a continuation of the tradition of practical Indian thought. As R.H. Robinson states, "(The Brahmins) underwent an intellectual reawakening, codified their school doctrines in *Sūtras*, and split into two schools, Mīmāṁsā and Vedānta. Vedānta borrowed from Buddhism, quarreled irreconcilably with Mīmāṁsā, and rose phenomenally to dominance under the Advaita masters."[4] Robinson continues to state that in South India, they "reacted strongly against the Buddhist, anti-ritualist, anti-realist character of Advaita."[5]

It seems to me that, non-dually, the Mahāyāna Buddhists and the Advaitins hold that reality is free from all diversity, beyond metaphysics or epistemology. It seems that they try to avoid the notion of differences and sameness. They hold that their reality is inseparable from (what appears as) duality. Their argument is not only to realize the nature of reality but to construct a philosophy of the human "game." This is a form of common sense with which Indian philosophy deals with difference and sameness, re-examining the sameness in itself.

The game is limited to two concepts: sameness and difference. However, Advaita Vedānta and Mahāyāna Buddhism introduced another notion—non-duality—free from diversity, as in Hegelian philosophy. It is clear that Advaita Vedānta is opposed to the Sāṅkhya and Rāmānuja (schools), whether they believe in absolute sameness (of *Brahman* in itself) and absolute difference (between appearance and reality) or not. Advaita Vedānta has a doctrine of two truths, (similar to) Śaṅkara. Because of this approach, Potter called this part of the system "unreal" or "do-not-do-it-yourself."[1] Potter explained that Advaitins and Yogācāra-Mahāyānists depend on the Lord, as described in the *Bhagavad Gītā*, who creates his own action and freedom and removes the suffering of man. Man himself cannot attain his own salvation (*mokṣa*). Therefore, the Lord is real and manifests the universe.

Advaita Vedānta introduced this theory to the *Upaniṣads*. It was the intent to complete the work of the Mahāyānists (Nagarjuna, Maitreya, Asanga, Vasubandhu), (arguing) that the reality of a consciousness-created world of mere appearances was not enough... that the world of appearances is God-created. What I mean here is that Ādi Śaṅkara's effort in developing Vedāntic thought was influenced by the two schools of Mahāyāna Buddhism.

Historically speaking, the first Mahāyānist, Nagarjuna, completely overthrew the early Buddhist form by (refuting) the Sarvāstivādin tenet (that existence is dependent on the real existence of all 75 *Dharmas*). His work was based on previous non-Buddhist forms. Apparently, the Sarvāstivādin school gave rise to the Sautrāntika, who established this school, being dissatisfied with the Sarvāstivādin. Hence Buddhism was (in this view) returning to Hindu forms based on the Vedānta and other *Brahma Sūtras*. Sautrāntika was divided into three sub-schools. The most significant of these schools was (that of) Kumāralāta, who primarily believed in the *Dṛṣṭānta* (school) before joining the Sautrāntika. Hence he also used a Hindu form as the name of a Buddhist school. According to the *Abhidharmakośa*, Kumāralāta was mentioned as the teacher of Harivarman, who was also a Hindu influenced by Buddhism. Harivarman later became a teacher of Nagarjuna, who developed his teacher's work in the *Satyasiddhi-śāstra*. In ultimate reality, both self and *dharma* are empty.

However, some later works resist this idea, stating that (the self) is empty, but *Dharma* is real. Nagarjuna took the position of the *Satyasiddhi-śāstra*, but argued against the later works that *both* self and *Dharma* are empty. (Vasubandhu) wrote the *Abhidharmakośa*, which shows his resistance to the "self-empty, *Dharma*-real" position. Hence, Nagarjuna emphasized more the problem of *being*—the real nature of all *Dharmas* as empty. In the long run, he was more interested in the problem of *becoming*... that is, how phenomena can come into existence. Thus, this reality is the reality of developing causation.

The notion of ***Śūnyatā*** in Nagarjuna's philosophy was primarily an extension of the *Prajñāpāramitā-sūtra*. Thus, Nagarjuna was influenced by the Vedānta, but also by the Buddhists. Nagarjuna strove to explain the Hīnayāna theory of origination by the force of *karma*. All things are empty. We cannot see emptiness because we have a relative mind, which is based on nothing more than the five *skandhas*. Hence, one can only know the truth by the *dharma*-mind. *Dharma* is in all being. All being is in the ordinary man, which is *Tathatā* (Suchness). *Samsara* and *Nirvana* are transcended in the mind of the *Bodhisattva*. Here, Nagarjuna brought Buddhist doctrine to the pragmatism of the Vedānta.

The later epoch, around the fourth or fifth century, of Maitreya, Asanga, and Vasubandhu, developed the Abhidharma and the ***Śūnyavāda*** Mahāyāna Buddhism, known as *Yogācāravāda*. They developed the Twelve-linked chain of dependent co-ordination (*pratītyasamutpāda*) which emphasized the third member, called *viññāṇa* (consciousness). The *Sandhinirmocana-sūtra* and *Dhammapada* describe the mind as the seed of existence and explain that the whole world of mind and matter unfolds due to the mind's unfolding. In other words, the Yogācāra school holds that the mind dictates all things, including the existence of God. This is why Potter named this school "non-do-it-yourself philosophy" (*ajātivāda*). According to this school, a man should be devoted to God (*bhakti*), which is described in the *Bhagavad Gītā*, as well as the ideas of *karma-yoga* and the grace of God—namely *Jñāna*, *Karma*, and *Bhakti*. Hence, through the Yogācāra school, Mahāyāna Buddhism brought Buddhism closer to Advaita Vedānta. As Sharma states, "most of the Post-Shankarites, following Shankara, do the same thing and repeat his arguments. But when Buddhism was ousted and the struggle died down, people began to think dispassionately about Buddhism."[2]

Ādi Śaṅkara himself was influenced by the Buddhist teacher Gauḍapāda, and both Gauḍapāda and Śaṅkarācārya had the same conclusion: that (which is not *Brahman*) is absolutely unreal. "Unreality is that which can never be an object of experience. By the criterion of subration, the unreal is non-being."[3]

Māyā, according to the Indo-Aryans, is the magic power of God... The Buddha identified himself with Māra (sometimes called *māyā*) after he was enlightened under the Bodhi Tree. Therefore, according to them, *māyā* is a magical power. Everything is created by the magical power of *Māyā*; *Māyā* is God. R.W. Brookes states that man's breath came to be regarded as his real nature and that which sustains... gradually evolving into the concept of ***ātman***. The inspiration (*Brahman*) of the early Vedas became elevated to the status of an impersonal principle that underlies all things; and the magic power of the gods (*māra*, *indrajāla*) in their specific actions came to be elevated to the status of cosmic, creative power—One God (***Īśvara-śakti***).

Śaṅkara never admitted that *Brahman* is identical to *Māyā*, or that *Māyā* is identical to *Brahman*, as the Buddhists did. He admitted that the world is the creation of *Māyā*, which is *Samsara* (which he called the "different truth," or conventional truth). But *Brahman* is not *Māyā*. *Brahman* is real, which he refers to as the absolute truth. God created man to be deluded. Hence, God knows what delusion is... but He is not deluded. The Sanskrit *kārikā* identifies the whole system of Śaṅkara:

Brahma satyaṁ jagan mithyā, Jīvo brahmaiva nāparaḥ.

Brahman is the only reality; The World is ultimately false; And the individual self (*jīva*) is not Different from *Brahman*.

Evidently, Śaṅkara borrowed the doctrine of the three natures from Vasubandhu and Gauḍapāda. The first two, *parikalpita* (imagined) and *paratantra* (dependent), are unrealty (the world), and the third, *parinispanna* (perfected), is real (*Brahman*). Hence, (the world) is not different in kind, but only in the degree of reality. Ādi Śaṅkara believes that *māyā* is a reflection of God—*māyā* is appearance or phenomena, not real. But God is absolutism. Whereas Sāṅkhya holds that the effect (*māyā*) pre-exists in the cause (God), Advaita Vedānta has had difficulty in explaining the synonymous terms among themselves, for example: *Brahman* is ***Ātman***; *Māyā* is *Avidyā*.

Śaṅkara used his own words for synonymous terms and distinguished between the two aspects of *māyā* or *avidyā*, which are called ***āvaraṇa*** (concealment) and *vikṣepa* (projection). The former is the negative aspect of concealment, and the latter is the positive aspect of projection. *Māyā* is thus not merely a negative designation, a privation of vision: "it is positive insofar as it produces an illusion (*bhāva rūpam ajñānam*)."[2]

Why does he believe that *Māyā* is positive? Because he thinks that God is truly free from diversity, which is to say, free from the power of *māyā*. God created *māyā* for the world. He is like a magician; only the one who watches the show is confused and deluded. When a magician makes something appear to be something else, or seemingly produces something from nothing, we are deceived by it. We mistake appearance for reality—but not the magician. For us, the illusion is caused by the power of the magician and by our ignorance; for the magician, there is no illusion.[3] Ādi Śaṅkara tried to slyly defend himself. Much like Christianity, he claimed that God is free from duality, free from *samsara*; He creates *samsara* and the world. The world is the object of his "game." What applies to his characters—*Anicca*, *Dukkha*, *Anattā*—does not necessarily apply to Him. To simplify this, he might say that *Brahman* can create anything He wants to. His creation is *Līlā* (divine play), which is only a temporary pleasure game. Therefore, one can(not) argue that "since the world is *māyā* or unreal, *Brahman* is unreal too."

God and the world are not in an object-subject relationship, since God is the creator of His creation, *Līlā*.

"*Līlā* thus removes all motive, purpose, and responsibility from ***Īśvara*** in his creation... Having no needs to create, and having no consequences attached to this action, ***Īśvara*** cannot be held responsible for actions that arise subsequently within the fields of his creation. *Līlā* thereby avoids any 'problem of evil' associated with Judaeo-Christian theism, and it sets aside as meaningless any question of 'why' ***Īśvara*** creates in the first place. There can be no 'why' to creation."[1]

He believes that *Brahman* is indescribable. The empirical and negative description of the Absolute by means of *neti-neti* ("not this, not that") "necessarily pre-supposes the affirmation of the Absolute as all-comprehensive and culminates in the transcendental Absolute which goes beyond both negation and affirmation. The *neti-neti* negates all descriptions *about* the *Brahman*, but not the *Brahman* itself."[2]

I disagree with Ādi Śaṅkara totally. I admire that he created an idea to avoid the unfreedom of God, stepping aside from duality, making God free from duality. But I think he ultimately loses the argument. His argument goes in a circle. "When it is maintained that pure and permanent consciousness, which is self-luminous and which transcends the subject-object duality, is the only reality and that the world is only its appearance, the criticism of Śaṅkara (against the Buddhists) falls off the mark because he believes in this view."[3]

I would rather believe and give credit to early Hīnayāna Buddhism, as it is more logical and consistent. Hīnayāna Buddhism would state that God does not take advantage of man, and man does not take advantage of God either. They are both working and sharing together in the center of *karma*; *karma* determines both God and man.

Māyā is sometimes called *Avidyā*, which is translated as "naive," "know not." However, analyzed by traditional grammar (Sanskrit, Pali), *Vidyā* is the last word of the compound *A-vidyā*. *Vidyā* means "knowledge," synonymous with *paññā*, *jñāna*, *abhisambodhi*, etc. But not merely knowledge... "going with knowledge, destroying desire, complete knowledge." Oftentimes *Jñāna* is used as *Vidyā*. The prefix *A-* is derived from *na*, meaning "negation." This analysis can be applied to the word *māyā* also. Hence, *Māyā* and *Avidyā* may mean "knowing-not," but not "not knowing" or "ignorance." *Māyā* (knowing) is not negative; that is, it possesses a positive sense. "Knowing not-ness" (*māyā*) is the implication of ***Ātman*** and *Brahman*. Philosophically speaking, "not knowing" is incomplete; it requires an object—a "what"—to complete its meaning. "Knowing not" implies "knowing not ***Ātman***," "knowing not *Brahman*": *Anattā* (Pali, *Anattā*). For Buddhists, this implies the *Dhamma*, the truth of knowing.

For the *Vedas* and *Upaniṣads*, *Māyā* is the primary and final cause. It is real: the *māyā* of *Dukkha*, *Samudaya*, *Nirodha*, *Magga*, or *Māyā* in the categories of ***Ātman*** (the five *Skandhas*), is real. Even *Brahman* falls into this category. Logically speaking, then, if one accepts *Māyā* as real, *Brahman* is real; and if *Brahman* is not real, then *Māyā* is not real either.

Ādi Śaṅkara believes that perception of reality is determined by unreality; that ***Ātman*** is determined by *Anātman*. He apparently pays a great deal of attention to the study of Vedānta when he preaches: "To get rid of ignorance, the cause of human misery, and to attain the knowledge of oneness of ***Ātman***."[1]

Remarkably, Ādi Śaṅkara had difficulty in understanding what *Māyā* is. It seems that *Māyā* is a concept in physics and identical to ***Ātman***. Buddhism holds that *māyā* is epistemological and *destroys māyā* as a part of real knowledge. It is epistemological and unreal. Buddhism makes the distinction that *māyā* is not ***Ātman*** (epistemology has nothing to do with ontology, as Hegel holds; being and knowing are two different states). In its doctrine, Buddhism categorizes ***Ātman*** into three categories: *Anicca*, *Dukkha*, and *Anattā*. Since *Brahman* is ***Ātman***, then *Brahman* falls into these three categories. Likewise then, *Brahman* is unreal. The *Upaniṣads* and Vedānta are considered the ultimate destination for things. His conclusion is that *something* must exist before *no-self* or *no-thing* can exist. He reverses the Mādhyamika Buddhist point of view, from unreal-to-real, becoming real-to-unreal.

Ādi Śaṅkara is, of course, a *Māyāvādin*, but he differs from Buddhism in that he turns the other way. If there were no water anywhere, there could be no mirages. If there were no snakes, one could not have seen a snake in the past and so no one could superimpose the memory of a snake seen on a path at dusk. He explains *māyā* in his own word, *Adhyāsa* (superimposition). He defines it as "the apparition, in memory-form, of something seen formerly in something else."[2]

Adhyāsa (superimposition) is equated with *avidyā* (ignorance), the cause of transmigration in all the material systems. Its opposite, *vidyā* (knowledge), is ascertaining the true nature of things by discriminating between the superimposition and its ground.

Advaitin thinkers hold that *Brahman* is fully real and anything else besides Him is unreal. One misleads "un-self" to be "self" and "self" to be "un-self," or "real" for "unreal" and "unreal" for "real," because of the power of *māyā*. It can be said that any appearance—all attachments, aversions, fears, dreams, memories, logic, etc.—is a result of *māyā*. *Māyā* is isolation from reality. Even the "I," "me," "mine" is *māyā*, which is created by God for man. According to Advaita, the "I-ness" is *māyā*. "Māyā is all the experience... that is constituted by and follows from the distinction between subject and object and between self and non-self."[2] This is why Advaita wants to remove or separate *Māyā* from *Brahman*. It is maintained that *Māyā* is real in the empirical world but not in the absolute world.

Brahman is absolutely real, but one misunderstands when *Brahman* is associated with the impersonal *Māyā*, since *Brahman* is impersonal and beyond dualistic relations. What he really believes is that *Māyā* is real on the one hand, *Brahman* is real on the other, and His reality is free from diversity. He fails to explain how the relationship between the reality of God and man applies. He holds that "the reality for A" is only for A in itself and does not apply to "the reality for B" (A is A and B is B), as does Kant. He describes creation as very similar to Buddhism: metaphysics and epistemology cooperate together. There are differences, however, in the relationship to scripture: Advaita is dependent upon scripture, while Buddhism is not.

It cannot be that only *Brahman* is real and *Māyā* is not real. A buffalo cannot be half an elephant at the same time; cause and effect must be the same. This is the major defect in the entire development of the doctrine of *Māyā*, as outlined in the earliest *Upaniṣad* tradition, including the later works of Advaita Vedānta. Perhaps the major failure was the lack of understanding of the use of language, or not knowing how the language employed *is* the essence of *Māyā* itself.

Basically, all of Indian philosophy is based on language and grammar rather than on metaphysics, including Buddhism and Advaita Vedānta.[1] Indian philosophy relies on linguistics and psychology rather than mathematics and physics. The pre-scientific investigations of the archaic period dealt with religious problems. Linguistics arose out of the need to accurately preserve and recite the Vedic texts. Secondarily, most of the Advaita Vedāntins took for granted the *status quo* of the earlier traditions, leading to dependence on the old *sūtras* of the gurus, *sanyāsins*, and *yogins*. Hence, in their minds, everything is sacred and to be worshiped, just as the Bible is to Christians. They shied away from developing their own thought. They usually returned to the traditions of the *Ṛg Veda* or *Upaniṣads*. Even the Buddhists and Vedāntins do this.

Hence, the concept of the *Māyā* doctrine in Advaita Vedānta is similar to that of other Indian schools. For example, the *Satkāryavādin* holds that the effect is not a new creation, but only an explicit manifestation of that which is implicitly contained in its material cause. There is nothing new that was offered by them.

CONCLUSION

Advaita Vedānta developed from the Mahāyāna teachers. Ādi Śaṅkara strongly believes that there is only one Self, not a plurality of selves. His denial of a plurality of selves brings him closer than anyone else to the Buddhist viewpoint. "The difference between Ādi Śaṅkara and the Mahāyāna doctrine is largely a matter of emphasis and of background. For, of course, (Advaita) non-dualism is orthodox and thus appeals to Vedic revelation, while the Mahāyāna does not."[1]

Advaita Vedānta is similar to Rāmānuja in that the notions of conceptualism and "effect pre-exists in the cause" (are central). Namely, the effect is only an apparent manifestation of its cause. Ādi Śaṅkara maintains that *something* must exist before *nothing* can exist. There must have been snakes in the past before we can see them (in a superimposition) in the present. His theory of causality is that the world is not a *transformation* of *Brahman*, but a *phenomenon* grounded in it. *Brahman* is defined by Śaṅkara as *saccidānanda*: *Sat* (being), *Cit* (consciousness), and ***Ānanda*** (bliss).[2] The phenomenal world is neither wholly real nor wholly unreal.[3]

Unreality is that which can never be subrated by other experience.[4] *Brahman* is free from diversity. *Māyā* is real in the context of human experience (empirical reality). *Brahman* associates with its potency (***śakti***). *Māyā* (or *mūla-avidyā*, root ignorance) appears as the "qualified *Brahman*" (*Saguṇa* or *Savikalpa Brahman*), or the Lord (***Īśvara***), who is the creator, preserver, and destroyer of this world, which is His appearance. ***Ātman*** is real in practical reality, but if one views it from the diversity side, it is unreal. Sharma asserts that (Yājñavalkya proclaimed) the identity of *Brahman* with the ***Ātman***; "denying that the world was outside the Supreme, he did not accept the description of the world as a pure illusion. Waking experiences are different from dreams and external objects are not merely forms of personal consciousness."[5]

Hence, *Māyā* or *Jīva* is the complex element of *Brahman*, according to Ādi Śaṅkara. The world is *Māyā*.

"The prime source of *Samsara* is beginningless... ignorance (*avidyā*), which is regarded as specific to each individual."[2] *Mokṣa* is attained through the mental-spiritual discipline of *jñāna-yoga*, according to Śaṅkara. The goal of man is to realize oneness with God. "*Brahman*, for Advaita, is a name for that fullness of being which is the 'content' of a non-dualistic spiritual experience in which all distinctions between subject and object are shattered and in which there remains only a pure, unqualified 'oneness.'"[32]

What benefit do I receive from Ādi Śaṅkara? That is, how can one live in a pluralistic world when there is really only the unitary *Brahman*? The explanation of Ādi Śaṅkara's entire system is that the world is an illusion, or *Māyā*. But I do not think that I always delude myself, since I know what the world is.

This is my major disagreement with the doctrine. I further see a most defective argument against Ādi Śaṅkara. He builds his argument in an endless cycle. He set up his argument that *Māyā* is beginningless. This applies to *Brahman* too. Since it is beginningless, there is no way for *Māyā* to be an exception for God and apply only to man. Therefore, *Brahman* is also (implicated in) delusion. Reality cannot be real in the whole and unreal in some parts; it cannot be real for God in some parts and real or unreal for man in other parts.

Therefore, the doctrine of *Māyā* by Śaṅkara is inconsistent and invalid, as he refused to acknowledge the practical reality of real life. It is difficult for me to believe in him, as it does not align with common sense and is not practical for daily living.

REFERENCES

1. Niriyanna, Indian Philosophy, p. 165

2. Deutsch, Eliot, Advaita Vedanta: A Philosophical Reconstruction, East-West Center Press, Honolulu. 1968, 13.

BIBLOGRAPHY

Deutsch, Eliot, Advaita Vedanta : A Philosophical Reconstruction, East-West Center Press, Honolulu, 1968

Hiriyanna, H., The essentials of Indian Philosophy, George Allen & Unwin, 1949

Koestler, Arthur, The Lotus and Robot, New York, Macmillan Press, 1961

Murti, T.R.V., The Central Philosophy of Buddhism. Ge Allen & Unwin, London Englewood cliffs, 1

Potter, Carl H., Propositions of India's Philosophies

Robinson, R.H., Classical Indian Philosophy, University of Wisconsin

Sharma, Chandradhar, Indian Philosophy : A critical

Philosophy, Barnes & Noble Inc., 1962

Adi Shankara, Introduction to Commentary on Brahma-Sutras. Sacred Books of the East, Vol. 1

Smart, Ninian, Doctrine and Argument in India Philosophy. George Allen & Unwin, 1964.

Sen., K.M. Hinduism, Baltimore, Penguin Press, 1

Thomas, E.J., History of Buddhist Thought, London, Kegan Paul

Appendix I

Summary Of The Basic Textual

Doctrine Of Mahayana Buddhism

The Six Main Treatises Of Nagarjuna

The six main treatises demonstrating the essential meaning of the doctrines, directly from directly from sūtras and other texts:

1. Śūnyatā-saptati and Mūlamadhyamakakārikā: Theory of relativity; the reality of origination from self and non-self.
2. Yukti-ṣaṣṭikā: Logic.
3. Vigraha-vyāvartanī: Antagonists.
4. Vaidalyasūtra-prakaraṇa: Controversy principle with adversaries and logicians.
5. Vyavahāra-siddhi: Absolute Truth (non-substantiality) and the empirical point of view (worldly practice) go along together.

Works on the Prajñāpāramitā.

1. ***Abhisamayālaṁkāra***: Dealing with the knowledge of the practical way—the omniscience of Buddha, etc.
2. ***Aṣṭasāhasrikā-piṇḍārtha***: Explains the subject of the *Prajñāpāramitā* in 32 paragraphs, i.e., faith, morality, etc.
3. **The commentary on the Śatasāhasrikā** (the *Pañcaviṃśatisāhasrikā* and the *Aṣṭādaśasāhasrikā*): An exposition of the "Climax of Wisdom"; includes "the medium of teaching in abridged form." This work became the basic doctrine of the Yogācāra school.

It is said that the works of Lord Maitreya are :

- *Sūtrālaṁkāra*
- *Madhyānta-vibhāga*

- *Dharma-dharmatā-vibhāga*
- *Uttaratantra*
- *Yogācārabhūmi* (which is divided into 5 divisions):
    1. *Bahubhūmika-vastu* (explains the 17 subjects on the 5 *skandhas* and cessation)
    2. *Viniścaya-saṁgraha* (commentary on the preceding volume)
    3. *Vastu-saṁgraha* (demonstrating that the first preceding volume should be combined, viz., *sūtra*, *vinaya*. "The subject of study," says the *Viniścaya-saṁgraha*, "is the Abhidharma, which is contained in the 17 subjects and in the four compendia.")
    4. *Paryāya-saṁgraha* (Explanatory of the preceding volumes)
    5. *Vivaraṇa-saṁgraha* (Enlarges the methods of teaching)

The work of **Āryāsaṅga** is:

- ***Abhidharma-samuccaya***: Dealing with the three vehicles, including the Four Noble Truths, etc.
- ***Mahāyāna-saṁgraha***: Deals with the elements of existence according to the Mahāyāna view.

The work of **Vasubandhu** on idealism is:

- ***Triṁśikā-kārikā-prakaraṇa***: All elements of existence are nothing but the process of consciousness.
- ***Viṁśatikā-kārikā-prakaraṇa***: Dealing with the means of logic.
- ***Pañcaskandha-prakaraṇa***: The 5 *skandhas* are the foundation of logic.
- ***Vyākhyāyukti***: Involves studying and preaching according to the theory of ideas.

- ***Karmasiddhi-prakaraṇa***: Dealing with acts of the three media (body, speech, and mind).

These five works are independent. The rest of the work is commentary on:

- ***Sūtrālaṁkāra***: Dealing with the practice of the six transcendental virtues.
- ***Pratītyasamutpāda-sūtra***: Dealing with the 12-membered formula of the evolution of individual life.
- ***Madhyānta-vibhāga***: The three aspects of reality.

Some believe that the *Daśabhūmika-sūtra* is also his work. Vasubandhu's work is connected with that of Lord Maitreya, specifically the five books of the *Yogācārabhūmi* and the two summary works based on the five books (by Lord Maitreya), as well as the eight treatises (by Vasubandhu).

The treatises elucidating the practical parts of the Doctrine are the *Bodhisattva-saṁvara-viṁśaka*, etc.[2]

REFERENCE NOTES

1. *Bu-ston. History of Buddhism, Part I. Heidelberg, 1931, pp. 50-53.*
2. *Bu-ston, op. cit., pp. 51-57.*

APPENDIX II: A COMPARISON: Western Phenomenology, Sāṁkhya, and Buddhism

In this chapter, I would like to draw a comparison between phenomenology, Sāṁkhya, and Buddhism. I am interested in writing this to my own satisfaction. Second, one of my primary interests is the philosophy of the phenomenologists. I do not wish to confine my writing to the comparison of particular philosophers, but to refer to Western phenomenology in general and its Eastern counterparts, Sāṁkhya and Buddhism.

As I have tried to indicate, it is difficult to treat or discuss any philosophical aspect as one single philosophy; it is almost impossible unless one is inclined to deal with only one philosopher and ignore the rest. There is one significant point to bear in mind when comparing Oriental and Occidental philosophies. The West, inspired by Jesus and championed by Kant and Hegel, also produced a counter-man-centered universe inspired by Nietzsche and Sartre. Similarly, in the East, led by its great mentors, the Vedicists, Brahmins, and orthodox Yoga were championed. It also has its revolutionaries, such as the great Buddha. I feel that the East and the West share this fundamental religious philosophy. As Richard Robinson states:

"If it seems surprising that God should be an optional element in religious philosophies, consider modern existentialism, with Heidegger and Sartre on the atheist side, Jaspers and (Gabriel) Marcel on the theistic side. In the Indian system, God and natural law (karma, the principle of physics, etc.) were rival candidates for the office of world ruler. The classical systems accepted the efficacy of karma. Consequently, the theists were posed with the problem of reconciling the roles of God and karma."[1]

It is clear enough that existentialism, phenomenology, Sāṁkhya-Yoga, and Buddhism share the major concern that their primary focus is on anthropological and historical chaos—the world of human society. This is one identity for both systems. Hence, it is plausible to claim that certain interests are parallel in both. There is apparently no rational connection between phenomenology and Sāṁkhya-Yoga. Both systems grew up under quite different conditions, and the ultimate answers to the problem of human existence in the two systems are opposite. I am, however, inclined to find a similarity between them.

Let us first take Sartre's phenomenological ontology, which is defined as a fundamental dualism of consciousness and being. To generalize his philosophy, he asks his fellow man: "Why worry about death? In the universe, there is nothing to be afraid of. One should realize that 'I am alone.'

No one can die for me. No one can help me. I am absolutely responsible for my own life. No one can stop me from death. No doubt I do not believe in Gods. I (love) my own life day by day. I hope that everything is alright. I remind myself to stop being afraid of everything. I am responsible for my own ideas. I want to live the way in which I am. I am as I have been and what I have not yet been."

The realization of man is not only in-itself, but also has a relation with things. Hence, the representation of things is nothing more or less than the things-in-themselves, which *are* the realization of man.

Sartre developed Hume's thought—namely, of resemblance, continuity in time, space and time together, and cause and effect (i.e., the assemblage of things).

The crucial phenomenological, ontological, philosophical, and methodological question which has arisen for all phenomenologists, including Sartre, is: "Is there any way that an object acts upon a subject?" Noumena-phenomena is an idea. The relation of subject-object is consciousness. What, then, is reality? Before I answer the above question in the sense of Sartre's argument, I will give precise statements and arguments from other phenomenologists, rather than give Sartre's point of view alone.

Reality is not dependent upon consciousness. Reality is dependent upon minds. Husserl was influenced by Brentano. For instance, Brentano believed that our mind becomes an object which contains a) content, and b) the activity of thinking, which is always directed toward something in the world. How is Sartre attached to Husserl?

Sartre holds that Husserl's true insight into the nature of intentionality was found in an early work, *Logical Investigations*. The "me" was a synthetic, transcendent production of consciousness.

To fail to distinguish the ego and consciousness, to posit a transcendental ego, and to make the object immanent contents of consciousness—as Husserl later did—was, for Sartre, to destroy the great contribution which he originally made. Husserl's later idealism, in Sartre's view, could do no justice to noetic experience. A proper study of the object of consciousness could only be conducted if objects were not part of consciousness, were not mental acts, but were transcendent *of* consciousness. If the latter were the case, subjects of consciousness could be constructed as the truly given—as transcending consciousness. The ego can be produced from consciousness *of* consciousness of the world.

At this point, I would like to return to the Sāṁkhya-Yoga perspective in order not to lose sight of the comparison.

The Sāṁkhya system maintains that dualism is understood in terms of *Puruṣa* (Consciousness) and *Prakṛti* (Nature) and represents an attempt to establish the ultimate basis of man's life apart from the determining forces of existence in the world. As Sharma says:

"Sāṁkhya means the philosophy of right knowledge (*samyak-khyāti* or *jñāna*). The system is predominantly intellectual and theoretical. Right knowledge is the knowledge of the separation of the *Puruṣa* from the *Prakṛti*. Yoga, as the counterpart of Sāṁkhya, means action or practice and tells us how the theoretical metaphysical teachings of Sāṁkhya might be realized in actual practice... Sāṁkhya maintains a clear-cut dualism between *Puruṣa* and *Prakṛti*, and further acknowledges the plurality of the *Puruṣas*, while remaining silent on the concept of God. It is a pluralistic spiritualism, an atheistic realism, and an uncompromising dualism."[3]

At this point, we can compare Sāṁkhya and Sartre's belief in the ultimate basis of man under the principle of consciousness. Sartre called this "being-for-itself," which is transcendent and infinite. To understand the world is to understand our consciousness. Phenomena, then, are that *of which* all consciousness is conscious.

Sartre does not believe in God, and Sāṁkhya is silent on ***Īśvara*** (God).

One should bear in mind that the conception of ***Īśvara*** in the Sāṁkhya system is completely different from the *Upaniṣadic* belief of *Brahman*. (In Sāṁkhya,) *Puruṣa* is limited to its own being. This point of view of Sāṁkhya-Yoga is relevant to Buddhism. They both agree that when man has realized who he is, who he will become, and who he has not yet become—in other words, man is not only who he is, but he is *beyond* himself—he can fully become himself. He can be free with his presence during the transmigratory state (*samsara*), reasoning that he is something more than his physical body's limitations (the five *skandhas* for Buddhism; *Puruṣa* and *Prakṛti* for Sāṁkhya-Yoga). In other words, he can be more than who he is at the time that his body confines him in that present time.

However, it may be pointed out that Sāṁkhya-Yoga seems not to prefer to call freedom in the *jīvanmukti* (liberated while living) state "real freedom," since man always depends upon his nature (*Prakṛti*). Therefore, he does not have his own choice, since his life is mastered by *Prakṛti* or *Puruṣas*, etc. Hence, there is no clear distinction of absolute freedom for man in *samsara*, even though the man has become fully enlightened. The Buddha prefers to teach that man can be free both *in* the state of the five *skandhas* and *without* it, as long as he has realized who he is. The Buddha's opinion, of course, makes more sense than Sāṁkhya-Yoga and has given man more hope in life, rather than hopelessness. He emphasizes that man has his own freedom to be made, rather than letting nature manage him, as is the case in Sāṁkhya-Yoga. Therefore, the Buddha became a teleological philosopher for all mankind in the East. In the same token, Nietzsche and Sartre preached directly to Westerners, helping man realize who he is. Likewise, existentialists, phenomenologists, and Sāṁkhya-

Yoga have, to some extent, shared the same point of view in the sense that they were all teleological in their approach, helping their fellow humans feel at home and find heaven on earth.

Sāṁkhya, to some extent, holds that *Prakṛti* is the primal cause of man. *Prakṛti*, the first cause of the universe, is thus one and complex; its complexity is the result of its being constituted of three factors, each of which is described as a *Guṇa*. *Prakṛti* and the *Guṇas* are equally beginningless. That means one cannot understand (how) *Prakṛti* has built the three *Guṇas* nor (how) the *Guṇas* are constituted in it... they are interdependent. They are so interdependent, therefore, that they can never be separated. In the same respect, Sartre believes consciousness and being pre-reflect together.

The three *Guṇas* are named *sattva*, *rajas*, and *tamas*. Each of them stands for a distinct aspect of physical reality. Roughly, *sattva* signifies whatever is pure and fine; *rajas*, whatever is active; and *tamas*, whatever is solid and offers resistance.[7]

As Richard Robinson says, "This theory satisfies superbly the rule that explanations shall posit the fewest possible entities. It's a very high-order generalization, a remarkable feat of scientific imagination... This theory may tell what happens very well, but it does not really explain *why* it happens, any more than the 'soporific principle' explains why the sleeping potion works."[8]

In my opinion, based on the description of each *Guṇa*'s function, they are not measurable. That is to say, they are working together harmoniously, yet their harmony becomes antagonistic in their own nature. Their function can be illustrated by the example of a lamp-flame; namely, one cannot say that the flame is separate from the lamp. The flame originates from oil and wick, or perhaps has no beginning at all, because their co-operation is beyond the judgment of the human mind to describe. Therefore, all of the effects of *Prakṛti* are essentially identical with their material cause.

My opinion is harmonious with Sharma's. He notes that "Sāṁkhya says that the disturbance of the equilibrium of the *Guṇas*, which starts evolution, is made possible by the contact of *Puruṣa* and *Prakṛti*. *Puruṣa* without *Prakṛti* is lame, and *Prakṛti* without *Puruṣa* is blind." ... "Concepts without precepts are empty, and precepts without concepts are blind." *Prakṛti* needs *Puruṣa* in order to be known, to be seen, to be enjoyed (*darśanārtham*); and *Puruṣa* needs *Prakṛti* in order to enjoy (*bhoga*) and also in order to obtain liberation (*apavarga*), to discriminate between himself and *Prakṛti* and thereby obtain emancipation (*kaivalyārtham*). If *Prakṛti* and *Puruṣa* remain separate, there is no evolution, only dissolution.[9]

Insofar as Sāṁkhya maintains *Puruṣa* and *Prakṛti* as dualistically interdependent, let us return to Sartre's point of view, which is different. There should be no mistake about what he has done: he has created a dualism as radical as that of Descartes—but the dualism is not between thinking and extended substances, but between consciousness and being (which includes the "I" of the *cogito*). Sartre wishes to keep the purity of consciousness and objects; they are radically distinct, though they cannot exist without each other. He conceives this as the essence of intentionality. Consciousness "finds" objects, except for the special object, the ego, which consciousness produces in reflection. A proper phenomenological reduction would leave only consciousness as absolute, with no parts; objects, whose existential status could be doubted, are other than consciousness. This existential interpretation of intentionality places "Being-in-the-world" (of objects) as that which is confronted by consciousness. This is opposed to an "Idealist" interpretation which places "Being-in-consciousness." The issue is of prime importance for epistemology. Here, Sartre's notion of duality is free from diversity and more similar to Advaita-Vedānta than to Sāṁkhya.

If Kockelmans (*Phenomenology, Transcendental Idealism*) is right, one who would be so dogmatic as to evaluate Sartre's phenomenological procedure by comparing it with Husserl would be engaged in a futile effort—for it seems that Husserl has both an existentialistic and an idealistic interpretation of intentionality. Only a critical understanding and resolution of the ambiguity in Husserl on this problem, it would seem, would allow for a genuine critical evaluation of Sartre. Indeed, this would ultimately (be more an) understanding of Husserl than an understanding of oneself. Therefore, I must become aware of what I am doing when I am conscious. I can say, in a brief and tentative way, that in my own experience, I am aware of no intellectual intuition; I do not confront myself with immanent objects or consciousness with transcendent objects. In truth, I find "looking into" myself rather unrewarding. I ask whether the notion that knowing is "something like" seeing is erroneous, is in fact part of the "Natural Attitude" which has not been phenomenologically reduced. I would anticipate that the problem of becoming aware of objects and their status is a task for a phenomenological (investigation). This would seem to require more attention to understanding and judgment than either Husserl or Sartre has given to them. However, it would seem that Sartre was at least heading in this direction when he postulated an act of reflecting consciousness; however much a departure it may be from the phenomenology of Husserl or Sartre, I cannot ignore what seems to be my experience: producing objects by acts of understanding and judgment upon the data of experience. While I am uncertain of the relation of these acts to all objects, whether real or imaginary, they seem to appeal to "thinking," in the usual sense of the term, and to reflection. This would seem to have important implications for epistemology.

Both Sartre and Sāṁkhya have the same problem. That is to say, there is suffering for Sāṁkhya because *Puruṣa* is "more than what it is not," and suffering for Sartre because consciousness of being is "more than what it is not." As Larson points out, "The fact of suffering arises because *Puruṣa* appears as what it is not."[10] Quoting from the *Kārikā*, Larson says, "*Puruṣa*, which is consciousness, thus attains the suffering made by decay and death, until deliverance of the subtle body; therefore, suffering (is an appearance)."[11] Furthermore, Johnston indicates, as Larson, that "suffering arises because the *Puruṣa* appears as what it is not—i.e., as part of the manifest world of suffering and death, yet it is the nature or function of *Puruṣa* to so appear and, as a result, suffering is of the nature of things (*svabhāva*)."[12]

In conclusion, I suggest that Sartre and Sāṁkhya, (like the) Buddha, see the existence of humans as suffering. Suffering is the result of *Puruṣa* appearing in the world as what it is not—i.e., as bound up and determined by the world.

Both the theories of Sartre and Sāṁkhya are concerned with the doctrine of freedom on the basis of an analysis of the nature of individual consciousness. In the Sāṁkhya system, the *Puruṣa* is, by its very nature, separate from *Prakṛti* and its manifestations. This realization of *Puruṣa* as separate from *Prakṛti* is the doctrine of freedom in Sāṁkhya. This realization ultimately leads to a condition of "isolation" (*kaivalya*). Sartre maintains that freedom is due to the fact that the individual's pure consciousness exists apart from the determining forces of the world and man's own past.

Man's freedom centers on his discrimination or realization that his consciousness is not determined by the world, but his freedom cannot exist apart from the world. Thus suffering is the basic, unalterable fact of existence, and man is condemned to be free within this suffering. Says Sartre, "Man is a useless passion."[13]

For both Sartre and Sāṁkhya-Yoga, this is the doctrine of viewing man's suffering in his own existence without God's assistance. To Sāṁkhya, God is *Puruṣa*'s manifestation to *Prakṛti*; to Sartre, God is only what man *tries* to become, insofar as consciousness strives to overcome the fundamental dualism of the *pour-soi* and the *en-soi*. Such an attempt is doomed to failure, however, and thus God is irrelevant from the perspective of human existence in the world.[13]

The phenomenological ontology of Sartre, Sāṁkhya-Yoga, and Buddhism deals with religious issues and supports humans in realizing their responsibility for their own lives, in the sense that man is not only who he is, but *beyond* who he is, and that he can be more than who he should be and who he has not been. Finally, Sartre, Sāṁkhya, and the Buddha preach that man should feel at home on earth and find "heaven on earth."

SUMMARY

I tend to believe that all existential and phenomenological science is based on the First Principle of the Four Noble Truths, which is suffering. The struggle for peacefulness in the realm of Human Society is to know the cause of suffering, which is the Second Noble Truth. To abolish that cause, to tell man to be happy while suffering, and to give hope for man's becoming a better man—that is the Third Noble Truth. To reach the utopia of human being here on earth is the last and Fourth Noble Truth. This is *Nirvana* in Buddhism—the aim of phenomenological science.

REFERENCE NOTES

1. Robinson, Richard H. Classical Indian Philosophy. Madison, Wisconsin, p. 156.

2. Larson, Gerald J. Classical Sāṁkhya. p. 230.

3. Sharma, Chandradhar. Indian Philosophy: A Critical Survey. Barnes and Noble, Inc., p. 138.

4. Sartre, Jean-Paul. Being and Nothingness. p. 74.

5. Sharma, Chandradhar. Indian Philosophy: A Critical Survey. Barnes and Noble, p. 151.

6. Hiriyanna, M. The Essentials of Indian Philosophy. London, England: George Allen and Unwin Ltd.

7. Hiriyanna, M. The Essentials of Indian Philosophy. London, England: George Allen and Unwin Ltd., p. 108.

8. Robinson, Richard H. Classical Indian Philosophy. Madison, Wisconsin, p. 202.

9. Sharma, Chandradhar. Indian Philosophy: A Critical Survey. Barnes and Noble, Inc., p. 146.

10. *Larson, Gerald J. Classical Sāṁkhya. Jawahar Nagar, Delhi-7, India: Motilal Banarsidass, p. 190.*
11. *Larson, Gerald J. Classical Sāṁkhya. Jawahar Nagar, Delhi-7, India: Motilal Banarsidass, p. 191.*
12. *Johnston, E.H. Early Sāṁkhya. p. 67.*
13. *Sartre, Jean-Paul. Being and Nothingness. p. 115. Ibid., p. 615.*

Conclusion

I wanted to emphasize this for the audience, given that I am a long-term Theravādin monk and scholar. I love two sūtras: one, the Buddha's first teaching, and the other, his last words before he passed away. Both sūtras profoundly and fundamentally contain all of Buddhist doctrine. I am presenting their well-written and amazing concepts as follows:

(Contextual Note: The author, during the Vietnam War era, and his dear, highly respected Buddhist scholar friend, Edward Conze, discussed three famous sūtras: the Sūtra on the Buddha's first teaching, the Sūtra on the Buddha's last words, and Conze's favorite, the Prajñāpāramitā Sūtra ("Perfect Wisdom"). We both held the ideal that the Buddha's first and last teachings are the best of all sūtras. Unfortunately, Conze had to leave America because he failed to renew his visa while engaged in Buddhist work, resulting in his deportation back to Germany. I greatly feel bad for my dear friend, so our joint printing work remains undone. Although we were both Sanskrit scholars, Conze was more interested in me because I am a Pāli language scholar. We both sought to apply politics to Buddhism, attempting to help audiences worldwide understand (the teachings.)

I love to write, especially focusing on humanity and kindness. In fact, there is no good, better, or best way to say thank you to the Buddha or to Jesus, or to anyone. The only kind way is to treat even the unkindest people—which is a trend across different countries—just to show them your kind attitude.

Buddhism is one of the great religions founded by Siddhartha. His Dhamma has spread all over the world. In the beginning, he sent his disciples to teach his Dhamma, saying, "Go separately, not together, and spread my words," similar to what Jesus told his disciples: to go separately. I feel I have carried the Buddha's Dhamma in the West. In the 1960s, I taught his Dhamma both in academic and non-academic settings on the campus of the University of Washington. Back then, there was a large hippie movement, some members of which were anti-academic tradition and dropped out from campus. I found a better opportunity to be their Guru, sharing the Buddha's teachings with my followers. Looking back, I was happy to help them find a direction in life. In the first sermon, the Buddha said, "I teach one thing and one thing only: suffering and the end of suffering," which is the ultimate goal of the Buddha.

Yet, the doctrine underlies the core Buddhist teaching: he taught the Four Noble Truths—the existence of suffering, the cause of suffering, that the cause of suffering can end, and the path to the end of suffering.

Even before he passed away, the Buddha's last teaching to the monks was: "Behold, monks, this is my last advice to you. All conditioned things in the world are changeable. They are not lasting. Work hard to gain your own salvation, or Nirvana."

Furthermore, he advised us that Dhamma is his representative treasure to us. One who practices Dhamma sees the Buddha because Dhamma is the Buddha. The Buddha never died as long as we practice Dhamma, which allows us to achieve complete freedom and the ultimate utopia of life, Nirvana.

Buddhism in Three Words: Sīla, Samādhi, and Paññā.

- Sīla refers to the code of precepts, known as the Pātimokkha (similar to the 10 Commandments of Moses).

- Meditation (Samādhi) is similar in both Buddhism and Christianity.

- Paññā is wisdom.

Or, the teaching can be summarized in another three phrases: Avoid doing bad Dhamma, do good Dhamma, and purify your mind. We both continue teaching these fundamentals and the proud foundation of Buddhist teachings.

To destroy delusion or Māyā is to achieve wisdom or enlightenment. The Buddha taught one thing and one thing only: suffering and the end of suffering, which is the ultimate goal of Buddhism.

In his first sermon at the Deer Park (Dhammacakkappavattana Sutta), he taught the Four Noble Truths: the existence of suffering, the cause of suffering, that the cause of suffering can end, and the path to the end of suffering.

The Buddha taught us to realize that the world is in truth fragile; there is nothing which is permanent. (He said:) "I will cast off my body just as if it were a disease; this condition, temporarily called a body, must be abandoned. It will submerge in the sea of old age, sickness, birth, and death. A wise man is extremely happy to get rid of it, just as a man would kill a robber. Monks, you must seek earnestly for the way. All worldly things, whether movable or immovable, are subject to destruction and decay. Stop thinking for a while. Stop talking for a while, too, for time is slipping away, and I am about to enter Parinirvana. These are my final words."

Dhamma

is Duty,

Duty

is Dhamma

Buddhadasa Bhikkhu

Dhamma
is Duty,
Duty
is Dhamma
Buddhadasa Bhikkhu
Published by
วัดอตัมมยตาราม
Atammayatarama Buddhist Monastery (ABM)
19301 176th Ave. NE Woodinville, WA 98072
Tel: 425-481- 6640 www.atamma.org
E-Mail ritthi @ yahoo.com
Sponsored by Sathit Pechmak

I have spent a lifetime practicing and experiencing various aspects of Buddhist life and have also gained knowledge of Western thought, thereby seeing the points of difference between the East and

West in modern Buddhist thought. However, most of my training and experience in Buddhism has been in countries where Buddhism exists, principally in Thailand, India, Sri Lanka, and Burma.

All my life, I have been a Buddhist practitioner. I am glad Buddhism has guided me to who I am and what I should do: practice doctrine, such as *Dhamma*. This is because *Dhamma* is duty, and duty is *Dhamma*. Being a man, if you do not know your duty, you are not (truly) a man. If you find your duty, that is acceptable, but it is not perfect. The completion of your duty is (not possible) without practicing duty according to the *Dhamma* way of life. *Dhamma* is nature; man is nature. The nature of man without *Dhamma* is not a complete man. Man must practice duty, or *Dhamma*.

One of my gurus taught me about duty when I lived with him, and that teaching I have taught to others in the Western world since the 1960s. I am proud to serve Buddhism with the gift of wisdom that my guru taught me, as the Buddha wanted him to be. I have followed his steps. Therefore, I am taking this opportunity to insert (an explanation of) what "duty is *Dhamma*" and "*Dhamma* is duty," in the way my guru has proposed it, as follows:

I want everyone to realize that *Dhamma* is duty, or to see that duty itself is *Dhamma*. Whether people in the past, or those living today, no one ever thinks that duty is *Dhamma*. Instead, we do our duties because necessity forces us. If we don't do it, we have nothing to eat. So, we do our duty by the force of necessity. This goes against our feelings, and we suffer at the same time that we do our duty. We call this "falling into hell while working." There is nothing cheerful about falling into hell while working.

Would all these people who have duties to perform please realize that these duties are the *Dhamma* itself. *Dhamma* is the thing that will help save people. And duty is the thing that will help save us, because the two are one and the same thing. If they say that God will save us, we must say that duty by itself is what saves us. If we do not fulfill our duty, however many Gods you wish, they are powerless to help.

When duty is done, that duty becomes the God that saves us. The meaning is exactly the same as *Dhamma*. Whoever has *Dhamma* is saved. Whoever does their duty is saved. Would you please observe carefully that any kind of saving duty is respected as a form of *Dhamma*.

You do not need to add anything to your existing daily duties. But be careful. If you are going to do something, see it as a *Dhamma* practice. With one's best mindfulness and clear comprehension, set one's heart and mind on performing those duties as well as possible, as accurately as possible. And then be content with those duties. That is how to be happy all the time, as long as one is doing those duties.

The result is that there is *Dhamma* in all movements. There is joy in all activities, because they are *Dhamma*. People do not need to undertake any additional duties beyond what they are already doing. However, please learn to be aware and recognize that duty is a form of *Dhamma*. We must do our best until satisfaction and contentment arise; that will be happiness all the time the duty is done. To do our duty all day long is to be happy all day long. To do our duty, we must be happy the entire month, and even the entire year. This is called being happy in all movements and activities, because we are able to turn our duties into *Dhamma* through correct understanding.

Before, we never felt this way. When we said the word "duty," we always felt tired. And we felt like doing it only to claim our right to get something in return. Even this is a kind of force, to be forced to do our duty, which makes it a burden most difficult to endure. We are miserable in doing such duties, just to have the right to demand something in return.

We no longer want it that way. We just do our duty and are satisfied, then we are happy. While performing that duty, we are happy; we are happy in that duty. Doing our duty all day long, we are happy all day long. By doing our duty throughout the year, we remain happy all year. These results, in short and simple terms, mean that "Duty is *Dhamma*."

Would everyone please feel this way about doing their duties. Then those duties will be satisfying and gratifying. We call this "being happy while working." This is the opposite of how it used to be, "falling into hell while working." Now we go to heaven while working. Please look at things in this way, understand life in this way, and transform your duties into a heavenly experience. Duty and heaven go together and become the same thing. You won't have to invest your money in heaven anymore. If there is satisfaction in doing our duty, there is happiness. When doing duty, that is true happiness. Thus, we refresh ourselves, we respect ourselves, and we honor ourselves. We have the best happiness through this cause.

The results of work, of duties, are not lost. They come as they always have, and they can be used as needed. If they are genuinely used correctly, there will be other benefits, but happiness is already achieved when we do our duties, including the little ones. Duties start with waking up in the morning, brushing our teeth, and washing our face. We are happy the whole time we are washing our face. But fools never get it. Their hearts are floating around who knows where. They have no intention of washing their face as *Dhamma*, to do their best, to be content and happy all the time when they are washing their face.

Fools cannot do it. Happiness and contentment are only for those who have the mindfulness and wisdom to see that even washing our face is a duty. It is a duty that is *Dhamma*. Be proud of washing your face as best as we can, doing it correctly, and being contentedly happy the entire time. If we go to take a bath, it's exactly the same. From the first second, it's duty, it's *Dhamma*. We are contented with doing it as well and correctly as possible. Satisfied every moment of bathing means one is happy the whole time of bathing, which is something that fools cannot do. One must know this oneself, but whoever thinks about it?

We continue in the toilet as we defecate or urinate, which are duties we must do. If we don't do them, we will die. So we do our best and are satisfied. Contentment is knowing we are correct in defecating and urinating. Make it satisfying and correct, then there will be joy the entire time one defecates and urinates. Fools cannot do it, because fools do not (act) with such a heart. Thus, they suffer the entire time they are defecating and urinating.

It is the same while we eat, throughout the whole activity of eating. Even while washing the dishes—if one must help with the dishes, if one wants to help with the dishes—be satisfied with washing those dishes. That is the duty of washing dishes. Be happy with washing dishes the whole time. If one helps to sweep the floor and clean the house, one is happy the whole time they sweep and clean.

The "Thick Ones" just cannot do it. All the fools who have these exact same duties cannot even do them. They don't have this feeling because they lack understanding. They don't know that duty is *Dhamma*. Once they know that duty is *Dhamma*, they are satisfied, content, and delighted. And that is happiness. Don't bother asking questions; we must know for ourselves. When we are happy with everything, from washing our face and taking a bath to defecating, urinating, eating, cleaning the house, dressing for work, and going out to work, especially at the office, we are correct and content. We do our best and are happy all day while we are working. Returning home, it's the same. To do anything, anywhere, the principle remains the same. Thereby, we are happy in every movement.

These are words that the Thick Ones won't accept. They don't believe that we can have *Dhamma* in every movement. They don't believe that we can be happy in every movement. That's up to them; they can suffer if they wish. However, please examine this carefully.

If you have seen this fact, you will be content, and being content, you will be happy. Farmers will work their fields and orchards with great satisfaction. Traders will do business joyfully. Civil servants will serve the people happily. Laborers working in the heat will be cool with happiness. Beggars will beg happily and coolly. No one will suffer if we see that duty is *Dhamma* and *Dhamma* is duty.

We do our best, our very best. We act as correctly as we can, we are as satisfied as we can be, and we are happy. The undeniable fact is that we can fulfill our duty in every movement, cultivate *Dhamma* in every movement, and be happy in every movement. There is only this matter. *Dhamma* is duty, duty is *Dhamma*.

Translated by Santikaro Bhikkhu

****

For Contact in USA

วัดพุทธธรรม Wat Buddhadhamma 8910 S. Kingery Highway, Willowbrook, IL 60527 Tel: 630-789-8866

วัดอตัมมยตาราม Atammayatarama Buddhist Monastery and Meditation Center 19301 176th Ave NE, Woodinville, WA 98072 Tel: 425-481-6640

วัดพุทธปัญญา Wat Buddha Panya Society 1157 Indian Hill BLVD, Pomona, CA 91767 Tel: 909-629-1771

วัดรัตนปัญญา Wat Ratanapanya Meditation Center 34550 Orange St., Wildomar, CA 92595 Tel: 951-245-1399

.... To contact in Canada ....

วัดพุทธปัญญานันทาราม (แคนาดา) Wat Buddhapanyanuntaram 4796 Canada Way, Burnaby, BC. V5G 1L5 Tel: 604-439-1911

BIBLIOGRAPHY

A. TEXTS (Abbreviations)

Aṅguttara Nikāya

- ***A.***
- *Dīgha Nikāya*
- ***D.*** *(number refers to Sutta)*

- *Dhammapada*
- ***Dhp.*** *(number refers to verse)*
- *Majjhima Nikāya*
- ***M.***
- *Saṁyutta Nikāya*
- ***S.*** *(Roman number refers to Samyutta division, arabic to Sutta)*
- *Sutta-nipāta*
- ***Snp.*** *(number refers to the verse)*
- *Udāna*
- ***Ud.*** *(Roman number refers to chapter, arabic to Sutta)*
- *Visuddhimagga*
- ***Vis M.***
- ***B. BOOKS AND ARTICLES***
- *Atthasālinī (Buddhaghosa's The Expositor). Tr. Pe Maung Tin. London: Pali Text Society, 1958.*
- *Beal, Samuel. A Catena of Buddhist Scriptures. London, 1871.*
- *Bell, Charles A. Grammar of Colloquial Tibetan. Alipore: 1939.*
- *Buddhadasa, Bhikkhu Indapanno. Another Kind of Birth. Bangkok: Buddhist University Press. (n.d.).*
- *________. Dhamma, the World Saviour. Bangkok: Buddhist University Press. (n.d.).*
- *________. Two Kinds of Language. Bangkok: Buddhist University Press. (n.d.).*
- *________. Key Book of the Human. Bangkok: Buddhist University Press. (n.d.).*
- *Bu-ston. History of Buddhism. Tr. E. Obermiller. Part One. Heidelberg: 1931.*

- *Cady, John. Thailand, Burma, Laos and Cambodia. New Jersey: Prentice Hall, 1966.*
- *Carus, Paul. Nirvana. Chicago: Open Court, 1913.*
- *Chaemyyasorn, Mrs. (Phin Niyomhetu) and Niyomhetu, Tipya. The Pali Chanting Scripture with Thai and English Translation. Bangkok: Bhagdi Pradis Press, 1966.*
- *Chalmers, Robert, Tr. Further Dialogues of the Buddha. Vol. I. London: Oxford University Press, 1926.*
- *Conze, Edward. Buddhism: Its Essence and Development. Oxford: B. Cassirer, 1951.*
- *________. Buddhist Thought in India. Ann Arbor: University of Michigan Press, 1967.*
- *________. The Prajnaparamita Literature. Reprinted. 'S-Gravenhage: Mouton, 1960.*
- *Daksinganadhikorn, Phra. "Adittapariyāya Sutta," in Buddhism. Bangkok: Thai Watana Press, 1973.*
- *Damrong, Prince. History of Buddhism in Thailand. Bangkok: Chatra Press, 1966.*
- *Davids, T.W. Rhys, Tr. Book of the Kindred Sayings. London: Pali Text Society, 1917-30. Especially Nidāna-vagga, Vol. II.*
- *________. Buddhism. New York: Macmillan, 1877.*
- *________. Buddhism, its History and Literature. New York: Knickerbocker Press, 1901.*
- *________. History and Literature of Buddhism. Calcutta: Susil Gupta, 1898.*
- *Dhananivat, Kromamun Bidyalabh. A History of Buddhism in Siam. Bangkok: Karnsasana Press, 1967.*
- *Diskul, Princess Poon Pismai. A Being that is Human. Bangkok: World Federation of Buddhists, Book Series No. 45, 1947.*

- *Dutt, Sukumar. Buddhism in East Asia. Delhi: Council for Cultural Relations, Caxton Press, 1966.*
- *Freud, Sigmund. Totem and Taboo. New York: Vintage Books, 1946.*
- *Geiger, Wilhelm, Tr. The Mahavamsa or the Great Chronicle of Ceylon. Colombo: Ceylon Government Information Dept., 1960.*
- *Hall, D.G.E. A History of South-East Asia. Ann Arbor: University of Michigan Press, 1973.*
- *Hiriyanna, M. The Essentials of Indian Philosophy. London, England: George Allen and Unwin Ltd.*
- *Iida, Shotaro. "The Nature of Samvrti," in The Problem of Two Truths in Buddhism and Vedanta. Boston: Reidel, 1973.*
- *Johnston, E.H. Early Sāṁkhya.*
- *Jung, Carl, et al. Man and His Symbols. New York: Doubleday, 1964.*
- *Kanakura, Yensho. A History of Hindu-Buddhist Thought. Tr. by Neal Donner and Shotaro Iida. Unpublished. Vancouver: University of British Columbia.*
- *Lamotte, Étienne. Le Traité de la Grande Vertu de Sagesse. Vol. I. Louvain: Bibliothèque du Muséon, 1949.*
- *Larson, Gerald J. Classical Sāṁkhya. Jawahar Nagar, Delhi-7, India: Motilal Banarsidass.*
- *Lester, Robert C. Theravada Buddhism in Southeast Asia. Ann Arbor: University of Michigan Press, 1973.*
- *Link, Arthur E. "Evidence for the Doctrinal Continuity of Han Buddhism from the Second through the Fourth Centuries." Unpublished. Vancouver: University of British Columbia.*
- *Mādhava. Sarvadarśanasaṁgraha. Tr. E.B. Cowell. London: Kegan Paul, Sixth Edition. Varanasi: Chowkhamba Sanskrit Series, 1961.*
- *Nakahara, Joyce and Witton, Ronald. Development and Conflict in Thailand. Ithaca, New York: Cornell University Southeast Asia Program, 1971.*

- *Nanamoli, Thera. Mindfulness of Breathing. Colombo: Buddhist Publication Society, 1964.*
- *Narain, A.K. The Indo-Greeks. Oxford: Clarendon Press, 1957.*
- *Niwano, Nikkyo. The Lotus Sutra: Life and Soul of Buddhism. Tokyo: Kosei, 1971.*
- *Nyanasatta, Thera. Basic Tenets of Buddhism. Rajagiriya, Ceylon: Ananda Semage, 1967.*
- *Nyanatiloka, Mahathera. Fundamentals of Buddhism. Colombo: Lake House Bookshop, (n.d.).*
- *________. The Word of the Buddha. Kandy, Ceylon: Buddhist Publication Society, 1959.*
- *Obermiller, E. "The Doctrine of Prajñāpāramitā as Exposed in the Abhisamayālaṁkāra of Maitreya," in Acta Orientalia, Vol. XI (1933).*
- *Pe Maung Tin and Luce, G.E., Tr. "Ordination and Initiation in the Three Yanas," in The Middle Way, Vol. XXXIV, No. 3 (Nov. 1959).*
- *Robinson, Richard H. Classical Indian Philosophy. Madison, Wisconsin.*
- *Sangharakshita, Bhikshu. The Glass Palace Chronicle of the Kings of Burma. Rangoon: Rangoon University Press, 1960.*
- *Sartre, Jean-Paul. Being and Nothingness.*
- *Sen, K.M. Hinduism. Baltimore: Penguin, 1961.*
- *Sharma, Chandradhar. Indian Philosophy: A Critical Survey. Barnes and Noble.*
- *Smart, Ninian. Doctrine and Argument in Indian Philosophy. London: Allen and Unwin, 1964.*
- *Stcherbatsky, Th. Central Conception of Buddhism. London: Royal Asiatic Society, 1923.*
- *Sunno, Bhikkhu. A Brief Guide of Meditation Temples of Thailand. Bangkok: World Federation of Buddhists, Book Series No. 44, 1972.*

- *Tepsiddhimuni, Phra. The Path to Nibbana. Bangkok: Prachandra Press, 1971.*
- *Thomas, E.J. Buddhist Scriptures. London: John Murray, 1913.*
- *Tillich, Paul. Christianity and the Encounter of World Religions. New York: Columbia University Press, 1963.*
- *Warder, A.K. Indian Buddhism. New Delhi: Motilal Banarsidass, 1970.*
- *________. "Is Nagarjuna a Mahayanist?" in The Problem of Two Truths in Vedanta and Buddhism. Boston: Reidel, 1973.*
- *Wilson, David A. The United States and the Future of Thailand. New York: Praeger, 1970.*

BIOGRAPHICAL INFORMATION

- ***Name:*** *Sompong Gunavaro Dumdeang Jr.* **Place and Date of Birth:** *Songkhla, Thailand, January 12, 1944*
- ***Education*** *(Colleges and Universities attended, dates, degrees):*
- ***University of British Columbia*** *(Aug. 1974 - present): M.A. Religious Studies*
- ***Seattle University*** *(Jan. 1974 - June 1974)*
- ***University of Washington*** *(Nov. 1969 - 1972): B.A. Philosophy*
- ***University of Washington*** *(1974): B.A. Political Science (post-graduate)*
- ***Abilene Christian College*** *(Oct. 1969 - July 1970)*
- ***Seattle Community College*** *(Sept. 1968 - June 1969)*
- ***Ministry of Education*** *(correspondent studies) (1962): Diploma in Ed.*
- ***Buddhist University*** *(1963): Highest Pali Degree*
- ***Buddhist University*** *(1964): B.A. S.E. Asian Language & Literature*
- ***Buddhist University*** *(1969): B.A. Religious Studies (post-graduate)*

- ***Publications:***
- *The Lord Buddha and his Great Disciple*
- *A Guide: How to Work Effectively with the Hill Tribes*
- *Village Life and Sangha*
- *Buddhist Rites*
- *How to Teach Dhamma to Children*
- *Early Buddhist Philosophy and Buddhist Meditation - A Work to a Happier Life*
- *The Noble Saint Pipetanna Dumdeang and Violence in the Union of Pattani*
- *Indian Materialism - Caravaka*
- *"The Northern Mountain Hill Tribes of Thailand"*
- ***Awards:***
- *Highest Pali Degree (First Class Honor Degree)*
- *Pramaha title (Great Pali scholastic and Buddhist Philosophic monk)*
- *Scholastic Achievement Award in Philosophy for the scholastic year 1971, University of Washington*
- *Highest Scholastic Award in Intensive English for foreign students, 1969, Seattle Community College*
-

POSITIONS HELD

- ***Philosophy Professor*** *(1977)*
- *Mahidol University, Graduate Faculty*
- *Bangkok, Thailand*
- *Social Sciences & Humanities, Department of Philosophy*
- ***Pali Language Tutor*** *(1974-75)*
- *University of British Columbia*

- *Religious Studies Department (for graduate students)*
- ***Teacher and Lecturer** (1974)*
- *Institute of Linguistics, Summer Program (SIL)*
- *University of Washington*
- *Subjects: Thai language, Buddhist Philosophy, Thai culture & Society, Thai Hill Tribe Culture*
- ***Designer & Coordinator***
- *Thai language textbook compiled by SIL staff*
- ***Teaching Assistant** (1974)*
- *Seattle University*
- *Department of Philosophy (Buddhist Philosophy & Psychology)*
- ***Instructor** (1971-73)*
- *University of Washington*
- *Departments: Philosophy, Asian Languages and Literature, Asian Studies (Sanskrit and Pali), General and Interdisciplinary Studies (GIS)*
- ***Teacher** (1971-73)*
- *Experimental College*
- *Subjects: Pali, Buddhism, Yoga and Mantra Meditation*
- ***Teacher (Yoga and Meditation)** (1972-73)*
- *Seattle, Washington (My home)*
- *For Professors & "Dropouts"*
- ***Teacher** (1971)*
- *Black Youth Center, Seattle, Washington*
- *Subjects: Yoga and Meditation, Comparative Cultures (African, Thai, Black American)*

- ***Supervisor of Teachers & Teacher***
- *The Orientation of Natural and Cultural Geography*
- ***Teacher** (1963-66)*
- *Buddhist University*
- *Subjects: Buddhism, Sanskrit and Pali, Asian Languages & Literature*
- ***Leader of Pilgrimage (Dhammacarik)** (1964-65)*
- *Thailand Hill Tribes*
- ***Preacher of Dharma** (1964-65)*
- *Buddhist Radio Program, Thailand*
- ***Teacher (Meditation)** (1963-64)*
- *Buddhist University*
- *For Retired Government Workers & Thai Youth Society*
- ***Editor** (1962)*
- *Attainable Dhamma Voice, Buddhist University*
- ***Assistant Secretary to the Principle Noble Governor Monk***
- *The Education Division in Buddhist Studies (Pali, Tripitaka, Dhamma, Vinaya, Abhidhamma)*

Dr. DANEY DUMDEANG
Author of the Book,
Founder, President, Chairman of the Board

DUMDEANG REALTY CO.
P.O. Box 2265, Portland. OR 97208 U.S.A.

Rev. Dr. P. YESU RATNAM
GSM Director
D.No. 9-419, Indira Colony,
Kakinda - 533 005 (A.P.) S. India
© 91-884-2341562, Fax : 91-884-2373607
email : yesu@calvaryprayerhouse.org
Web : www.calvaryprayerhouse.org

OUR MINISTRIES :
Orphan Homes • Church Plantation • Adult Literacy
• Film Ministry • Children Bible Clubs (V.B.S.)
• Health Care & Sanitation • Leprosy Rehabilitation
• Floods - Cyclone & Fire Relief
• Counselling by Phone & Persons
• Sewing *Tailoring) Training Centres • Tribal Ministries
• Community Development
• Construction of Houses & Community Halls
• Help the Aged & Widows • Bible Schools (I.C.T.)
• Literature Distribution • Leadership Trainings

Appendix

Sherman's Wilderness

What happens after a Christian minister comes out as transgender

Why Me? Would I Be Blessed?

Posted on January 1, 2012 by David Weekley

Dear Friends, this was in place of my sermon this New Year's Day 2012. Daney Dumdeang is a member of the Capitol Hill UMC. He grew up in Thailand. It is a privilege to share his testimony with you all. Blessings and Peace, Deborah and Rev. David Weekley

Why Me? Would I Be Blessed?

I do know God... I have been with Him long before I realized it, while I was a Buddhist monk practicing the *Dhamma*. I know Jesus... Jesus is the Son of God... God is His Father. God is everywhere, even in *Dhamma*. God is in Buddha... God was showing me His quality in the *Brahma-vihāras* (the sublime attitudes, as ordained in the *Metta Sutta*: *mettā*, *karuṇā*, *muditā*, and *upekkhā*), and that is God inside Him... (which) has come through me. It is such ignorance for me to ask the question, "Does God exist?" Yes, God does exist in this quality: love, kindness, sympathy, equanimity, and all forms of humanitarianism. God is there for everyone, including you and me... one and all, and all for one.

On December 22, David sent a message that I should publish my Christmas book. ... It will be the best day... It will be fine with me. I have not yet coordinated the message that was given to me to deliver. Mountains of messages were given to me by Him this year. I do not know where to start, where to be in the middle, and where to end. The inspiration of God's word has come after the Holy Spirit rested upon me. My daughter, Dona, gave the essential key words before the Thanksgiving Holiday. "Papa, we have so much to be thankful for, don't you think?" asked Dona. Upon hearing her words, it came to my mind that this is what we are always missing: thanks to our Lord and His people.

To tell the best story is not to start at the beginning, but in the middle of our story... Buddha achieved his enlightenment and taught us his *Dhamma* when he was in his middle age, and his middle age was significant. So did Jesus. He gave up his life to repay our sins when he was in his middle age. So too, other spiritual leaders, like the Dalai Lama... and John (Smith), who discovered Mormonism in this country when he was in middle age. (Think of) some of our presidents, like J.F. Kennedy, who was loved by us when he was in middle age, and our President Obama now... and many more young and middle-aged leaders in world history. This is the age God (calls) us to serve Him, because it is more profoundly and effectively well done in the eyes of GOD.

God knows when His children are getting old, they are not as energetic. It is true. Many times Chin asked me, “Don't you know that you can't do things that you used to do, maybe because you're getting so old?” Of course, we feel our old age and our energy is decreasing daily... we must accept it... birth, growing up, decay, old age, and returning home with GOD, as Buddha might say.

My love life story began in August 1961, when I was 16 years old and was sent to Buddhist religious affairs in Burma. On the way, on my flight in the white sky, I saw an angel. She put me in her wings... she showed me my sweetheart and future soulmate. I could not believe what I was being told and what I was seeing... that beautiful young girl, who was shown to me by the angel, would be my lovely wife.

I was asked by Allen and Mary, “How did you meet your wife?” When I told them, Allen said that was the best story of all.

Later, I was awarded a Fulbright Scholarship and Asian Foundation grant to continue my graduate studies in Philosophy, Political Science, and Asian Literature in 1966 in the USA at the U of W. In August 1970, I saw that most beautiful girl in college at Parrington Hall in the Philosophy Department at the U of W. I was connecting with the girl who had been introduced to me by the angel. I fell in love at first sight. I saw sunshine in her eyes. She was a gorgeous, blue-eyed blonde with a beautiful smile... and I said, “Hi.”... I knew in my heart that she was the beautiful girl with whom I would spend the rest of my life. I was stunned when I first saw her. I asked my angel, “Is this the same girl you introduced me to in my vision in Burma?” “Yes, this is the one.” I said, “She is angel-like but more hippy-style, in 1970.” “Yes, she is the same.” I was so amazed and accepted it in my heart. Two years later, we were married, after we had already lived together for two years.

True love is knowing someone so well, so deeply, so completely, and feeling connected to them. True love goes beyond anything that can be described in human words... something that touches my heart as an eternal song for life, and that woman is my true wife today... True love has not gone away, even today and forevermore. She is not only my wife, but she is my soul mate, my sunshine and sunset, the grace that filled my soul and the wind under my wings. Our love continues even beyond everything, and the phenomenon of the loving life story that I am sharing with you. You are even part of the story. My wife's story is part of you all. She loves all people in the church and others, and that is her nature. Just know that God asked me to share this story with those who care enough to share the loves and losses they have experienced. Our friends who lost lovers or loved ones, please know that the body does not last forever, but the spirit does.

As for my wife and I, we work as a team. We have three children, we are happily married, and we are building our spiritual life day by day with each other. Of course, I am not lying to you. Our lovely married life's journey has ups and downs, just like everybody else's. It is not extraordinary. After all, love connects and reconnects on a spiritual level more than a physical level. One fights in a mundane, everyday sense (in the sensual world) and continues to live in the spiritual or super-mundane world; then happiness, joy, and peace are fulfilled. A friend's love says, "If you are in need of anything, I'll be there." A true love says, "You'll never need anything; I'll be there." This is the love: "Steadfast love and faithfulness will meet; righteousness and peace will kiss each other" (Psalm 85:10). We are called to speak the truth in love (Ephesians 4:16)... "to those who call upon HIM in truth" (Psalm 34).

Besides having each other, we have three wonderful grown-up children and four grandchildren. We have many God-children. We are happy with who we are. This is the story of the restoration of our love, from the one Angel... the angel is one, and one for all. Thank God for making our international marriage work and last forever. God's gift is the best, and beyond the giving of the gift, that is our life together. Happy one, one for all, all for one. So, that is my story, with a fairy-tale ending... that I have dreamed of, and I'm savoring every minute of it, happily ever after. May I have a song of the angel, "Angels We Have Heard on High," that I love to hear with our friends in the church, if I may, if time allows, to cherish in my unforgettable memory.

Life doesn't get any better than being married to your own soulmate.

God promises to be with my family, just as He promises to be with all of us. "Therefore, having these promises, beloved, let us cleanse ourselves from all filthiness of the flesh and spirit, having perfect holiness in the fear of God. Open your heart to us. We have wronged no one," said Apostle Paul.

Another year is dawning, Dear Father, let it be; In working or in waiting, another with thee; Another year is dawning, Dear Father, let it be; On earth or else in heaven, another year for thee. —A beautiful, anonymous poem

Let's start a new life this new year. The beginning of the new year is a time, in a certain sense, when everything can be about as it ought to be; a time when we aim higher, reach further, dream bigger and stronger. As Henry Ward Beecher said, "every man should be born again on the first day of January. Start with a fresh page... on the first of January, let every man gird himself once more, with his face to the front, and take interest in the things that are past."

Last year in my Christmas testimony, I raised the question, "What do we do for ourselves?" I never gave the fullest answer. But I have told a story of part of my life, as Mel used to tease me, "Daney, you should write more fully about your life." Here, Mel, I did as you requested. Next time, I want to hear from you; it is your turn, as you promised me, Mel. Hope my story will convince you to do the same... take care of your loved ones. "Love is actually stronger than death." Our beloved can and do (live on) beyond the grave.

Thank God for Peter, our son, who is the coach for young children around the state, both in Washington and elsewhere. He sincerely devotes his life and his time to those children whose parents need him. Peter knows the worst thing for our children in the community: Children who have so much free time will join gangs and drop cut from school. Peter has a heart of love for his teams. He trains them and lets them enjoy themselves and have a lot of fun. Peter has no intention of allowing evil forces to harm the children, and the parents trust him. Peter has come along so perfectly well. Thank you, God, that you changed Peter and turned his life around. Peter knows he has not lost his identity anymore. He has been deeply involved with the Boys and Girls Club for many years, motivating kids and influencing them for a very bright future. Parents and kids have looked to Peter as their role model and mentor. Peter has realized that to give all positive thoughts for the future does not take only parents alone, but also some real mentors like him to motivate them in their future life, to have a beam of shining hope out of the darkness... We are supporting him 100% for what he has done for the community, for young children. As one Sunday, David asked for us to pray for the young after I announced we lost a young friend, Allen, who was stabbed to death after a confrontation.

Thank God for Myla, who is the best mother to her three children (our grandchildren), and who has also given a great deal of help to her nephew, Dylan, while supporting Morgan, who does not have very good energy. Myla has gone the extra mile as a mother to support Peter at the children's games, without saying one word of complaint. She gives Peter 100% support. She is our daughter more than our daughter-in-law. She is the perfect person for traveling as a spiritual pilgrimage in Thailand, especially when we all honored my mother on the day of paying our last respects at her funeral. She is taking part in my family out of her own heart. Thank God she is part of my family. Please, God, protect her from worrying about her brother's health. After all, Patty and I feel closer and closer to Myla. We enjoy listening to her and being with her. She is a very bright young lady in our family.

We must love them unconditionally, as God loves. Without faith in God, who can we trust around us, around our children? Building faith in our heart through Jesus is the only way (Proverbs 3:5-6). I would like to remind the so-called leaders in our society that acknowledging the Lord in all our ways means keeping HIM in every "event," no matter if private or public, at all times of our lives.

To me, Godly living is not confined to worship, for God is involved in each moment of each day. God's instruction covers our lives from waking up in the morning to going to sleep at night. God wants us to remember Him at all times and to trust and obey Him, allowing Him to guide our conduct in everything we do. That "He shall direct your path" suggests that God will "smooth" or "make straight" the road of our lives. I do know from my heart that God promises His children, like you and me, that He will go before us and He will remove many of the obstructions from our path.

For example, among us, Patt McConnell testified on Sunday that she didn't know if she would ever feel joy again after losing her dear son and for all the sorrow she carried in her heart, but that she did feel joy upon hearing the beautiful music from the concert, upon seeing the Christmas tree ornaments and remembering the women who made them in years past, and also upon enjoying one another at the Christmas party. "Here I am, full of (joy) and starting the new beginning of my life," said Patt.

I am so happy for Patt, to see the new world and begin to enjoy her life again. The most pain in my life is to experience life's pain from my dear friends in Capitol Hill Church. This is why I try to follow God: to help others, so that others can see and help others, and give them hope and shining hope in their hearts, shining their hearts and their souls from dark hope to shining hope. I am asking all of us to do this for each other, to "love thy neighbor as thyself," as it is endorsed by our Lord Jesus. Why? Because he wanted to unite humanity... the more unity we have, the more power we gain, and that is what God wants us to have as we live godly lives. Besides, God wants us to be successful and have a happy life. So, if we trust Him and follow His instructions, He will lead us forward, sweeping many of our problems aside. How encouraging is our Lord and Savior, Jesus Christ (2 Peter 3:18). This is a most vital part of God's will which HE gives to us as spiritual empowerment. "He strengthened us with all Might... Glorious Power." "I can do all things through Christ who strengthens me." (Philippians 4:13).

I would like to share with you here what I am unable to (comprehend). Why does God let bad things happen to good people like me and my wife? And why me? Why us?

Last night at 12:15 a.m., "The house is on fire," cried one of our tenants. "What house?" asked Patty. "The rental next door." Patty and I ran out of the house quickly and went out to (meet) the fire trucks and related people. "I am sick of it," said my wife. I said, "It is beyond us." I got butterflies in my stomach, too... my whole body was shaking and I just about fainted. My wife called to see if anyone was inside the house. Knowing all tenants were out, I felt better. Thank GOD. Later, we found out that one cat did not survive. I felt terrible... I imagined how much he struggled to fight for his life. Poor cat (named Mr. T). Today we found out one more cat died in the fire. They are now resting. I know how much I love animals. They are part of the family.

The whole night I could not sleep, thinking of losing the cats, losing the property. I have to go through the recycling of this life: fire, insurance, and mortgage business. I am sick of asking myself why, why me, why does God let it happen to me over and over? This is the third house in my life on fire, nearly one every three years. If you were in my shoes, what would you be thinking? Where is GOD? This question arises at some point in our lives, especially in mine, for a long time. I believe that God created all men in His image and gave us His free will. It is beyond question, and yes, there is a God; there is no doubt in my mind. Next, then, since He exists, where is He when we or I want Him? When we need protection from HIM, like from the fire on the house last night? Why does He even bother to create us? He knows that by giving us the choice we could and would choose to ignore him. Is it not feasible that by allowing us the freedom to choose, we please God when we choose to believe Him?

Ultimately, I have rested my mind to believe that GOD is, and I will live my life accordingly... Well, if GOD is all-loving, why does he allow suffering and bad *kamma*, bad fortune, pain, and death for us? To this essential point, I have experienced it myself and have wondered about it. Why does God allow for so much suffering? Our son's friend who was stabbed to death a few weeks ago, someone's son who committed suicide a few months ago... I have a lot of neck pain and a degenerative (disc problem)... There is so much violence in my country, Thailand, causing my older brother to be murdered. (One can) count the suffering that causes us to face... human suffering, or *dukkha*... it happens, like when we had the fire at our rental house last night (Dec. 27, 2011). We lost over half a million dollars... Why? Why do those unpleasant things happen repeatedly to me, to us, among HIS children? You, all or each of you, please help me to answer for our GOD. I will leave it to you to share with me... Does God let bad things happen to good people like me and you?

On Thursday, at 10 a.m., on December 29, David sent me an email message: "No, Daney, God is not punishing you... you and Patty are good people." Thanks, David, for being aware of my troubled heart... and for being there for me when I need you, and for each of us when problems arise. After listening to David's voicemail, in which he and Deborah showed their concern for us over the fire, tears filled my eyes and fell all over my face. God makes me realize that when bad things happen to me, such as a house on fire, it is a demonstration of immeasurable love from others, like the Liberty insurance company staff, calling nonstop: "If there is anything we can do to help, we are more than happy to do it for you, Daney. ... Sorry for your loss... sorry for the death of two cats." Trauma Intervention volunteers came over and stayed until the last minute... sharing their love and empathy on behalf of the spirit of Americans, and they offered some of my (tenants) help finding a place to stay. There were a lot of clothes given, and a lot of calls offering help. I am crying but I had the greatest joy of this miracle love from my fellow Americans. It touched my heart deeply that they showed love to my wife and me. Otherwise, I would have no chance to experience this love from others. Our dear friend said, "God will work out something for you for sure, Daney. Do not worry." I corresponded to Bob that, in the end, what is God going to do with me next, and what is God going to do with people who trust my faith in you?

It surprised me that some neighbors did not even express the word 'sorry' to me... what kind of neighborhood do I live in? Am I not good enough for them, or did I not do enough for GOD? I do know I need no sympathy from them, but where is our heart (that says), "love thy neighbor as thyself"? Are we truly Christians if we don't practice this, or do we just recite the words? This message keeps coming to my heart and bothering me during difficult times like these. Of course, I am not a pastor or spiritual leader, but I am tired of so-called Christians and fake Christians. Why do we fake it so much? Why do we spend so much time trying to please everyone else and make so little effort trying to please God? When I am asking myself these questions, I cannot come up with good answers. So this is the time we must decide to drop the act and start getting real. With that one choice, our lives will begin in a big way, and we all, as real Christians, can do this... this is the Gift of all gifts for 2012... At this point, I realize that this year is the year of the awareness of friends within Capitol Hill and outside. To me, friends are like a page in my (book) of life. Every page features different subjects, but you are my index page, covering every aspect of my life. A friend is a friend forever, from the day I was born until the day I'll be in the graveyard. I am in the hand of God... God gives the reason for hiding love behind His purpose: what more can I ask from Him? "I will wipe away every tear from your eyes." (Revelation 21:3-4). "The poor man cried and the Lord heard him, saved him... the angel of the LORD... saved him out of all trouble..." (Psalm 34:6-7, 11).

OUR GOD is pleased when we honor HIS grace and seek his perfect love.

"You are the light of the world. A city built on a hill cannot be hidden. No one after lighting a lamp puts it under a basket." (Matthew 5:13-16).

I am so thankful that GOD turned my life around from the bad, bad direction where I was heading as a gang member among Muslim men in Thailand. I became a Buddhist monk, and now I am a true Christian believer. Thank you for turning Chin's life around and saving him.

Jesus wants us to love one another as a demonstration of unity in love. As he loves God, Jesus gives us life to pay our debt of sin. His is our glory. His investment is in us, and we receive Jesus' spiritual life. He gives life to one God and to all men. Therefore, we are to walk in Him. If we are not yet walking in Him this year, we will, and we must walk in Him. The only way to receive HIM is by grace. We must walk by grace. We were born again by spirit. We must walk by spirit. Remember when we first received Christ, He was our only hope. Now, we are to walk with HIM the same way.

My best wishes and prayers to you. May this Christmas and New Year season draw you into a spiritual embrace with our Emmanuel, for unto us a SAVIOR is born. May God bless you, your family, and every man and child in the world.

Daney Dumdeang The President of Dumdeang Foundation

Image credit: Christ et Bouddha by Paul Ranson 1890. Reproduction in "Le Monde de la Bible", No. 184. (via Wikimedia Commons)

Posted in Blog. Tagged Sermons and Writings. permalink (http://www.shermanswilderness.org/why-me-would-i-be-blessed/)

About David Weekley Reverend David Weekley is the author of "In from the Wilderness," a clergyman, and an advocate for transgender equality and acceptance. Connect with David on social media at Twitter, Facebook, Google+, or LinkedIn.

www.ingramcontent.com/pod-product-compliance
Lightning Source LLC
Chambersburg PA
CBHW080839120626
46553CB00009B/2500
* 9 7 9 8 8 9 3 2 4 9 6 8 2 *